A TRIP DOWN THE RABBIT HOLE

My 10 Year Journey with a Brain Tumour

by

Matthew Carpenter

Grosvenor House
Publishing Limited

This book is published by
Grosvenor House Publishing Ltd
Link House
140 The Broadway, Tolworth, Surrey, KT6 7HT.
www.grosvenorhousepublishing.co.uk

A CIP record for this book
is available from the British Library

ISBN 978-1-83975-951-2

Introduction

At the age of twenty, after obtaining a head injury, I was sent for a CT scan to check for any skull or brain damage and sent home with the all clear. I didn't know it at the time, but doctors had completely missed a brain tumour.

This book is my story about the highs and lows I have experienced over this ten-year journey I have been on since then.

Being misdiagnosed and then formally diagnosed with a brain tumour, understandably comes with many ordeals including; handling my emotions, dealing with the consequences and difficulties presented by a brain tumour and the benefits as, believe it or not there has been some.

I want to share my story from the beginning in the hope of helping others who may have had to deal similar struggles in life.

Where to begin?

How do you even start a book like this? I guess the answer to that is the same answer as "What's the correct way to react when you're told you have been living with a brain tumour for the past eight years that had been missed on a previous scan."

Apparently, there's no real answer to that, so I guess the best place to start is here and now.

In 2018 I was diagnosed with a brain tumour. I would later find out that this brain tumour of mine had been missed during a CT scan in 2010! After having vital brain surgery, I would soon find myself in a life-threatening position that would see me lose more of my skull than I care to think about. Only for the tumour to later grow back resulting in even more treatment.

Over these next twenty five chapters, you'll get an idea of how life was for me pre and post diagnoses and all the weird and wonderful stories and adventures that occurred in between, but also the tragic and damn right heart-breaking bits too. You'll see the gradual build-up of symptoms and side effects that were missed and ignored by me as well as the doctors. You'll see what life with a brain injury is really like and how trying not to accept it, only serves to make the final part of recovery, so much harder than it needs to be.

Over the course of this book, I truly hope you, the reader, finds some form of lesson to learn from the good, the bad and the ugly sides of this ten-year journey of mine. I hope that by showing how and where I feel I went wrong, you can follow better and healthy paths should you ever find yourself on a similar journey.

Thank you, from me...

This book is written for and dedicated to the two most important people in my life. My son Jack and my daughter Billie.

Always know that not a day has gone by since you were both born that you haven't been on my mind and in my heart. I truly wish things up to now could have been different and that your mums and I could have separated on more amicable terms to allow us to better co-parent but I hope this book offers you some answers for the questions in life you may find yourself asking.

Whatever this weird and wonderful life throws at me; I will always love you both.

Now, a huge thank you to the amazing army of friends, family and acquaintances that I have been lucky enough to have in my life over the past ten years.

I wouldn't be the man I am today or even be alive long enough to write this book, had it not been for the selfless actions of the amazing people mentioned in this book. I truly hope that I am able to convey my love and appreciation for you all and for all that you have done for me over the course of this book.

A particular thank you to Michelle. This book would not have been possible without you. Thank you, from the bottom of my heart.

Happy Reading!!

CHAPTER 1

Here We Go.

It was March 1st 2010, I was twenty. Me and my best friend Kris had gone out for "a couple of pints"

After an entire day and night of drinking and getting up to god knows what, I woke the next morning on Kris' bedroom floor. After a quick look in the mirror, I soon realised I had a rather nasty looking head injury. My previously white t-shirt was covered in dried blood as was my face. I later discovered that I had ran into a concrete post during the night and face planted the floor. I have no memory of that happening at all, but I looked a complete mess! Apparently after somehow making it home from Kris' I had collapsed.

I was taken to hospital with a suspected concussion and sent for a CT scan to check my skull and brain for any potential damage. A nurse came to me soon after and said "Congratulations Matthew! You actually have a brain!" after which I was soon sent home with the all clear.

By 2010 I'd spent a couple of years bouncing from job to job thanks to never being motivated enough to stick things out when they got hard and as a result I'd found myself unemployed and on benefits. In order to remain eligible for benefits, I had to prove I was actively looking for work or training. So one day I found myself in a library using a "job search machine" to see if I could land a job that might actually last more than a couple of months. While using said machine, I spotted a poster just above it with a logo that stood out like a sore thumb. It was a poster about The Princes Trust. It wasn't so long ago that I had completed their TEAM Program while living in Camborne - Cornwall.

This poster was advertising a retail program with work experience. Hell, the last time I did something with these guys I ended up with a decent job so thought if this short course worked well, maybe this would too.

I called the number on the poster and spoke with a lady named Lucy. She explained that they had already done the sign ups and induction but that she could get me a last-minute place starting the next day. Perfect I thought.

The course itself was only a three week stint. Two weeks in a classroom and one week work experience in a shop attached to the local shopping centre. There were about ten of us all aged between seventeen and twenty-one. Most of the group were only there to make sure their benefits stayed in place. I think in all, three of us (including me) were there because we genuinely wanted to get back into work and were willing to do whatever we needed to do in order to make that happen.

Week one was all about learning certain rules and regulations around the retail sector. Basic stuff really. In week two, me and another lad took on Tesco for our work experience. Nothing too technical. We were essentially shelf stackers for the standard 9-5 routine. Even so I made a point of turning up in a shirt and tie for each day that I was there and went out of my way to talk to customers as if I was actually employed by Tesco. I would always ask for extra jobs to do when I'd completed my set tasks as if there was any chance of me getting a decent reference out of this, I was taking it with both hands. I had no interest in remaining on benefits any longer.

Despite having worked so hard to make a good impression, on the last day of the work experience myself and the other guy working there decided we would ditch work in favour of the pub. We didn't even call in and pretend to be sick - we just never bothered turning up. Looking back, I'm annoyed with my thought process there. I'd put so much time and effort in to making a good, lasting impression of myself only to piss it all away for a couple of pints with a guy that I barely knew.

We came back to the start of week three, back in the classroom for the final week - Jan, the tutor took me out of the class that afternoon to ask what had made me ditch the last day of work experience without bothering to tell anyone at Tesco. I gave her some lame excuse that she clearly saw right though. Jan then explained that a manager at Tesco had reached out to her to say that they wanted to offer me job (something that would have been announced on the final day of the course) but thanks to my little pub trip, they had decided I wasn't worth the time after all and changed their mind. Jan actually seemed really disappointed in me. She told me that she thought I was the only person in the group that seemed genuinely interested and wanted to finish the course by making something of myself. Any respect she had for me prior to that had gone and she made that very clear. I took what she said to heart. She actually hit a nerve.

On the final day of the course, everybody had to take part in a mock interview with a 'big wig' who came over from Boots. She was some kind or corporate manager. Just like the work experience and with Jan's disappointment taken to heart I decided that, mock interview or not, I would put 100% in and nail that "interview".

I turned up that day suited and booted and with a freshly printed out CV to hand. Everyone else took the piss, reminding me that it was only a mock interview with no real job offers but I didn't care. I'd taken Jan's disappointed words and Tesco's repealed job offer to heart. This "Job" was mine even if it was only pretend.

I smashed the interview and was the only one to get "an offer" That in itself was a much-needed confidence boost!

The final part of the retail program involved all of us doing a short presentation to talk about what had made us decide to sign up, what we had done during the course and what we had learnt. In my speech I spoke briefly about my ambition to join the army a few years earlier and about how I'd been rejected at the selection medical due to having scoliosis (a curve in my spine) and how said rejection had impacted my mental health. After we'd all finished a man came over and introduced himself to me. He told me that he was an ex-army officer and asked why I hadn't put an appeal in to get a second chance at a medical at least. Truth be told, I'd never even thought about it until then but he told me I should maybe try.

The rejection by the army occurred when I was seventeen and at the time it hit me hard as it was all I had ever wanted to do. Not long after, I started binge drinking, barely eating and self-harming. This escalated to the point where I ended up trying to kill myself twice. To say the least it was a pretty messy affair overall - but we will come back to that in a moment.

For two weeks solid after the retail program, I was out every day until late afternoon, walking wherever there were businesses that may have any jobs I could apply for. I must have handed out almost a hundred CVs over those two weeks before eventually bagging an interview for a shop at a petrol station - working night shifts. The interview was pretty bad and lasted all of ten minutes give or take. I left the interview pretty certain I hadn't got the job and I was right.

As a result I found myself taking up a job at Burger King; it certainly wasn't what I aspired to but it allowed me to earn my own money and meant I could finally come off benefits. It turned out not to be for me though and just a stepping stone as a couple of months later I landed that job at the garage after all. I did try and work both jobs for a while but after a disagreement with management at BK over time off to have my beloved dog put to sleep I decided the best thing to do was leave and focus on just the garage.

A few weeks into that role Lucy (the Princes Trust rep that got me on to the retail program) reached out and asked if I would be up for volunteering for them as a "Young Ambassador" I had no idea what that meant or involved but took her up the offer anyway and soon found myself at a one-day public speaking workshop in Manchester.

It turned out that a handful of people who had previously completed Princes Trust programs would sometimes be asked to become Young Ambassadors for the Trust as a means of promoting what they do and gaining more funding and awareness for the charity.

As well as allowing me to do some really great things for the charity I was able to learn a lot about my mental health issues through things like the public speaking events and later they helped open a whole new avenue for me professionally in which I feel I was able to help others – again, more on that later though.

So.....that takes me nicely back to the failed army selection and subsequent mental health issues in my earlier years.

After failing my medical at selection, over the next couple of months, my weight dropped to around 7 stone and I started self-harming quite badly. I felt as though I had messed up the one thing I was supposed to do in life.

I found myself drowning my sorrows and eventually after getting completely shit faced one weekend I decided that I'd genuinely had enough and wanted to end it all. As a result I necked a stupidly large amount of pills.......sixty to be exact. Strangely - I knew how many I had taken but not what they actually were.

At the time I'd thought taking the pills would be an easy exit, that I'd just pass out and die in my sleep but that turned out not to be the case. I have very limited memory of that day but do remember feeling as though I was extremely drunk. One thing that does still sit with me now - fourteen years later is a memory of lying down on the floor with my face in a pool of my own vomit unable to move. I remember thinking to myself.

"Just let me die. I want to die"

If I had known dying by overdose was so messy and horrific I might not have taken all of those pills.

The next day, I woke up in my bed with what felt like a nasty hangover. My first thought upon waking up? "Fuck, I'm still alive - Plan B it is then"

Plan B was to find a nice quiet spot in the middle of nowhere and slit my wrists. I even found what I thought would be an ideal spot and started the process. Fortunately (or at the time I thought unfortunately) I was discovered by the police. After a brief chase they caught up with me and called an ambulance. I was taken to the local hospital where they treated the wounds to my wrists.

At the time I was fairly angry with myself as I felt it was just another thing I had botched.

No sooner was I discharged by the hospital I was arrested due to being found in public with a knife. Although I felt this was a little harsh I knew that I had broken the law and so I never questioned the arrest – in fact I still agree with the decision to this day but this is where things started to get a bit weird.

Whilst in custody I kept passing out but only after I'd drunk water or been to pee. At one point, I remember being in a room feeling very strange - everything was a blur and I could barely speak. I remember asking for water before everything suddenly turned black.

The next thing I remember is being dragged across the floor by the custody sergeant who was taking me back to my cell. He was telling me to stop acting like a child and that he knew I was attention seeking even though I genuinely couldn't walk.

Soon after, I was taken to see the on duty doctor who quizzed me about what had happened in the run up to being arrested. I remember thinking to myself that maybe the overdose hadn't failed at all and was just taking a damn sight longer to kill me than I thought. I didn't let on though and told her that I'd spent an entire weekend drinking without eating which was why I was so ill. She saw right though the lie though and called me out on it so eventually I caved and admitted that I had, in fact taken sixty pills the day before but that I didn't know what they were. She took blood for testing and I was taken back to my cell. Although much of this is quite foggy I do have a vague recollection of her coming back to my cell and telling me the results had come back showing something may be wrong with my kidneys.

Eventually I was taken to be interviewed, I still felt "drunk" and not quite with it so when I was offered a solicitor I refused. Being only seventeen though I had no say in the matter of an adult being in the room with me as legally I was still a minor. I was asked to explain my actions the day before-the why's and how's etc. In short I just explained that I'd gotten a little too drunk, felt sorry for myself and took myself somewhere I knew nobody would be before trying to kill myself. The officer pulled out a clear plastic tube which contained my knife, it was covered in blood which actually made me cringe. I was asked to confirm it was mine which obviously I did.

After the interview, I was told I'd be given a reprimand (a formal slap on the wrist essentially) but when it came to being released, during another grilling from the custody sergeant about needing to grow up etc, I passed out again. The few police officers that were in the room were pretty nice and helped me up. They even managed to crack a couple of jokes all while the sergeant continued to waffle on about whatever it was he felt I needed to hear.

Mum and Dad had been contacted to come pick me up - neither of them said a word in the car on the way home. I think they were still trying to come to terms with what had actually happened.

I hadn't been home long before the phone rang and Dad picked up - the call was short; maybe a minute at most.

"Right, ok we're coming now" he said before putting the phone down.

He looked over to me and told me to get dressed and put my shoes on with a real sense of urgency. I asked who was on the phone and in return he snapped at me telling me to get dressed now!

In the process of trying to get ready I remember collapsing another couple of times and I don't actually remember getting into the car. When I did come around Dad was speeding towards hospital and I still had no idea what the hell was going on.

When we arrived I was placed in the waiting area and remember thinking that I was now going to have to sit and spend a stupid amount of hours in a packed waiting room for naff all. Instead within two minutes of being there I was called into a room; no sooner had I sat down I was having my bloods taken before a cannula was stuck in my arm - still nobody explained to me what was happening.

After much poking and prodding I finally found out that the bloods that had been taken while in custody had in fact shown my kidneys were dangerously close to failing.

The phone call that Dad answered while at home was to see how quickly they could get me to the hospital in case an ambulance with blue lights needed to collect me. That explained why Mum dragged me off the floor when I collapsed instead of doing the normal recovery position stuff - I was quite literally dying and only just starting to comprehend that.

It's a strange thought process really - to go from being determined to die to then finding that you're now ok and in fact do want to get things sorted and to live only to then be told that you're in a life and death situation. I'd say it's a strange feeling but I what actually mean is - it's fucking terrifying.

I ended up needing a six day stay in hospital, hooked up to a drip the whole time, having my kidneys flushed. I vowed I'd never let myself fall prey to any kind of suicidal thoughts again.

But it wasn't until I became an Ambassador for Princes Trust that I really decided it was time for a fresh start and new outlook.

But we will get to all of that in due course – for now we will pick up where we left off.

CHAPTER 2

Army selection, Relationships and early symptoms

The petrol station job was pretty straight forward, all I really had to do was keep the shop clean and tidy, keep the shelves stocked and make sure the place ran smoothly. As it was only a small store it was mainly lone working and I'd work two or three night shifts a week with plenty of overtime to keep me going.

After a few months of being there I finally felt ready to kick start an appeal for the army. So after an appointment with an independent physiotherapist I had myself a letter to send off with the appeal giving me a clean bill of health. I wasn't sure what I expected but it certainly wasn't for my appeal to be granted so quickly so in no time at all I was back in the career's office working my way through the BARB test and interview process.

In order to complete the selection process I needed to travel to Scotland but as 2010 was a bad year for snow in the north my selection date kept being pushed back due to travel issues.

Every couple of weeks, my best friend, Kris would come home on leave from the army and we'd go out for few drinks. Sometimes it was just a few pints at our local and on other occasions we'd go into town for a few more. For some reason I found that if I had been out, drinking only Corona soon after waking up the next day I'd collapse. It was so bizarre - I could go out and get completely wasted, drinking pints of lager minus the Corona and I'd be fine. I never really had to deal with hangovers but add a couple of bottles of the Corona and boom, I'd be hitting the deck hard by the time I was up and about the next day. I never did work out what that was about but as I am writing this in the Great Corona pandemic of 2020 and 2021 I certainly see the irony now.

During those days Kris and I got up to some pretty crazy stuff that we both look back on now and cringe. Things like climbing into a construction site in the middle of the night, wasted and deciding it was a good idea to climb the scaffolding. I will admit that I am ashamed to admit things like that now but I did say this book was about the good, bad and ugly after all.

Only working a couple of night shifts a week in the garage meant I had plenty of opportunity to get some time in with my new volunteer role with the Princes Trust and I got a call in November 2010 offering me my first gig. I was told it would be a short presentation in front of a small group of people from different businesses for an event called "Million Makers". What was meant to be "only a few people" turned out to be at a formal black tie, champagne reception event with over fifty people who were all business owners and CEOs. Luckily for me, I managed to snag a cheeky glass of champagne before I took to the stage which helped calm my nerves. Slightly.

I'd written my speech down and brought it up on stage with me. I don't know why, because I didn't look at it once. I was so freaking nervous. I'd never been in a position where so many eyes were on me before. The speech lasted about five minutes and, well....it was pretty bad. I'm pretty sure the clapping I got when I'd finished was more from sympathy than anything else.

Over the next few months, I got quite a few more different public speaking events. I was even asked to meet with some CEOs from Pepsi Co. to deliver a speech on one occasion. It ended with jaws on the floor. I never realised just how important "my story" was. People would actually come to me and thank me for being so open about my mental health struggles. I guess hearing someone talk so openly about it helped them as much as talking about it helped me.

I grew to love public speaking and eventually, I'd perfected my speech and the art of delivering it. I'd be up on stage talking openly for a good fifteen minutes; talking about how I'd grown up set on joining the army, how I knew I was going to be in the army not long after leaving school and how getting in the army soon became an obsession and of course, my mental health struggles when I was rejected and how The Princes Trust had helped kick me up the arse and help me see that there was more to life than getting one dream job.

Around late 2010, I'd been to town and bought myself a camera. Nothing flash just a basic camera - cheap and cheerful. As I was walking home, I decided to cut though Pearson Park that has a police station just inside. As I got closer to the entrance I could see a protest was underway outside the station. The protest happened to be an anti BNP one (British Nationalist Party) a completely racist group filled with vile thugs and bullies.

I decided to get my camera out and take some photos and video. If anything I was curious and just wanted to see what was happening. I've always hated racists, homophobes and bullies in general, so to see a large group of people that also shared the same feeling was pretty cool, or so I thought...

While stood there filming, I could see people from within the protest staring at me. Those that were looking at me seemed to be glaring. There was a man at the front of the protest with a megaphone, screaming this, that and everything else that was wrong with the BNP, but while doing so, he kept looking directly at me, making eye contact. I didn't pay much attention at first until I felt a tap on my shoulder. I turned around to find a police sergeant who asked me to follow him to the back of the protest, well out of sight of the protesters.

"Can I ask you what you're doing here?" He asked.

I told him that I was just passing, that I hadn't realised there would be a protest and that I had stuck around out of curiosity as I too hated the BNP (like most normal people did) so I thought I'd stick around. The sergeant pointed at my hoodie which was a Help for Heroes one. He went on to explain that because the BNP publicly supported the charity, a lot of people, especially those that actively protested against the BNP, viewed those that wore Help for Heroes merchandise as either racists or members of the BNP. He explained that me being there in that hoodie was making some of the protesters angry, which explained the looks I was getting.

He made it very clear that I either left the area immediately or stay at the very back out of sight and amongst the police. Obviously, I chose to leave.

As I was walking away, a few lads were walking towards me, they began to start chanting "Fuck the BNP" at me over and over. I couldn't believe it - I was being viewed as a racist thug, because I was wearing a hoodie that showed I supported a charity that helped men & women who had been injured while serving this country.

To this day, I believe that those protesters and anybody else with that thought process, are just as bad and pathetic as the very types of people that they were protesting against.

Eventually in early 2011 I finally got a solid army selection date. My selection had been booked and cancelled a few times up to this point – once while I was halfway there as the centre had to close due to snow.

So it felt good to finally be on a train heading to selection again. This time I knew I was safe. I'd met a couple of lads on the way there, who were also heading to selection and we all stuck out like a sore thumb. Tracksuits on, rucksacks and a suet bag to hand. I'd gone for dog handler as my priority job and Main Battle Tank (MBT) driver as job choice two. I already had experience working with dogs so knew I had a very good shot at getting it.

This time around during the medical I noticed one of the team staring at my wrists. She could obviously see the scars on both of my arms from my previous self-harming and suicide attempt but I didn't think much of it at the time. Soon after, I was asked to do a Peak flow test (to check my lung capacity) No matter how hard I tried, I kept getting far below the minimum score needed to move to the next stage of the medical. I was taken aside by part of the medical team and told that I needed to be deferred. I'd not failed selection this time I just needed to improve my lung capacity and prove it before being allowed to come back.

Although disappointed I wasn't really worried about the decision as I knew I'd be able to sort the lung capacity "issue" in no time. I called my GP the next day and got myself an appointment for that week.

I explained what had happened at selection and what had been said. The doctor got me to go a few times on a peak flow machine and soon realised the problem was my technique. Basically I was an idiot who clearly didn't know how to breathe.

My GP wrote me a letter with proof of my actual peak flow score and sent it to the selection centre. Two days later, the army replied. In short, they had reviewed my medical records (again) and found that there was an overdose on my records. It was obvious now, why that medical examiner at selection had been staring at my arms and the fairly noticeable scars up and down them. She had noted it on my records. Knowing that if I was to try and appeal the deferral, it would be flagged up.

The letter explained that not only had I failed selection, I was now permanently barred from joining the army due to "more than one act of deliberate self-harm"

Obviously, I appealed the decision straight away. Surely this must have been an oversight, a mistake maybe. The reply I got just re-enforced the first letter. The army had no interest in me at all.

There wasn't much I could do after that. I was beyond gutted. I'd been given hope and once again it had been taken away from me, for what I felt was a ridiculous reason. But as hard as it was to accept it, I'm the one who had taken the first rejection so badly, the one who chose to self-harm and eventually overdose and so I had no one else to blame but myself.

Later that year I got another call from the Trust offering another Ambassador gig. The call came from a new member of the Ambassador team, Les who had never managed Young Ambassador's before which explained the lack of detail he gave me for the gig. He offered me a public speaking event, I asked how many people would be in attendance and he told me one hundred at the very most. That was one of those out Loud "fuck me moments" I took a moment to think about it. The biggest audience I'd had ever done a speech for was between sixty or seventy. The thought of having one hundred people staring at me, while I waffled on about my story was pretty intimidating to say the least but I decided to take the offer. It was only going to be around thirty people more than I was used to so it can't be that bad I thought to myself.

Imagine my surprise when I turned up for said event only to find that it was a formal clay pigeon shoot which was attended by the kind of people who are multi-millionaires. This was not an average day and definitely not an average gig! It was THE biggest fundraising event that the Trust hosted, once a year. Hell, one guest decided to show up in his helicopter! I was so, so underprepared for this. One hundred people max I was told would be there... Try almost three hundred! I was very seriously considering disappearing before I heard the words.

"Can I offer you a glass of champagne, sir?" Yes, there was even a champagne reception! Without thinking about it, I accepted. I downed it and was soon offered another glass. Once again, I downed it and again, had another. I was barely a mouthful into of my third glass when I heard somebody shout "what an earth is he doing with alcohol!"

Before the same lady snatched the glass away from me. Turns out Young Ambassador's weren't allowed to drink at events. It's rather unprofessional, apparently.

Not long into it was time for lunch and the meal was amazing. One of those fancy meals where you have three of each piece of cutlery. The trick is to start from the outside and work your way in for each part of the meal. I have no idea how or why I knew that but I was right. I felt rather posh being able to explain how that worked to the others on our table.

I was still slightly tipsy when it came to doing my speech. To say I was nervous would be a huge understatement. Just imagine for a moment, standing up in front of nearly three hundred people (most of which being millionaires) and then spending fifteen minutes talking about some of your most personal moments.

Before I knew it, I heard my name being mentioned by the host. I walked up to the stage with my heart was racing. I may still have been tipsy but that definitely wasn't helping. I got to the podium, stood there for a moment, looked around the room and took a couple of deep breaths - in through the nose and out the mouth. It sounds a little daft but for me it's an effective method for calming the nerves (especially in that kind of situation!)

Within a couple of minutes of talking, I could see that I was on a roll. The nerves had all but gone and it looked as though I had everybody's attention.

About halfway into the speech I hit a snag. I was reading from my pre written speech that I always brought it with me just in case I needed it. It was a pointless aid really. Instead of just having key points written down I had the whole speech. Key points are definitely best for a speech like that as they make a great prompt if and when you need it. A full speech on paper with you while you're talking can act as a distraction and just kills the flow of your talk.

No surprise then that at the halfway mark I lost my place. I was stumped for a good few seconds and could feel my nerves coming back. There's three hundred people sat staring at me, probably thinking I'm a complete twat who's forgotten what I'm talking about so I went back to basics. I took a couple of deep breaths, looked around the room and remembered where I was in the speech which allowed me to continue. When I finished, the room erupted with applause. I spotted a table full of older ladies, all in tears. I had people coming over to me before I could even get back to my table, shaking my hand and hugging me.

Christ! What the fuck's happened here? I'd never had this kind of reaction before. I sat back at my table only to be met by another couple of ladies who were crying. I gave them a hug; still slightly confused as to how people had gotten themselves so upset by my story. I was quite embarrassed really.

It wouldn't be until a few weeks later that I'd find out what had really happened. I met the photographer from the event at an Ambassador workshop and we got talking about the event and the speech. She called me a dick (in jest) for leaving her with tears in her eyes during the event; once again, I was stumped. I asked what about the speech it was, that was so upsetting, as I'd never seen that kind of reaction before. Especially as I'd cocked up.

It turned out that the moment I'd lost my place during the speech was a key moment. Essentially, I'd just spoken about failing selection, the self-harming and finding myself in a position where things felt like they were getting worse and worse. I said something like "I waited for my parents to leave the house for the weekend. I then locked the doors, closed the curtains and turned off the TV..."

Obviously I knew what happened next but I'd forgotten how I was meant to word it. It turns out that was a key moment to pause. It left the audience in suspense, desperate to know what happened next. Basically, it was a metric fuck ton of drama added to an already dramatic story. A complete accident, but a technique I would make a point of using for other public speaking events from that point onwards.

2010 through to 2011 seemed to fly by quite fast. My job in the garage was going smoothly, my Young Ambassador role was only meant to last one year but thanks to me being so effective with the public speaking and Les being a little bit sneaky, letting me go at the one-year mark had become something that was conveniently overlooked. I certainly wasn't complaining. I found talking about my story was quite therapeutic and the fact it was helping others see that they weren't alone, made it all the more worth it.

I was eventually asked to start attending the inductions for new Young Ambassador's as a means of showing them how to deliver a good speech confidently and effectively and to give them an idea of what to expect when they were at events. I loved this. I was starting to feel useful and the fact that I was meeting more and more staff within the Trust was ideal. I didn't know how, but I knew that knowing some of the team could be beneficial for me at a later date. It's always handy to have a good, long list of contacts.

That same year, I began to help out with the retail program that had helped me get back on track in the first place. Whilst I was there, I met a girl named Katie. She seemed nice and we seemed to hit it off pretty much straight away. We soon found ourselves together in a relationship. She already had a daughter but that didn't bother me at all.

After being together for only a couple of months she called me one day to tell me that her mum had told her she wanted both her and her daughter to move out. The way she explained was that she had been kicked out and had until the morning to go.

My Mum and Dad both decided that the pair of them could come and stay with us so that night both Katie and her daughter moved in with us. Things seemed to work out fairly ok at first. I would take her daughter out for walks to the park and for days out to give Katie time and space to relax and give me chance to bond with her.

Shortly after this I received a call from the Trust to tell me that I'd been nominated for two awards - part of the Prince's Trust Celebrate Success Awards. One was for The Flying Start Award - for overcoming challenges in life and the other, for the Young Ambassador Award for all the work I had achieved as a Young Ambassador.

I'd never heard of the Trust doing award ceremonies before so did some digging. It turned out that these were quite high-profile events held once a year. There were the regional awards and then for a select few, the national award ceremony held in London. London was the big one. Hosted by high profile celebrities and of course, the founder of the Princes Trust, HRH Prince Charles.

In the run up to the ceremony I was interviewed by a reporter from the Yorkshire Post -it was the first time I had been interviewed by a reporter. They wanted to know some of the details about my mental health journey - from being rejected by the army, the self-harming and the eventual suicide attempts, but more importantly, how the Princes Trust had helped me though it with their TEAM program and "Get into Retail program."

A few weeks before the award ceremony, a camera crew came over. They had been asked to interview some the nominees for a short video for the ceremony. Part of the filming was to be done in the place of work. I had to go to work and act casual so they could get footage of me working. Once they had a bit of footage of me serving a couple of customers, my boss, Elaine needed to be interviewed. In short, she was asked a few basic questions about me and what I was like to work with. Interview and filming done; it was just a case of waiting for the award night in mid-November.

A couple of weeks later, it was time for the Celebrate Success Awards and I invited Katie and my best friend Kris along as my guests. Kris had been out the night before so was suffering from a pretty nasty hangover.

His plan was to hit the bar when we got to the venue which was in a posh hotel in Leeds. Which was exactly what he did as soon as we arrived. I remember seeing Kris walk away from the bar with no drink.

"Matt, there's no alcohol being sold here!" he said rather unimpressed but I was too nervous to care, if I'm honest.

After a few short hellos with some old familiar faces, it was time to grab our seats. There was about three hundred people in attendance. There were five categories in total, each with three nominees with me being nominated for two of them. When the first of them, Flying Start, came up I felt sick with nerves. The names of the three nominees were read out with a brief description of why we'd been nominated. "And the winner is... Matthew Carpenter" Fuck! I shouted, I genuinely thought that I had no chance. The competition was tough, so hearing my name caught me off guard.

While the audience sat clapping, I had to make my way up on stage. Shaking like a leaf with all eyes on me, the video that had been made a few weeks prior began to play on an enormous screen behind me. I suddenly turned bright red with embarrassment! I was given my trophy and a framed certificate and made my way back to my seat, again with everybody clapping.

The last award of the night was the Young Ambassador of the year award. I had been nominated and made it to the final three but I didn't win. I was just grateful, that my work and effort had been recognised to be quite honest. The fact I had already won something was the main take away for me and again, I was just grateful to have even made it that far.

Seen as though we couldn't get a drink at the ceremony after staying for a few photoshoots Me, Kris and Katie took to Leeds, for some much-needed celebration drinks. This night is one of my proudest memories and certainly a high point for me in my journey.

Eventually though, the cracks started to show with mine and Katie's relationship. The pair of us were becoming stressed and the living situation with me, Katie and her daughter all living with my mum and dad in a small house didn't help.

In January 2012 I had arranged for us both to have day and night away together in a hotel as a way to de-stress, unwind and relax.

Despite my best efforts though it wasn't long after our mini retreat that I started to realise this wasn't a relationship I wanted to be in. Neither of us were happy and I wanted to end it, I just didn't know how. You could say I didn't want to hurt her or that I just didn't have the guts to call it a day.

A few days after I had started to run ideas of how to end things as painlessly as possible Katie called me upstairs. As soon as I walked in the room she almost screamed at me "Matt, I'm pregnant!" her words full of joy and excitement. I had absolutely no idea what to say; she'd certainly stumped me. Seems we both got more from the hotel stay than we bargained for -well, I did at least.

I know many of you will say that I should have been more responsible and practiced safe sex but in my dim witted and naïve head – I was. Katie had always told me that she hated the feel of condoms but that it was OK anyway as she was on the contraceptive pill.

At the time I had no reason not to believe her but having later found out she had always wanted to have four kids I do now question this. Despite my doubts over the relationship I decided to do what I felt was the right and stay with her.

Obviously adding the stress of a pregnancy on top of the issues we were already experiencing didn't improve the relationship and three months later we were both struggling again. I'd started to not only feel unhappy in the relationship but also trapped. I felt I had no choice but to stay with her and I wanted to give us a shot and be a dad. I couldn't just bin her off when she was carrying my child. I was fighting every urge I had to leave her, essentially forcing myself to be with her which I know now is clearly not a healthy relationship especially when kids are involved but at the time I felt I was obligated to do it.

A few weeks before the first scan though I couldn't take anymore and I called it quits for both our sakes – I mean she had already moved back in with her mum by this point anyway. I later discovered that her mum had never told Katie and her daughter to leave at all, she had just wanted to move in with me to help start the family she was so desperate to start and had therefore made the whole thing up.

Katie's immediate response to the breakup was to ban me for attending the first scan, but after a lot of petty arguments (something I'm just as guilty of as she was) she caved and allowed me to see our baby for the first time. I came away from that scan so freaking happy! The baby was perfectly healthy and there were no issues and I got a copy of the first ever image of my first child.

Soon after the scan though my happiness was destroyed when Katie vanished. It was almost like she had disappeared from the face of the Earth. No matter how hard I tried, I couldn't find any trace of her. No Facebook, no contact number, no address. I even went and spent a few days in Beverley (the last place she'd been seen) hunting but still couldn't find her. I just wanted a chance to talk to her, tell her that even though I didn't think our relationship worked I was on board to help and support her and our baby. Both, in person and financially.

The run up to the due date was extremely hard for me. I had no idea if the baby was ok or if anything had happened. All I knew from that first scan was that she was due in November 2012.

During that time Kris was a welcome distraction though even if we did get up to some rather stupid antics. This included not only turning up to my sisters 21st birthday party in massive Snoopy (me) and gorilla (Kris) costumes but also travelling to it on the bus and wandering around Tesco's.

22

In our defence it was a fancy dress party but these were something else – the big full body things with fake heads that certainly earned us some rather strange looks (and a free bus ride).

I remember one day in March that year, Kris had come home on leave from the army. It was Mother's Day weekend so we planned to head to town, grab some food and a couple of drinks before picking up some bits for our mums.

I was working the night shift that night and had a strict two-pint rule when it came to work. I'd happily drink during the day if I was working that night but would always stick to a maximum of two pints and be sure to have a few hours' kip before my shift started.

This particular day would soon change that rule... Me and Kris had gone to MaySum (a Chinese all you can eat restaurant) We were sat there having our lunch when I noticed in the shop opposite us (Chinese Laundry) a very brightly coloured Hawaiian shirt on display in the window. I looked at Kris and just said "Any money says you don't have the balls to go and buy that shirt over there and wear it for the rest of the day". He laughed and just like that as soon as we had finished eating we were soon in the shop. Kris agreed to buy and wear the Hawaiian shirt for the rest of the day, just so long as I did the same.

We both bought our funky new shirts but before leaving, we noticed some trilby hats on display. Ok, we need to buy one each! Sure enough, we both changed into our new shirts, put on our trilby hats and proceeded to go and pick something for Mother's Day which was the next day.

Obviously, we got more than a few funny looks. I remember a group of girls walking by, all staring at us and shouting something like "Woooowwww, you guys are so cool!" I didn't know if they were being sarcastic or serious, but I definitely wouldn't have used the word "cool" to describe our look!

We soon found ourselves in another bar. It was about 4/5pm at this point. I needed to be at work by 10:30pm. I decided to grab a couple of shots before I left to help kill the embarrassment. I don't remember much after those shots. I vaguely remember being in a bar with Kris, telling him that I needed to go to work but the rest of the night is a blur. I do remember waking up in my own bed in the early hours the next morning with a string of missed calls from work and a few very angry voicemails from the assistant manager. It turned out; I'd called in "sick" 10 minutes before I was due to start. The manager was really pissed off because she was the one on call and therefore had to cover my shift.

Although it was fairly obvious what had happened, the night was brushed under the carpet. I was lucky I didn't lose my job for that. That particular day is now referred to as "the Hawaiian shirt day" and to this day, I still have my Hawaiian shirt!

Looking back I guess you could say it was around that time in 2012 that things started to change.

"Hawaiian shirt day"

CHAPTER 3

Working towards that "Fresh start"

2012 was definitely, a big year for me.

On November 4th, after working all day, I arrived home to be greeted by my Mum who told me that a mutual friend of Katie's family had contacted her to say that Katie had given birth to a healthy baby girl. Now, I had already accepted that when the day came I wasn't going be there, but that didn't make it any easier to take when it actually happened. Initially I was angry. Thanks to what I felt was Katie's unwarranted selfishness, I had just missed the birth of my first child. That hurt me more than I'll ever be able to describe.

As our friend had told us which hospital they were in I called them that night to see if I could at least get an update on my daughter.

When I finally got through to a midwife on the ward where Katie was, I explained who I was and that I just wanted to know how my daughter was. They asked for the full name of the mother which I provided but I was informed there was nobody there by that name. I was confused, angry and so upset, I mean it didn't make sense as I had been told that was the hospital where they were. I was grateful that my daughter was healthy, but gutted that I hadn't been there.

The same friend who had told me about the birth eventually told me that my daughter had been named Billie and they were even able to get me a picture, although Katie was none the wiser.

Katie was still off the radar and I was spending more and more time either at work or working with the Trust. I couldn't afford to pay for a solicitor so eventually decided to put a claim in to child maintenance against myself. I knew that even though I had no idea where Katie was, being able to pay towards Billie's care might have some form of positive outcome. Besides, what kind of parent would willingly shy away from supporting their child?

Eight weeks after I'd put the claim in, I received a letter from CSA. (Child Support Agency) stating that a parent earning what I was at the time (about £500 a month) should be paying about £68 a month. However, in this case, Katie had refused the offer of any money from me, so the case had been closed. I couldn't believe it - Katie had never worked a day in her life, was on benefits and was being offered money to do absolutely nothing. Why would she refuse that? The only realistic reason I could think of was that, if I was supporting Katie and my daughter financially, I'd have more rights which it seemed she didn't want me to have. The flip side to this though was that the letter contained my daughter's full name which I hadn't known up to that point - Billie Lillie Abbie Maria (and then Katie's surname).

I found it extremely tough not being able to see my daughter or have any information on how she was doing and it was definitely having an impact on my mental health. Looking back, it was around this time that my behaviour also started to change. I can't really say I ever noticed it at the time though but I was starting to become moody for no reason. I wasn't sleeping and I'd often find myself in very depressive moods getting myself completely shit faced and continuously considering killing myself.

I remember towards the end of that year getting a call from the Trust asking me if I wanted to go to London the next day and give a speech to a company named Activsion Blizard. I didn't even need to think about this one, after all this was the gaming company who published most of the PlayStation games I loved. I had a night shift the next day so it meant I'd be doing the event and then coming back home for an hour or two before going straight to work but for an event like this, not sleeping before work was worth it!

The speech went far better than I expected. There were about sixty people stood listening to me talk. By the time I got to the end a couple of the women were in tears. I'd nailed the speech - helping to secure yet another large donation for the Trust in the process.

After a tour of the studio and seeing how the developers made some of their games I was given a huge bundle of games and merchandise as a mark of appreciation. Unlike the box of port I had been given at the clay pigeon shoot, I was permitted by the Trust to keep this.

The following year Les, the man in charge of Young Ambassadors for The Princes Trust in Yorkshire & The Humber, moved to a new role and was replaced by somebody who was intent on following the rules to the letter. No more turning a blind eye which meant he realised that, although I was only supposed to be a Young Ambassador for one year I'd actually been on the books for three. As such me and a few others that had completed their year were brought over to Leeds one evening for a thank you and farewell get together. It was nothing special just a bit of cake, some chit chat and a few photos before we all headed out to town to celebrate properly.

During the night, one of the lads from Sheffield told me about a new job he had been offered within the Trust. A paid job. Something called a "Job Ambassador" This was a new role created within the Trust specifically for those who had been a Young Ambassador. The role itself only came with a one-year contract but it was a role that paid a damn sight more than my job at the petrol station and it seemed like a career boosting role.

The next morning, I made a point of digging up some info about what this job might involve in the hope something similar would be available in Hull. I loved the Princes Trust, so I was determined to snag a job with them if I could.

It was towards the end of 2013 though before I got word that they were now looking for someone to do the role in Hull. As I already knew a Job Ambassador I got in touch with him to get every ounce of information about job I could. We spent a good hour on the phone talking about what the job is and what it involves. Essentially the role would be a one-year contract with the aim to help unemployed 16 – 30-year-olds get back into work, education or training or help them start their own business. A job that I felt had a real purpose and would allow me to help people - I didn't just want the job, I needed it.

During this time I started chatting to a girl named Amy though Facebook. It wasn't long before we were chatting daily and began to talk about a possible first date. One of my friends knew her quite well so I told him that we had mentioned heading out on a date at some point soon. He nearly choked on his drink when I told him.

"Mate, no! Stay well clear of her trust me." He went on to tell me various different stories about her, none of which shed her in a great light. I was fed up of being single though and she did seem genuinely nice to me so I decided not to take his advice – after all they were just stories.

And so Amy and I arranged our first date; just a simple night at a bar with a few games of pool. It went really well and we soon found ourselves in a serious relationship. My family and friends all really liked her too.

In November 2013 things were going so well that Amy and I decided to get our own place. We'd been together for less than six months but it just seemed right and so we moved in to a flat in Old Town. Considering it was only a one bed flat, the place was huge. It wasn't perfect but it definitely served our needs well. Things seemed to be on the up for me.

CHAPTER 4

A fresh start doesn't always bring happiness

In January 2014 I landed an interview for the Job Ambassador role. There were about ten people in all who were selected to attend the full day interview. The morning was spent being briefed by the Line Manager and Supervisor for the role about the job and what it would entail, with the afternoon set aside for interviews. This was by far, the most nerve-racking interview I'd ever been too. I knew that if I failed this, I'd probably be stuck working in retail for the rest of my working days. If I was successful, my options and opportunities would open up greatly.

Everyone being interviewed had already been a Young Ambassador. Hell, I'd even trained and mentored a few of them. I knew that I had a decent shot thanks to being the only person in the country that had already spent three years as a Young Ambassador, with everyone else serving less than a year; but that wasn't enough to give me true confidence. This was a completely new job role. Nobody had ever done this in Hull and the role itself had only existed for a year. This really was anybody's game.

I was the first to be selected for interview in the afternoon. I had a quick can of RedBull before being called in, thinking and hoping that it would kill the nerves. It didn't. If anything, it made them worse!

The interview was surprisingly laid back and quite straight forward, lasting around twenty minutes. I felt that I left on a good note however, when I got out, I quickly noticed that my bloody trouser zipper was wide open. There was no way the pair that interviewed me didn't notice.

I got home and spent the next few hours constantly checking my phone. Had I missed any calls or texts? How long had it been since the last interview would have been?

It was around 4 - 5pm that day when an unknown number called and I knew that this was them. I was almost too scared to answer as getting this job meant the world to me. It would have felt like a lottery win if I actually got it. Failing, however, would have been a huge blow.

I took a few deep breaths to try and calm my nerves and answered to find the caller was the manager, Steph.

"Hello Matt, it's just a quick call about your interview this afternoon." My heart sank.

The way she had started that sentence was pretty clearly the opening to a "you did really BUT..."

She continued "You did really well and I would love to offer you the role of Job Ambassador if you're still interested?"

My response? "

"Holy shit! Yes, I bloody am still interested, thank you!"

Definitely not the best way to make a first professional impression but luckily, Steph saw the funny side and laughed.

I was asked if I could start immediately; I'd been interviewed on the Wednesday and was due to start a week's training in Manchester on the following Monday. The Trust even booked me a hotel for the week to save me rushing about. This meant it was time for an awkward conversation with my boss at the petrol station.

I'd have to tell her that not only was I quitting but I wasn't able to work my notice. I decided to soften the blow by heading to Thornton's and picking up a nice big box of chocolates and a thank you card.

When I turned up at work to tell her what was going to happen she was far from impressed. It's safe to say that the chocolates did not help soften the blow. She tried telling me that I wouldn't be able to just walk out with zero notice. She wanted me to call Steph at the Prince's Trust and ask to be allowed to skip the induction but I couldn't and wouldn't do that. After a very heated conversation, we managed to work out a plan which would see me work the next four Friday and Saturday nights after my induction to try and at least give them some time to replace me.

Monday came quickly and I headed out to Manchester for my one week's training where all food and accommodation was paid for by the Trust. I was the only person in Hull that had the role of Job Ambassador so out of the five of us attending the training, I was the only person outside of Manchester to be there so the training itself was aimed at those working in and around Manchester. I was expected to learn everything that I could and try to adapt it to Hull. I found it quite hard to understand the role itself and most of what was being mentioned about it. I thought it was just a case of being in a new job role and needing to learn something completely new. Looking back, with the benefit of hindsight, I realise that I had been struggling to understand, interpret and remember instructions for tasks for a little while at this point.

With my week of training completed, I came back to Hull to start my new role. For the next month I would work Monday to Friday, 9 - 5 and then work the Friday and Saturday night in the petrol station. During my last shift there, the boss came in to say good luck and goodbye. She handed me a goodbye card and a pen as a parting gift.

The first few months of my new role seemed to go extremely well and I was determined to make something of this opportunity. The job was only for a year so I needed to prove myself to make sure I had a shot at a new role after that within the Trust. This was my first step on the ladder to a much better future.

I was earning more than double what I was at the petrol station and with Amy getting herself a job we decided to start looking for a much bigger and nicer looking house.

For a while, things really did seem to be going great.

Most of my role with the Trust was outreach and networking with the odd day a week spent in the office, catching up with admin and completing reports.

I'd spend most days heading out and about, looking for anywhere that offered 16 – 30 year olds training opportunities so I could link in and identify ways I could help get them into opportunities that would help them in the same way that I had been helped by the Trust. I'd often find myself linking up with places like youth probation and local colleges.

One day, after being with the Trust for a few months I found myself sat in the office, quite bored with nothing that I really needed to do. I jumped on to our intranet and looked through the fundraising challenges page to see what I could take part in.

The Prince's Trust were part of the reason I had any kind of opportunities in life so I wanted to give something back and I felt like I owed them something. There was few of generic things like bake sales and walks and small things like that but none of this really stood out to me at the time. Then all of a sudden, I noticed skydiving.

I'd always said that I would NEVER go skydiving, no matter the reason. I'd never even been in a plane and hated heights so why the hell would I do a skydive? I scrolled on but something about skydiving suddenly stuck out to me. I mean maybe I could just pay the deposit and think about it; I could always change my mind I thought.

I called Kris and mentioned it to him as he'd once mentioned that he'd thought about joining the parachute regiment in the army so I knew he'd definitely be game. He said he'd consider doing it if I did so I spent the next few hours weighing up the pros and cons. The only pro I could think of was money being raised for the Trust but there was a stack of cons.

I called the skydiving centre to see how things worked and what would happen if things went wrong. The guy I spoke to somehow managed to convince me that being pushed out of a plane in mid-air was perfectly safe (apparently) and so within an hour of the call, I bit the bullet and paid the deposit.

I booked it for my birthday, in September which gave me about six months to fundraise and mentally prepare myself and by prepare, I mean watch a stack of YouTube videos about skydiving accidents. It's safe to say, that wasn't my brightest idea to date.

By the time June came though I'd started to lose motivation for my work. It turned out the Trust had not thought about how to make the new Ambassador role work as effectively in Hull as they had in other parts of the country. My line manager was based in Leeds and I had only seen her three times over five months and my senior was based in Gateshead so I was lucky if I saw her more than twice over the year. There was very little support and the lack of direct management made it easier for me slack off and do as I pleased. I needed someone to kick my arse into gear but it seemed that the Trust had almost forgotten about me and Hull in general. It started to feel as though that there was a huge lack of support for Hull within the Trust compared to most parts of the country.

It was during that year - 2014 that I first started to notice my speech was on the decline. I would sometimes forget how to say a word mid-sentence or would occasionally slur my words even when sober however, it was barely noticeable and something I would soon put to the back of my mind.

In July, thinking that our relationship was perfect, I decided it was time to start planning a proposal to Amy. I decided to wait until my next payday go to a fancy jewellery shop and pick out an engagement ring. The funny thing about fate is that sometimes it likes to sneak up behind you and give you the shock of your life in the weirdest of ways.

The week before I was meant to pick up the ring, I was at work in the office, quite happily catching up with that month's reports when out of the blue, I got a message on Facebook from Katie, my daughter's mum. It simply read "Do you want to meet your daughter?"

The message knocked me for six. My mind started racing with reasons as to why she had suddenly decided to make this offer. I was dumbstruck and didn't quite know how to reply and in the end I went with a simple yes before sitting back in my chair and waiting to see what happened next.

"Meet me in 30 minutes at East Park and you can meet her. If you're not here I won't offer again"

I'd never mentioned that I had a daughter to my team at work before. I looked at the person I was working with that afternoon and very briefly told her what had just been said and then told her I was leaving work and wouldn't be back until the next day. I then dropped Amy a quick text explaining what had happened. She was at work but saw the message and simply replied "what the fuck!" I had no idea what context she meant that to be read in, but at the time, I couldn't have cared less. I was about to meet my nearly two-year-old daughter for the first time.

The meet went better than I thought. Obviously, Billie had no idea who I was and was fairly shy at first. We had a little play with a ball while Katie, her mum and her sister watched over us. After about an hour Katie called time on the meet and we spoke briefly about a plan moving forward. Money for her, contact times and dates for me and Billie etc. What annoyed me was the fact that not once did she apologise or offer an explanation for vanishing the way she did.

As angry as I was with her and as much as I wanted to call her every bad name I could think off, I had to bite my tongue and suck it up. I couldn't risk pissing her off and losing Billie, not now.

A few days later, on a Saturday morning, it was time to pick up the engagement ring. Obviously, Amy had no idea what I was planning. I told her that I was heading to town to pick up a new game for my PlayStation and asked her if she wanted anything picking up.

"Yea, I need you to pick up a pregnancy test…" We'd had a pregnancy scare or two in the past and they all came back negative so neither of us were particularly worried so I agreed thinking nothing of it. I went to town picked up the engagement ring and then a pregnancy test. I dropped the ring off at a friend's house so it wouldn't be found by Amy at any point then headed home.

Amy did the test and a few minutes later it actually came back positive. Ermmm..... Nope. I quickly made my way back into town to buy a few more tests as there was no way that test was right - it was wrong, it had to be. I got home and after three more tests when we got two more positives and one unreadable we both realised that we had a baby on the way. In just one week, I was connected with a daughter that had been deliberately hidden away from me, only to then find out I now have another baby on the way, both of which occurring the same week that I had decided to pick up the engagement ring for the upcoming proposal!

Trying to contemplate all of that together at the same time left me with an expression that would resemble a deer in headlights prior to becoming roadkill.

Once the shock of the moment had passed, we were both happy; right up to the point where Amy called her mum who was far from happy to say the least. Disappointed would probably better sum up how she seemed to feel at the time. I get that she was probably just in shock - that or she just didn't like me. Either way, once the shock and emotions calmed, we were both happy.

What had started out as the perfect year was becoming slightly intense. Work was starting to take its toll on me and my mental health and I was starting to think that I wasn't ready for a role like this after all. The Trust very rarely had its own programs running in Hull and I was struggling to find local opportunities that could help the people I was working with. Either that, or I was just really bad at the job.

The run up to the skydive was starting to freak me out too but people had already donated money to see me jump so I was committed whether I liked it or not but I was having plenty of sleepless nights and nightmares about it going wrong. Carrying on watching YouTube videos of skydiving accidents definitely did not help.

As time went on I realised I needed a plan B for when my contract with The Princes Trust ended so I decided to sell my PlayStation so I could pay for a security course. If I couldn't get a job with the Trust before my contract ended I needed something that I could jump straight into because there was no way I was going back on benefits. The company that I used to do the security course with (RDS Training) actually worked out to be a perfect opportunity for me. The owner, Sharron was a great person and ended up becoming a very handy contact for me and the young people I was helping at work.

Around July, I was at a Princes Trust TEAM Program final day presentation that I'd been asked to attend as a speaker with the aim of showing some of those who had just completed the twelve week program that they had a heap of potential. Coming from someone who had been on that very same program and had been through some struggles in life proved to be quite effective. I gave them the same speech that I would use back in my Young Ambassador days.

Once the presentations had finished and the afternoon was completed I was approached by a lady who had come to see one of the young people she supported do his own presentation. She explained that she worked in a local young person's hostel and that my story had struck a chord with her. She asked if I would mind popping over to the hostel and giving that same speech to some of the residents in the hope it would inspire them. I agreed. The idea of using my story to once again help people that may be in a similar position to what I was back when I was their age seemed great!

I'd been asked to do said speech during an evening as that was the best time to catch everyone when they were up and about. With it being late in the day, I wasn't going to be paid for my time, this was strictly voluntary but I didn't care. I loved the idea of sharing my story in the hope it would help people.

When I turned up that evening I was met by one of the workers who seemed genuinely nice. He made a point of making sure there was a good number of people to hear me speak and stuck around to make sure that all eyes and ears were on me.

The speech seemed to go down quite well, there were around fifteen people who turned up to hear me speak. After some time spent chatting with some of the residents about parts of my story, the why's and how's etc. I went home but something about that place had struck a chord with me. I had never thought to work with homeless hostels before but I soon found myself spending a couple of evenings a week at the hostel as a way of being able to catch some of the younger residents and talking to them about some of the upcoming courses the Trust had or some other local opportunities that I could get them involved with.

The more time I spent at the hostel the more I'd get to know how the place ran and what the staff were like. Some evenings, I'd be there for a couple of hours and not meet one person but would be stood having a good old chin wag with the staff instead.

Eventually during one of my quieter evenings, the two staff on shift both mentioned that there were jobs available at the hostel and that I should apply. They made a point of saying that if I were to apply for a job I'd have to have an interview but would most definitely get the job. I was known to all the staff and management in the hostel and was liked. The job was a zero-hour contract which meant I'd be able to work there, promote the Trust and help support more young people that would roll over into my main job and I'd still be paid for it; to me it was a no brainer. I applied for the Locum role, had the interview and bagged the job after what was by far, the easiest interview I'd ever had.

I soon sound myself working seven days a week; five with the Trust, doing 9am - 5pm and then I'd work the Friday and Saturday night shift at the hostel before heading back to do the Sunday 2pm - 10pm shift. It worked out to be around 70 hours a week with no days off.

Amy had left her job due, in part to being pregnant and I didn't mind picking up the slack. If I worked seven days a week we'd easily have more than enough money to keep us going comfortably until March when our baby was due.

Before I knew it September arrived and the skydive was looming. I was genuinely terrified and the night before I didn't manage to get any sleep at all. Amy and I took the train over to Bridlington and met the rest of my family at the jump site but, after about six hours of sitting around waiting the instructors called the jump off due to the clouds. I was almost relieved. It was rebooked for the next weekend, (Saturday 28th) I remember on the Friday before the rescheduled jump, I'd started working in a new hostel owned by the company I already worked for. This hostel, unlike the one I had started in and was for adults only rather than young people and was a completely different kind of set up.

I got talking to an older guy who had worked there for years and had been showing me the ropes throughout the day. Towards the end of the shift I told him that I had my skydive booked in for the next day; the weather was meant to be perfect for the whole day so it would be extremely unlikely that it would be called off again. I told him that I was at the point where I was tempted to call it off myself and that a part of me really didn't want to do it. He looked at me and without any hesitation he said.

"You only ever regret what you don't do in life." I'm not sure why but those words stuck with me. To this day I firmly believe that and do my best to live by it.

The next day was jump day and the nerves were very much still an issue. Regardless of repeating "you only ever regret what you don't do" over and over in my head I really didn't want to be lobbed out of a plane and still couldn't work out why I thought booking it in the first place had been a good idea.

I spent the morning watching other people doing their jumps and nobody seemed to be nervous or worried apart from me. A couple of jumps in front of me a girl landed and came running over to her family, she was so happy that she had done it and was obviously very excited. Trailing behind her was the instructor she'd been attached to for the jump. As he was walking over he looked at another instructor, blew a sigh of relief and said.

"That was a bit too close, that one mate." I had no idea what he meant by that and he walked away with the other instructor before I could hear the rest of the story so I could only imagine what had happened to him and the girl to seemingly worry him. Twenty minutes later, my name was called. It was go time!

I'd paid extra to have a cameraman do the jump with me. Obviously, for a first timer - skydiving is done as a tandem with an experienced skydiver. Just to make things a little more interesting I'd decided to do the jump in a bear onesie.

I'd done some of the fundraising wearing it so decided to roll with it or in this case - fly with it! Hell, it looked a lot better than the overalls I'd have had to wear instead.

My pre jump interview

Before we got in the plane there as a quick interview with the instructor for the video. Just a quick, how do you feel and why are you here doing this kind of thing.

Watching the video back now you can see just how nervous I was and my terrible attempts to hide it. Interview done; it was time to jump in the plane. I'd never in all of my life set foot in a plane before.

Imagine knowing that the first time you get into a plane, somebody is going chuck you out of it at a height of two miles!

As I was first in I was to be the last one to 'jump' out. Just before we took off a woman jumped in, sat in front of me and started talking me through what was going to happen. I think the other instructors had realised just how terrified I was and had asked her to calm me down as we flew up to the jump zone. Something I was pretty grateful for to be honest.

Take off wasn't as bad as I thought it would be – in fact it was quite smooth. When we hit 2000ft, the lady looked at me and said.

"Don't worry Matt, now that we're at 2,000ft, if anything happens to the plane we'll jump out and use our reserve chutes. You'll only break your legs."

I knew she was joking but that was exactly the opposite kind of conversation I wanted to have on my first plane ride!

When we hit 5,000ft she opened up with a similar line.

"Don't worry Matt, if anything happens to the plane now, we'll jump out and use the main chute and we should be fine!" Seriously, first time in a plane that has no seats or seatbelts a conversation about said plane getting into trouble bad enough to warrant jumping out is not the kind I really wanted to have.

As we approached 10,000ft (two miles high) Sarah told me that as soon as I realised the door to the plane was open I should start shouting and swearing as much as possible. She then explained that my instructor would be placing his hand in front of my eyes to stop me seeing the first few people jump out.

No sooner than she had told me that, the instructor I was attached to blocked my sight with his hand. I then heard a couple of people shouting "DOOR OPEN! DOOR OPEN!" followed by the sound of a surreal amount of wind blowing into the plane, before being edged forwards towards the door. As we were moving closer, I kept saying very loudly that I needed to stop and think this through! Like a true wuss, I had my eyes firmly closed all the way to the door.

Prevented from seeing the plane door open!

Obviously they ignored me and the fact I was strapped to the instructor meant it didn't really matter what I said - one way or the other, I was "jumping" out of that plane. I remember feeling my legs dropping out of the plane all the time me telling the instructor to bring me back in. Suddenly the plane tilted, with my eyes still closed I instantly thought that we had left the plane so I opened my eyes only to find that we hadn't yet left the plane! As I opened my eyes, the instructor jumped and with that, my eyes closed up tight again! (with me screaming like a child all the way out).

As we were falling, I suddenly felt an overwhelming urge to open my eyes and I am so glad I did.

Try as I might, I just can't seem to find the words to describe just how incredible free fall is.

We were plummeting to the ground at over 120mph and rather than screaming like I was back in the plane I was hit with this incredible feeling of euphoria. I felt invincible, nothing could kill me. Hell, as hard as it is to believe, it actually didn't feel like I was falling, more like I'd been suspended in mid-air. It was an incredible feeling that I honestly believe everyone should try to experience at least once in their life.

Once the parachute had opened there was some time to glide, taking in the views of Bridlington - again just a really nice, surreal experience.

Coming in to land was actually scary, out of nowhere, the instructor started screaming "LEG'S UP" over and over as we

were coming in. When coming in to land during a skydive, you're falling at around 30mph. Imagine falling to the ground at that kind of speed only to land on your legs, your walking days would come to a short sharp end! The idea is come in with your legs up in the air, so you come in on your arse with a slight skid. It's honestly not as bad as it sounds.

Once we'd landed and I was unhooked, the lady from the plane came over and hugged me, gave me the whole "well done and congratulations speech" before we all headed back to the waiting area.

Another skydiver came over to me and said that he'd just heard that this was my first time in a plane. He looked genuinely shocked and asked if it was true. When I told him it certainly was, he shook my hand. Suddenly, I realised just how ridiculously crazy what I had just done was.

In the end, I raised £550 for the Princes Trust. Not a great figure but I was and still am actually proud to have done so.

Unfortunately life didn't continue on that high though and by December, my life was starting to fall apart. I had a new manager with my Princes Trust role and it was becoming more obvious that I wasn't the right fit for the job - both to me and to management.

I'd gotten to the point where I was almost terrified of going to work. Every time I spotted an email or text from my boss, I'd be too scared to open it. It turns out that anxiety is a fucker. It's even more of a fucker when you think that dealing with it on your own is the best way to get through it. Spoiler alert - it's not.

By mid-January 2015 I realised that I couldn't actually maintain both the job with the Trust and the one at the hostel and I decided to call it quits with the Trust. I only had about 6 weeks of my contract left but I left without completing it with no real notice which I hated myself for. The Princes Trust had done so much for me in the past and had helped shape me to be the man I was but I knew that I had to go sooner rather than later. Looking back, I do wish things had ended on a better note though.

CHAPTER 5

First life saved and the break up.

Within days of leaving the Trust I found myself another job working in a petrol station and once again working night shifts. No sooner had I started the new job, I was offered an interview for a full time role in the hostel. Not only was it full time it was salary pay and much more than I had ever earned before. There were about five people being interviewed for the job - all with a damn site more experience than me. As I did for every interview I'd been to I brought a CV with me and all my past training certificates.

I didn't think I would get the job but I wanted to make good impression either way.

While I waited for the call back about the interview I continued to crack on with my new job at the petrol station. It was a 15-mile bike ride there and back but not only did it mean I could support me, Amy and Billie, it was also a much easier job with a lot less stress than the one at the Trust. Less stress of course meant less money and with Amy not working we soon lost the house but luckily we managed to get a house though the council last minute thanks, in part to Amy being pregnant.

I'd finished my training/shadow shifts at the petrol station when I got a call to say that I'd passed the interview at the hostel for a full-time night role with an immediate start. After a very awkward phone call with the boss at the petrol station which played out quite similar to the other petrol station I left, it was time to get some sleep in preparation for my first shift at the hostel. A job that came with more money than I'd ever earned, more opportunities and of course, a real purpose!

In March 2015, not long after we'd moved into the new house Amy went into labour. It wouldn't be long before I'd finally be able to meet my little man.

The birth was fairly straight forward, Amy had opted for a water birth and after a few long hours Jack arrived. Watching him enter the world and be pulled out of the water was quite possibly the single most amazing thing I have ever seen and is a feeling I don't think anybody can describe in words. It's a moment I'll never forget!

Jack was born at 23:46 on March 19th 2015 and I remember "Uptown Funk" was playing on the radio. Thanks to it being so late when we were all sorted, around 3am I was sent home and told to come back later that morning.

Getting Jack home was a surreal moment. Just seeing him and being able to actually cuddle him was a feeling I can't describe.

A couple of days after Jack was born, it was Amy's birthday, her 21st birthday in fact and so I decided to go all out and bought her a spa day package for her and her mum and a sunset hot air balloon ride with champagne for the summer.

After months of holding on to the engagement ring trying to think of the best way to propose, I finally came up with what I thought would be the best kind of proposal.

Amy and I had one of our best dates in The Deep - a sea life Centre in Hull. I reached out to the managing team at The Deep and told them that I was planning to propose and that I wanted to do it there. After some planning I opted to pay them to send a diver down during one of the shark feeding shows and hold up a sign with her name on it, asking the question.

It was our two-year anniversary and the plan was for us both to be at The Deep by 11am. We'd walk around with Jack, before sitting down to watch the shark feeding show. Something I hadn't thought about was that it was a bank holiday and the place was rammed! There was around fifty people all sat down watching with Amy and I close to the front. About ten minutes in to the show, one of the divers pretended to struggle pulling food out of his shark food bucket and I knew this was my cue to get ready. The diver then removed the sign and held it up for everybody to see - a huge gasp came from the audience. With that, I was down on one knee, ring in hand and asking that all so famous question... After waiting for what felt like an eternity, she said yes. I thought I would finally be getting my Happily Ever After....... again though – that turned out not to be the case......

Not long after I started working full time at the hostel an opportunity for a promotion to a night shift supervisor came up and I soon had an interview date set. There were only two people in the running, me and a guy I worked with called Mike. To me Mike was an absolute legend. It was thanks to him that I stood a chance in the interview for my current role in the first place, so I felt like a bit of dick going for the same job as him but knew that it would be a great leg up for me within the company. Plus, I needed the extra money so it was a no brainer really.

I was working the night before the interview but my slot was scheduled for late the next afternoon which meant I'd have plenty of time to sleep beforehand. So I decided there was no real reason to book the shift off, plus not only did it mean I could hammer out some revision for the interview but I was also on shift with Rachel who I had become good friends with and she'd offered to run me though some practice questions to help me prepare. It was a win win.

I remember walking into work that night after handover and sitting down with Rachel reception, I looked at her and said "easy night tonight, mate!" She agreed. It didn't take long before we both knew it wouldn't be the quiet shift we'd hoped for. Around 12am just as things would normally start to get quiet, a resident came down to tell us that he had been robbed. He explained that he had been in someone else's room and left his door unlocked. Living at the hostel and in receipt of benefits, he had been working full time - something we all knew but turned a blind eye to. He was working so he could save enough money for a deposit/first month's rent for a house as he didn't want to wait for the council to sort him out. Over six months he'd managed to save £1000 and had the entire amount in his room in cash. Had any of the other residents come and told me this I wouldn't have believed them but having seen this guy get up and go to work every morning I knew he was being truthful. I checked the CCTV and found that one of our residents had in fact let herself in to his room. Obviously, we couldn't see what she had done in there but you could clearly see the big smile on her face as she left his room. She'd left the building an hour before this guy even realised what had happened. He knew it was her, I didn't need to tell him that. He and a gang of about ten other residents wanted blood, they were ready to kill her. Literally.

Not long after things had calmed down, I started to type up a report of what had happened when out of nowhere we heard a loud bang from above us. We put it down to a resident just moving things around in their room but we turned out to be completely wrong... A minute later one of our female residents came down, smiled at us and said "see ya later guys."

We thought nothing of it at the time, I mean why would we? A few more minutes went by before we started to hear something outside. It wasn't overly loud but it was enough for me to step out and have a nosey. There was a big pile of broken glass on the floor, I looked up and saw that a resident's window was completely shattered with bits of glass falling from the window.

It turned out that the woman who had left with a smile on her face, had in fact chucked a fridge at the window. Had the window not been a reinforced, the fridge would have gone straight through but it had still caused several hundred pounds worth of damage. We never did get a solid answer as to why she had done it though.

I called it in to our maintenance team as an emergency repair and began to start writing an incident report. No sooner had I started typing when another resident came down and started heading out of the front door saying the resident in the room next to him wouldn't shut up and if we hadn't sorted them out by the time he got back, he would. He made it sound like whoever he was talking about was having a party. I looked over to Rachel and told her that I'd sort it if she finished the smashed window report and the report for the stolen money.

I took my time heading up to the room I needed to check out on the second floor. As I approached the room, I realised that this was the same room of the man who had been robbed earlier. At the same moment I realised whose room it was, I heard a woman screaming for help.

"Fuck, this guy is attacking a woman in his room!" Instead of knocking on the door, I slammed it open. I thought that I was about to find him pinning her down on the floor or against a wall with the way she was screaming. Whatever I was going to do, it had to be fast. I was ready to have to crack him over the head with my radio if needed. As I got through the door, instead of seeing this woman being attacked like I thought, I found that the guy was on floor with a needle in his arm and his lips turning blue. The woman was slapping and shouting at him, trying to wake him but he was unconscious, unresponsive and not breathing. It only took me a couple of seconds to realise that this guy was close to death and I instantly went into auto pilot. I dragged the woman out of the way, called 999 for an ambulance, and gave a very quick rundown of what I could see and where we were before starting CPR.

After a few seconds I heard a crack and stopped, panicking that I'd done something wrong before realising that I'd just broken one of his ribs. Ok, carry on I thought. After what felt like hours but was barley a few minutes, three paramedics walked in. I handed over to them expecting them to start using a defibrillator on him. To my surprise, their first reaction was to grab a needle from their kit - I didn't have a clue what they were doing. They jabbed him with something I'd later find out is called "Naloxone" in short, a simple drug that counters the effects of all opioid drugs. After two shots, nothing happened. I was stood there thinking I must have done the CPR wrong, maybe the pause cost him his life, was this my fault? After the third shot of Naloxone, the fucker shot up, screaming like he'd just been electrocuted! Truth be told, I shit myself but he soon calmed down. After a few questions from the medics and a once over, they told him that he'd need to be taken to hospital which he refused saying he had no intention of leaving. I was ready to punch him.

"You are fucking going, mate! After what I've just done for you, you can at least get checked over!" He didn't even realise that he had been given CPR until I told him.

"Ohhhh! Is that why my chest hurts then?"

"Yes mate, I broke one of your fucking ribs!" I was quite pissed off now but thankfully he soon changed his mind and agreed to go to hospital.

Thanks to the resident who stormed off complaining about the noise in that guy's room, had I not given him CPR and the medics not injected him with the Naloxone when they did he would have probably died that night. It's really that simple although I never did get a thank you from him.

Once he'd been taken away I went to the office, locked the door and closed the blinds before breaking down and crying my eyes out. The shock and adrenaline from what had just happened hit me like a train. I was crying and shaking when Rachel checked in over the radio. I told her I was having a breather and she seemed to know that I needed a minute so left me to it.

Of all the first aid courses I'd done prior to that incident, not one of them warned about the effects of dealing with life and death incidents. I couldn't wrap my head around the fact I'd just saved a man's life. The thought of seeing him lying there, almost dead and then suddenly alive and kicking just sent my head into a spin. I eventually managed to pull myself together and cracked on with the rest of the shift. In all the time I worked in that hostel up to that point, I'd never heard of anyone having a shift like that. It really was the definition of the shift from hell but somehow, both me and Rachel nailed it!

The morning after the shift had finished, I got a call from work. My boss had obviously read the reports from the night before and couldn't believe it. She offered to let me come in a week or so later for my interview but I was determined to get it done.

It ended up becoming more of a debrief than an actual interview. Over two hours, my manager and area manager spent about 80% of the time talking about how the previous night went and how I felt, congratulating me on saving a life.

Once the interviews had concluded for some reason it took two months for a decision to be made. It turned out that the area manager had decided to offer it to someone he felt was better suited who had just started working for the company and offered the job to them. I was disappointed to say the least and felt that was a bit of a shady move but I soon realised that the company's values and integrity were not exactly aligned with my own.

Over the next few months things between me and Amy started to become toxic. She banned me from taking Jack out on my own as she'd decided that I would leave and never come back with him and soon after she stopped my family from having contact with him too. If I told her that any of my family would be visiting, she'd disappear with Jack, always having a place to be or something else important to do. There would also be nights that she would take Jack out for long drives with her friends. I had a strong suspicion that she was seeing somebody else but, like a mug I never acted on it.

There was one afternoon, I'd just finished work and had been invited out to a coffee shop with Rachel and her partner. Some of my friends were starting to see things weren't going well so would try to get me out of the house to talk about what was actually going on. It wouldn't be long before Rachel and her partner got a real insight into what was happening at home. Within ten minutes of being in the cafe, Amy called.

"Where are you?"

"Just in town at such and such a cafe with Rachel and her boyfriend." No sooner had I finished answering her, she started screaming down the phone, shouting that she knew I was fucking Rachel and not really in a cafe. I tried talking, but couldn't get a word in - she sounded possessed, screaming, shouting and swearing. I put her on speaker so the two could hear what was being said – even when Rachel's boyfriend spoke up and said "Matt is definitely not having sex with my girlfriend in this cafe" (it was quite hard not to laugh at that point!) she still refused to believe me.

Moments like this became all too common over the next few months. At the time, I put it down to hormones and stress but looking back I think there may have been more to it. I probably should have left much earlier than I did but that's the thing about hindsight. It's always a "shoulda, coulda, woulda" kind of deal.

By the time October came things hadn't even come close to improving. If anything, we were only together for Jack's sake. I was worried about leaving her though because I had a sinking feeling that she would play the same kind of game as Billie's mum and disappear with another one of my children. One night in late October, we were caught up in yet another argument. Jack was sat in the living room so it was an argument without the shouting, just snide comments and the usual rubbish from the pair of us. During said argument, Amy looked over to Jack, then me and said.

"I can't believe I had something as beautiful as him (looking at Jack) with something as vile and disgusting as you..."

There was something about how she had said that and the way she had used Jack as an example that just made my blood boil. I snapped back.

"Ok, we are finished" I left before either of us could say anything else. After a walk and a chance to think I came home and told her that I had had enough. Neither of us could carry on like that and it wasn't fair on Jack. A few days later, I moved out and went back to my parents.

CHAPTER 6

Monkey

When I moved back in with my parents, I felt like I'd taken a few steps back, like a failure. Twenty-six years old and having to live with my parents. I felt quite pathetic actually. As time went on, I began to sink lower and lower.

Me and Amy, we're on good terms. Not long after I'd left her, she was soon in another relationship. She later admitted that she had been seen this person for a while, while we were together. It didn't matter by this point. We both knew that weren't right for each other anyway. One way or the other, we both needed to move on...

I remember being at work one night with a fairly new locum worker. A call came in saying that one of our residents had just text his friends a "goodbye text" telling them he was going to kill himself. He was on the third floor so I figured the main risk was that he may try to jump out of his window.

I remember getting to his door, realising that his door was locked I put my key in his lock and announcing that I (staff) was coming in. With that, I heard.

"Open that fucking door and I'll slash your thought, cut my wrists and jump out this window!

"Fuck, now what!?"

I backed off, radioed down to the other staff member I was on shift with and told her to call the police and let them know that we had a possible active suicide attempt in progress.

I stayed by the door, keeping the guy talking. He was about twenty so still a kid. I started talking about my own mental health struggles and how I found life during and after my last three suicide attempts. It was a risky move but I wanted to show him that I had a genuine understanding of the position that he was actually in. It worked, even though he still wouldn't open the door to me, we talked though the door. It took the police at least half an hour to show up. They tried to walk in the way I had by telling the kid who they were before putting the keys in the lock. Once again, he warned what he would do if anyone tried to enter. The officers backed off and called in their sergeant. He was met with the same response so decided to call for a negotiator.

This had been going on for almost two hours by now and even with three police officers there, nothing had changed so I decided to carry on talking to this kid as I had a decent enough rapport with him by now. After another half an hour of talking, I asked him if I could come and sit with him. Finally, he agreed! I wasn't worried about myself as the police were there. I knew I was fine; I just needed this kid to be safe. Once we had gotten into the room, the police removed a large knife. He wasn't messing about. We spent some time talking that night and soon had a plan for him to move forward with helping his mental health. This was the first time I had ever been faced with a situation like this. I may have saved a life but just like before, with CPR I found processing the incident quite hard. Those kinds of situations are actually incredibly mentally draining.

In fact the job was fairly mentally draining most of the time. So when I had things like momentary lapses in memory that's what I put it down to – being tired and drained.

In November 2016 I decided to do my CBT so I could ride a motorbike up to an engine size of 125cc to make getting around easier for me and I brought myself a motorbike a month later, although I soon started to realise just how much of a bad idea me being on the road was. Seriously, I was shocking - I couldn't seem to grasp how road signs worked or what they meant no matter how much I read the Highway Code. It turned out that I was better at stalling the damn thing than I was actually riding it and I lost count of how many times I nearly crashed it!

Exactly 4 weeks after I'd brought the bike (and somehow not ended up dead) I came home from work in a stinking mood one day. I was drained, run down and just genuinely pissed off. I parked up in front of the house and being in the rush I was to get to bed only applied the steering lock. I actually left the main chain, lock and alarm in the seat box.

Obviously, it was stolen overnight and because I was stupid enough to admit to the insurance company that I had voided my insurance by not locking it up correctly or placing it in the garage, they wouldn't pay out. Just to add insult to injury though the police eventually recovered my bike – or should I say what was left of it which was more or less just the engine and I ended up with a bill for its "recovery"

None of this was a great time for me, I found that within weeks of the break up and moving back to my parents, I fell back in the deeper side of depression. I'd started self-harming again at every opportunity I could too so before long I was back to wanting to kill myself.

The ironic and quite destructive thing about depression is that you quickly learn to become an amazingly great actor when you're around those that care. You learn how to let those around you only see what you want them to see which, in my case was the "normal, happy go lucky, Matt". I also hadn't told many people about my change in circumstances or living condition which made hiding my depression a little easier as nobody had any reason to think there were any issues.

One day, my boss Jo, walked passed me and asked how I was in passing. Something about my face must have given her an inkling that something was wrong and before I could even answer, she invited me into the office to talk. I don't know what it was about that instance but before I knew it I was telling her everything.

She seemed more shocked than anything; suddenly, part of her team was in a similar position to a lot of our residents. We ended the conversation with her setting me up with a counsellor via work and making sure I took a couple of weeks off work to "de-stress" and get some R&R.

I left work later that day and got myself an appointment with a doctor. After a quick conversation about how I was mentally, I was hooked up with a course of anti-depressants. I was given a month's supply but once I'd finished them I decided not to go back for more as I felt they weren't working for me.

It wasn't long though before I started my counselling though work. I'd always stuck my nose up to the idea of counselling, to me the idea of sitting in front of a complete stranger, talking about the shit that's making me feel crap just didn't appeal to me, so I turned up for my first session not really expecting much.

The counsellor was a guy named Dom, he was in his early 50s and studying counselling at university. Part of the final part of his course required him to get "contact hours" with clients. He'd chosen to work with the homeless as a means to help with their journey moving forward in life. Jo had arranged for me to have six sessions with him to try and help get my head in shape.

To my surprise there was something about Dom, the way he spoke and came across that made it so bloody easy to talk to him. Over the first session, I managed to talk about so much and felt like so much weight had been lifted from my shoulders. All the fears of being judged, patronised and otherwise just made to feel like an idiot soon went away.

The six sessions came and went quickly and on the last session, Dom offered me the chance to keep coming in and continuing the sessions - I was so relieved. During most of the sessions it felt like I just waffled on and talked about shit but Dom didn't seem to mind. It was almost like he could listen to me talk rubbish over an hour and still manage to see what I was actually trying to talk about and offer practical solutions to some of the issues I'd mentioned over the hour.

Just when I was starting to get my mental health back under some level of control Katie decided to go off the radar again. It appeared she had decided that she didn't want me in her or Billie's life - I didn't and still don't understand why as to me there didn't appear to be any real reason for it.

After months of trying to get her back on side and let me see Billie again, Dom recommended that I send Katie a letter which was something I'd never thought to do before. I wasn't overly keen on the idea but I trusted him so decided to give it a shot, after all I had nothing to lose at this point. I told Dom that I was dyslexic and that my handwriting was terrible so he offered to write the letter as I dictated it to him. It was a small gesture but it meant a lot to me at the time.

Surprisingly the letter actually worked and Katie got back in touch a week or so later. I didn't get any explanation but she was happy to move forward again.

Things after that with both Amy and Katie stayed fairly mutual for some time. I would finish a night shift, head to Amy's for around 07:30am so I could wake Jack up, feed him and get him ready for the day to come – I was happy to do whatever was needed as it was nice to be able to spend some real time with him. In fact many of those mornings are some of favourite memories of that year.

I had every other weekend off work so I'd take advantage and have Billie. We'd go to Amy's and both spend some quality time with Jack. I loved watching the pair of them play and laugh together. Looking back at moments like that even now, always puts a smile on my face.

Around June, I remember being sat in my room one day thinking about where I was in life. What I had and didn't have and I realised that I needed to do something. Something had to give way and change as I couldn't keep going round in circles any longer. I realised that I needed to change my perspective and it needed to be a drastic one at that if I was going to sort my head out.

I started thinking about my bucket list. Something that had always been on it was volunteering abroad. I have no idea where the idea came from and no idea why I decided to spend any time thinking about it but there I was, typing in "volunteering overseas" on Google. The first option that popped up was volunteering in a monkey sanctuary in South Africa. Boom, perfect I thought to myself. Working between five and seven days a week overseas with people who didn't know me and wouldn't judge me on any of my past fuck up's.

Without even thinking about it, doing any research or even booking the time off work, I booked and paid for a three week trip there and then to leave in August which was a couple of months away. I'd been in so much of a rush to book the trip, I'd not even stopped to think that I didn't even own a passport. Luckily for me, I managed to get one sorted not long before my departure date.

I'd never left the country before, I knew nothing about South Africa hell, working with monkeys? What the hell had I let myself in for? As nervous as I was about being in another country, there was also the fear of actually flying. The only plane I'd ever been on I was chucked out of mid-air. It's safe to say I was slightly fucking petrified! Looking back, I can't help but laugh at myself for such an irrational fear but there I was, more worried about flying than I was about the whole monkeys in South Africa thing! This turned out to have a massive impact on my life though which we will come back to shortly.

While I waited for my departure date I carried on looking for other things to occupy my time and give me a feeling of purpose. Around July I spotted an opportunity to do my first Tough Mudder - all I knew about it at the time was that it was a 10-mile obstacle course that involved getting fairly muddy. I signed up for the closest event in Skipton which would be held a couple of weeks before I would leave for SA. I chose to take the opportunity to raise some money for charity and went with the one the meant a lot to me and was also their partner charity - Help for Hero's.

I decided to take the opportunity to do more fundraising in the run up to the actual event - a bake sale and a few pies in the face later and I'd raised about £200. Not too much but every bit helps and it was for a good cause.

With everything I was doing to keep busy my Tough Mudder event seemed to come around quite fast. I'd managed to do absolutely zero training. It'd be fair to say the thought of hitting the start line alone and feeling so underprepared had left me pretty damn nervous – I had no idea what I'd let myself in for. Nevertheless, I made it to Skipton and hit the start line.

A quick selfie before hitting the start line

I nailed the first few obstacles on my own with no issues and I soon realised that although most of the people I was coming across were also solo runners. Even so everybody was helping each other get over, under and though every obstacle. Strangers going out of their way to help other strangers. I loved this! I remember getting to an obstacle called "Blockness Monster" in short, it's a long deep pool of water (neck/chin deep for me) that you swim/wade your way across before you are met by a long, thick and heavy rectangular shaped block that covers the full width of the pool. The idea is to work together as a team with a group pushing the block form one side and pulling from the other while a few hold on to the top moving them over to the other side.

On the first of the two blocks I must have stayed for about twenty minutes just helping to push the block round and round, getting more and more people over. Eventually an older guy came by, he helped for a few minutes and then out of nowhere he shouted at me to hold on and get my arse moving!

Eventually, I hit a rather large log carry. Clearly, I couldn't do this on my own so I waited to see if I could spot any other solo runners. Within in a minute, two girls appeared out of nowhere. "Are you on your own!?" They asked. "Sure am!" "Do you want to join our team?" Sure thing! I couldn't believe it - I was now part of an actual team!

I soon found out their names were Elizabeth and Katie and that Elizabeth had already done one TM the year before. Over the rest of the course me and Elizabeth managed to get some really good conversations going and I mentioned that I was due to go to SA later that month. Elizabeth told me that she had been to Cape Town not that long ago. She gave me a quick rundown of what to expect and what it's like over there which I really appreciated. When we came close to the finish line I realised what the last obstacle was. "EST" (Electric Shock Therapy) Essentially, the idea is to run through a long corridor that has electric wires dangling from the top of a frame. You run though hoping that you miss the cables that carry up to 10,000 volts but deep down, you know you're going to get shocked.

"Just run as fast as you can!" I shouted at Katie! It was only as I was running though that I noticed there were some hay bales at the half way point intended to make you stop and step over or run and jump. Just as I prepared to jump, I thought to myself it was odd that I hadn't been shocked at the exact moment that I heard a crack, followed by an instant shock down my arm. I'd been shocked by one of the cables as I tried to jump the hay bale and I ended up face planting the extremely muddy floor! Once we cleared EST it was time to head on over to the finish line and collect our headband, t-shirt and of course, a free "finishers cider" (which tasted absolutely disgusting, I must say!) After a few photos with my newly formed team and a quick wash it was time to head home.

I felt absolutely amazing having completed the whole course. For me, it was an achievement and for probably the first time I my life, I was actually proud of myself.

At the finish line with my new team

The few weeks between my Tough Mudder and my departure for South Africa I'd often find myself feeling guilty and worrying about how my kids would view the decision to go when they grew up. There were a few occasions where I found myself questioning what I was actually doing and whether I should just cancel the whole trip.

I spoke to Dom about it in almost every session. He always managed to remind me that the kids were too young to really understand that I had gone away. He also reminded me that I would be gone three weeks and that it wasn't really that long. Hell, this wasn't a holiday, it was a working trip that was going to hopefully kick me back in to normality.

I remember trying to sort my kit out the week before I left. My niece had come to stay at my parents for the weekend. She had left all of her toys all over the place and I remember seeing a little PG Tips monkey amongst her toys. I instantly realised that this little monkey would make the perfect little travel mascot so I quickly nabbed the monkey and strapped it to my luggage giving him the imaginative name of "Monkey" and with that it was almost time to leave for what would soon become a life changing experience!

CHAPTER 7

Riverside - A Life Changing Experience

Departure day came around much faster than I expected. The flight was from Manchester Airport, I was flying to Doha then from there I'd fly out to Johannesburg -a total flight time of about 18 hours. The flights weren't nearly as bad as I'd expected minus some rough turbulence on the first flight - looking back I'm not sure why I was so scared of flying.

I remember clearing customs and not having a clue where I was meant to go in order to catch my shuttle over to a hotel I'd pre booked. Thankfully though it wasn't long before a porter stopped me and offered to show me where to go. Obviously, he wanted a fee for the privilege of helping me though. It took him a grand total of two minutes to walk me where I needed to be for which I ended up paying him about £15, essentially all he did was walk me out of the airport while also trying his best to convince me to buy weed from him. (In a bloody airport of all places).

Once I'd made it to the hotel and settled in I decided it was time to head out and explore. I asked the hotel receptionist which direction I'd need to walk in order to get into the local town. She looked at me as if I'd asked the most ridiculous kind of question.

"You can't go to town on your own sir! I'll get you a driver".

I wasn't too sure why she was so worried about me taking a half hour walk to town but figured a cab wouldn't be too much money.

When the driver arrived, he introduced himself "Hello, my name is Welcome".

I miss understood him and thought he was greeting me by saying welcome. A few minutes of awkwardness later, Welcome explained that he would be willing to drive me around Jo'Burg for the next few days. He was essentially offering to be my personal driver which seemed pretty cool.

As we drove into town, I soon realised why the receptionist was so set on me not walking into town. The area on the way seemed to resemble rough looking shanty towns that I'd have had to walk through to get where I needed to be - I would have stood out like a sore thumb. In a city with one of the highest crime rates in the world, a city that's regarded as one of the most dangerous in the world, I had wanted to take a stroll in to town on my own.

The three days in Jo'Burg seemed to be just what I needed, I managed to catch a movie (Suicide Squad) and head out to "The Lion Park" - essentially a Centre dedicated to caring for lions, cheetahs and giraffes, funded by tourists. The place was amazing – over the course of a day I managed to grab some cuddles with lion cubs who all seemed hell bent on biting and scratching the hell out of me. then take an hour out for a Cheetah walk. This was an opportunity for just a few people to go on a walk with one of the adult cheetahs. For this walk, we would be with Judie - a one eyed cheetah - she had been found trapped in a giant thorn bush with one of her eyes stuck in a thorn.

I remember being sat in a truck waiting to head out for the cheetah walk when a man approached me.

"I bet you're from England, aren't you!?"

"Yes mate, I am, how did you know?"

"Well, nobody has a pair of legs that white and skinny unless they're from the UK. It's pretty obvious".

He had a good point to be fair. We got talking and he mentioned that I might have seen him on TV (I hadn't) and asked me if I'd heard of a show called "Wild at Heart" I had but never really watched it. He told me that he was the vet on that particular show.

I think he was trying to name drop his own name hoping that I would ask for an autograph no doubt which I never did. I actually thought he was taking the piss and that he hadn't been on TV at all. I later googled him (Stephen Tomkinson) and it turned out he actually was telling the truth. He seemed like a pretty cool guy to be fair but I'd never really watched the show he was in so there wasn't much I could say to him other than the general stuff that we talked about.

There was a moment during the cheetah walk when Judie randomly walked off so I seized the moment and followed her, I mean I wasn't supposed to but the workers never stopped me. After a minute she stopped, sat down and just stared into the distance, I knelt down beside her and began to stroke her and she soon started purring. It was just a special moment between me and a beautiful animal.

A special moment between me and Judie

After those three days it was time to fly out to Limpopo and get to work. On the way over to the airport I got talking to a couple of Americans who were both teachers at a university. They asked what I was doing in SA so I told them where I was heading. They asked if I was a student or vet.

"Nope, I just want to try something new" I said. They gave me a kind of confused look before swiftly looking away and talking between themselves.

The flight over to Limpopo was only an hour but it was almost like a theme park ride, the turbulence was freaking terrifying. I remember looking around the plane to try and gage how the other passengers were reacting but nobody else seemed bothered by it, seemed I was just being your typical wuss!

Soon after landing, I met another volunteer at the airport named Mary, we'd both flown in together but didn't realise we were heading to the same place.

A long-term volunteer, Luke that was there to pick us up and take us across to the sanctuary.

I'd turned up thinking that I'd be put to work as soon as I got there so had dressed accordingly in green shorts and a hiking shirt. Overdressed would be an understatement, I mean I looked like a bloody Steve Irwin wannabe and I soon found out that nobody works their first day there.

After a quick tour, some brief introductions and dinner it was time for an evening of chilling where everybody got to spend the night socialising and drinking. Luckily for me, I'd picked up a bottle of Jack Daniels while in Jo'Burg. I woke up the next morning with the mother of all hangovers and an empty bottle of JD next to my bed but, hangover or not come 6am it was time to crack on and get to work!

I soon learnt that this "monkey sanctuary" as it was advertised on the agency's page was actually a lot more than a place which only dealt with monkeys. The actual name of the place was "Riverside Wildlife Rehabilitation Centre" but I never realised it at the time as the agency's who promote trips like this seem to go out of their way not to name the place they advertise in order to stop people from booking directly and paying a few hundred quid less.

The Centre had Vervet Monkeys, baboons, Ostrich's, a pair of donkeys and bush babies, hell they even had a pair of geese but I definitely wasn't complaining - this was much better than I thought it would be.

We'd start the day by doing "morning chores" which were normally something like cleaning out one of the two main enclosures, clinic or quarantine although the main task after that would be "food prep" which was essentially prepping the all of the food for the morning feeds and all the related tasks that go with it. Whatever the task was you'd always work through to 9am before somebody would stand and ring a bell to let everyone know it was time for brekkie. After two hours of hard, fast labour I honestly can't describe just how good it was to hear that bell ring!

At some point during day two, I remember looking at the main baboon enclosure "Monty" that housed the young baboons aged one to three years and deciding that, having once worked with dogs in a rescue centre I would be capable of entering an enclosure that housed fifteen baboons by myself.

As I walked in a couple of volunteers looked over and asked if I was ok going into Monty on my own.

"Yea course I will!" I said, thinking that I'd just walk in, sit down and let the baboons come to me, show them respect and try not to piss them off. The first few minutes went quite ok, the baboons didn't seem to pay attention to me; until that is, Ron came along. Ron, a fairly big greyish coloured baboon decided to come over and check me out, after having a quick sniff and giving me a look up and down he decided to bite my stomach - hard. I pushed him away - not too hard because I didn't actually want to scare him. Initially he walked off before coming back and biting me again. I did the same as before, pushed him away but this time I told him to piss off.

The third time he came over and bit me, I lost my patience and pushed him back so hard that his feet left the floor and with that he began to scream. Before I had any time to react every single baboon in Monty launched themselves at me.

It's pretty hard to describe what it's like to have fifteen young baboons all screaming at you while biting and scratching you but in short, I'd say it's pretty fucking scary. I just pulled my arms up and covered my face - for what little it did. After what seemed like an extremely long bloody time, another volunteer managed to get into the enclosure and screamed at the top of his voice "wahoo!" Just like that every baboon dropped to the floor and left me alone. Ryan, an American that had come in and helped me was apparently seen as an "alpha" by the baboons in Monty which certainly worked out in my favour at that moment in time.

The baboons definitely fucked me up good but the worst of the damage was to my ego. I mean - what kind of idiot walks into an enclosure full of baboons that they've never been in with before and assumes that they can just sit there, consequence free? Looking back, I can't help but laugh but at the time, I'd be lying if I said I wasn't scared. I ended up being mobbed three more times that day – seems that I'd really pissed them off.

During the first few days I met a couple of girls called Mary and Charlotte who were both amazing people - Mary was American and Charlotte was a fellow Brit. We soon became a great little trio and I loved spending time with them but unfortunately Charlotte didn't have much time left there before she was going back home. Mary and I still spend quite a lot of time together though, sharing stories over drinks etc. we were just good friends making the most of our time there.

Me, Mary and Charlotte

Every day we would take the baboons out for a "baboon walk" to allow them some time away from the enclosure but, more importantly, a chance for them to play in the open and forage. Here they would learn the basic skills they would need for when they made their next steps in their rehabilitation journey. It basically involved a half mile walk down to the river and back, during this time the baboons would find volunteers that they liked and jump up on them. They'd often sit themselves on someone's head, cling on to their legs or just sit on their shoulders, you'd often find five or six young baboons all clung on to one person at a time. It's quite the sight to see; somebody trying to walk with baboons wrapped around both legs, sat on their head and around their belly.

For the first week the baboons would all avoid me during the walks, I didn't mind but would have loved to have had at least one trust me enough to sit on me while we walked down to the river.

There was one baby baboon, Darwin (or "baby Darwin" as he was known) who absolutely hated everyone and men in particular. If anyone tried to grab him without his bottle to hand, he would run away.

By the end of the first week during one of the baboon walks, as Darwin left the enclosure with all the other baboons he charged right me, leapt up and wrapped himself round my belly giving me a bear hug. This was the first time a baboon had come to me and I put it down to a fluke, just a one off. He stayed with me all the way down to the river before running off with all the other baboons to have fun, forage and play. After an hour or so, we all headed back up and once again, Darwin came to me and clung on to me for the rest of the walk and I realised that Darwin had chosen me as his human.

The day Darwin "choose" me

After a week of not knowing if I'd made the right decision in coming to South Africa, this moment suddenly made me realise I had indeed made the right decision.

From that moment onwards, Darwin and I were inseparable. Nobody but me could feed Darwin his bottle and he wouldn't let anybody else get close enough to feed him – I felt unbelievably honoured.

A week or so into the trip I found myself down at the dorms having a shower. They were all outdoors and open plan - no roof or doors. You'd just walk in, pick the shower you wanted and crack on and if it rained, you just had to deal with it. Normally, you'd go down in groups but on this particular day I was on my own. I got in the shower and began to wash - obviously, completely naked. I looked up and noticed, in the tree hanging over my particular shower there was a wild Vervet monkey just sat there, watching me wash myself and probably trying to figure out what the hell I was doing. The cubicle I was in happened to be in the far corner which meant if I needed to get out fast I'd have run down a narrow corridor, then across an open area before I could even get to my dorm and even then I'd have to unlock the door - all while completely naked. I turned away, hoping that this wild monkey would just move on but when I turned back a minute later one wild vervet monkey had now become a dozen. I was pretty fucking worried now - imagine the kind of headlines you'd see in the paper had I been attacked. I was naked, in the woods covered in soap.

All the monkeys just sat in the tree watching me, I decided it wasn't a good idea to hang around so I got out of there in double time and locked myself in my dorm. Looking back I highly doubt anything would have happened, they were probably just curious and wanted to know what I was doing. This was just one of many random yet funny moments I find myself looking back on and laughing about.

I remember around halfway into the trip, I met a girl named Silke from Belgium who had the most infectious smile. She spoke good English but seemed to struggle with my accent.

I remember trying to explain how the Hull accent works and that generally people from there don't pronounce their H's. We spent the next few minutes going over words without the H while she tried to copy my accent - it was just a random but funny conversation that to this day still makes me smile.

For all the good, amazing and surreal moments I experienced in those three weeks I still struggled. Before I left for the trip I found myself constantly worrying about the kids. I felt like some kind of jackass who was abandoning my kids for a bit of a jolly. Regardless of what Dom, my family and friends had told me I still couldn't get used to the not being able to give them both a cuddle. Luckily, we had Wi-Fi so I could at least video call them. We had days where the Wi-Fi would go down though or we'd have power cuts etc. No matter how good a day I had those were the worst, not being able to see them both, not being able to do bedtime stories, not even a photo of them during their day just made things so much harder.

I'd booked the trip there to coincide with my 27th birthday. When the day came it started like any other with two hours of morning chores before brekkie. When I walked into the dining room though there was a huge banner with Happy Birthday from all at Riverside written on it with some pictures of baboons, Bob & Lynne (the owners of the sanctuary) and a couple of the dogs. As soon as I sat down a huge cake was brought over and I was given a card and a Riverside T-shirt. I was quite happy with that but what really made the day was an excursion had been booked; Me and most of the other volunteers were going to go out to a small mountain area and do the "tree canopy tour" which meant using ten different zip lines to work our way down a mountain. It was incredible! The views and overall experience definitely made that birthday a particularly memorable one!

During my last couple of days there I met a new volunteer named Hannah who had come over from the U.K. and was a returning volunteer. We got talking and seemed to click just like that. We had a lot in common, she was the kind of person you could talk to for hours with ease and not have to worry about looking a tit, talking too much or having to deal with those long awkward silences. We were sat outside of The Hide one afternoon, (a dedicated volunteer building for general down time, kind of like a staff room) Hannah was sat down on the floor with her back against the wall. Mid conversation, I looked up and noticed a pair of birds just sitting there right above Hannah's head.

"Seriously, if those birds shit on your head now."

Before I could even finish my sentence, I was interrupted by a "splat" sound and Hannah looked at me in horror. At least one of the birds had explosively shit right on her head and not just a small amount either – It was all over her head and face! Obviously being the kind and supportive friend that I am, my first reaction was to do the right thing - I told her to stay still, whipped my phone out as fast as I could and took a photo. How could I not? It was genuinely a hilarious moment!

I met some amazing people at Riverside but Mary, Charlotte, Silke and Hannah are four friends still I'm grateful to have met to this day. They really did help make that trip all the more fun!

Leaving Riverside was harder than I thought - I'd fallen in love with the place. Bob, Lynne and Mias each played a part in helping me move forward. Remember - I'd been struggling since the breakup with Amy and Riverside made me feel like I had a purpose in life again. Once on the plane to Jo'Burg, I cried; words can't describe just how powerful the impact Riverside has on you actually is. There are so many memories from my first trip at Riverside that come with so many stories which I will always be grateful for and cherish until I take my last breath.

CHAPTER 8

For Stu

For all the good that came at the beginning of 2017 it also came with moments that try as I might, I'll never forget; one of which was in March.

I believe everyone has a story; regardless of who they are, where there're from or how they've lived their life - we all have a story to tell. Obviously, working in a homeless hostel you see and work with people from all works of life, nobody just wakes up one day and decides they're going to become homeless. No. There's a long list of things that can and do go wrong in somebody's life that leads them down particular paths. There's a common saying that I firmly believe to be true and accurate - You are never more than three pay cheques away from becoming homeless. It's true – take it from someone who knows.

Stu came to us at the hostel in early 2017 addicted to heroin and it was rare you'd see him sober. I remember coming to work one night and being told during handover that at one point he had a roast dinner in front of him, it'd only just come out of the oven and covered in hot gravy. He had only just shot up (used heroin) so was in no state to eat so ended up face planting the food but because he was so high he couldn't then pull his face out. It might sound funny to some but he ended up with some fairly nasty burns over face.

Stu had started using heroin when he was around fourteen or fifteen. He never went into details as to why he started using such a horrific and life changing drug, only saying that he had family problems. The problem with a drug like heroin is, it only makes a problem worse and it's an easy trap to fall in to. You hit a hard point in life and suddenly you're offered something that can help make things that little bit more bearable. From what I've seen and it's normally a dealer that'll groom you into using, leaving you hooked and dependent.

By the end of this book, you'll realise that I hold a particular dislike for those that choose to sell heroin. They worm their way into a vulnerable person's life, offering to help and make things better and then before you know it, they've successfully ruined another life and that of a family, all for the satisfaction of making a few quid.

One evening just as I was about to leave work Stu came over to me.

"Matt, can you tell me what this Facebook thing is?"

He was almost 40 and had never found himself in a position where he would need or want to use social media so the idea of something like Facebook was alien to him. He explained that he wanted to get off drugs and get in touch with his son who he'd never been able to meet thanks to his life on hard drugs and he had been told that the best way to reach out to him would be though Facebook.

Stu was sober when he came to me and asked about it and he seemed genuine so I decided to stay and help him. I took him into one of the back rooms with a laptop and explained how Facebook worked and that he'd need to get signed up with an account. Obviously, you need an email addresses to sign up to Facebook so I helped him create one and we then moved over to Facebook which took us all of five, maybe ten minutes to get set up. I took a photo for him so he could at least have a profile picture and asked him for his son's name which I typed into the search bar while Stu looking on and found him almost straight away. Stu's face lit up when I turned the screen around and showed him. "Oh my god! Matt, that's my son!" He was so excited, the look on his face said it all. He'd never met his son or even seen a photo of him so this was the first time he'd seen him. He was mesmerised by the photos of him and just kept repeating.

"Matt, that's my son" with the same look of excitement on his face.

Something about his reaction and sheer joy reminded me right there and then just why I loved my job, it was such a feel-good moment. I suggested that he shouldn't add him as a friend or message him until he'd at least spoken to the mum first which he agreed to. That was when he told me that from that point on he wanted to give up the heroin and wanted to be given a chance to meet his son - to be some form of role model. Normally, when someone in his position said something like that I'd smile and nod, knowing deep down that they probably wouldn't stick to it but with Stu it was different. Two weeks on, he had a new addiction - our gym. He had completely stopped the heroin and was spending what even I would call, an unhealthy amount of time in the gym and that's coming from someone who would soon be banned from said gym for my own health........

One weekend in March, I was booked on for two doubles shifts 7am - 10pm both Saturday and Sunday where I'd be working with the same two people over both days. For both mornings I was with an experienced staff member that had spent years with the company and for the afternoon, a completely new member of staff that had been with us for a week.

On the Saturday morning a guy walked in to the hostel who immediately seemed suspicious. Neither I nor the person I was on shift with challenged him because no matter what we thought we couldn't just assume he was a drug dealer but we were concerned as he seemed to be talking to Stu. They both remained in our line of sight for the duration of the guys stay, as soon as he left Stu came straight over to us.

"Did you see that?" he asked us excitedly. He explained that the man who had just left was in fact a dealer just like we thought and that he had been Stu's dealer who was trying to give him free gear (heroin) in a bid to get his former customer back. He failed miserably and Stu couldn't have been prouder of himself and rightfully so. It was a fairly special moment; to see someone who had spent almost their entire life dependent on a drug like heroin turn it down because they want a fresh start and a chance to be with their family, even when it's handed to them on a plate for free. That's something that not only takes a metric fuck ton of strength but also some big brass balls! I take my hat off to and respect anyone who can do that.

The rest of the morning shift went fairly quietly. Our new member of staff turned up for the afternoon shift and swapped over with the previous worker. She was new but definitely quite competent. I ran her though how the shift was going to go and a few basics that nobody had bothered to explain and then just cracked on with the rest of the shift and before I knew it 10pm came. It had been a long day but other than the incident with Stu it was uneventful. The next day, I was working with the newbie first. I explained that the best way to learn (for me at least) is to get stuck in and do the job yourself; you can't beat hands on experience so I let her take the ropes for the majority of the shift. During every shift, we were required to tick off any residents we'd seen; the idea being that if they hadn't been seen for a while we'd know that we needed to check their room and do a welfare check. If morning staff hadn't seen a resident by 2pm it was down to them to do said welfare check.

I told our newbie that normally it's better to do them in two's but as there was only two of us on that morning, I'd let her do it with me monitoring her on the CCTV. She was more than happy to get stuck in and do something practical rather than sit and watch.

There were ten people who we hadn't seen that the morning spread over the three floors. Before she left to do the checks I ran her though the safest way to carry them out. Number one, always have a radio with you and never leave reception without making sure it was charged, working and connected to the radio on reception. That way if you get into trouble and you're in one of the stupidly large number of blind spots you can call for help. (Plus, it can make a handy weapon to defend yourself with if you're ever attacked).

Number two, always have your mobile phone with you when you leave reception. If you need to call an ambulance the in-room phones may not work and trying to relay the message via a radio doesn't work. She'd been told not to have her phone with her during shifts though and decided that she'd follow that rule regardless of my advice. Each to their own, I guess.

I watched her go to each room, knock on the door and get a response from nine out of the ten. When she got to room thirty-eight on the third floor I watched her knock on the door, wait a few seconds and then when she didn't get a response knock again. After a few more unsuccessful attempts she radioed me to let me know she was entering the room – it was Stu's room. I watched her walk in and turned away to look at my computer screen. Before I had time to think I heard "Matt, Emergency!" through the radio. I grabbed my keys and sprinted up the three flights of stairs to her with no idea what I was running into.

As I got closer to the room I saw a small crowd gathered around Stu's door all looking in. Completely out of breath I just about managed to shout "clear the area now!" The group moved away and I walked through the door to find my colleague staring down at Stu while he was on the floor lying on his side with a pool of blood around his head. I shook him while shouting his name. "Stu! Come on mate, can you hear me!?" As I grabbed his arm I knew something didn't feel right but I didn't have time to think about it then. This could well have been an overdose or just a simple slip or trip with a concussion but I had to treat it as life and death until I knew he was ok.

With no response I tried to do top to toe, a quick check to see if I could locate any obvious issues (other than a head injury). As I started, I shouted over for my colleague to call 999. "Matt, I don't have my phone" she said. I went to grab mine and realised I'd left in such a hurry that I had also left my phone at reception.

"Ok, fine, use that phone there" I said pointing to the in-room phone but second later she told me that it wasn't working. I stopped, gave the room a quick scan and spotted Stu's phone on the side.

"Chuck me his phone, I'll sort it" She chucked me his phone but no sooner had I dialed 99 the battery died. This was fast becoming a cluster fuck of a situation. With no response from Stu and no working phone the only option left was for one of us to run down to reception, grab my phone and call an ambulance while the other person stayed and began CPR. I'd given CPR twice before so was the obvious choice but I was also a much faster runner. Without a moment's thought, I ran off shouting at her to start CPR as I left. As I ran downstairs I stopped every resident I saw and asked for their phone but nobody had one to hand. I must have cleared the three flights of stairs, grabbed my phone and been back with Stu in around a minute. When I got back to Stu's room I found my colleague still stood where I left her. I put it down to shock and told her to go back to reception and wait for the paramedics then continued to deliver first aid. I still couldn't shake the feeling that something about the feel of his arm just didn't feel right. It was frozen solid in a room where the heating was on full blast.

As the 999-operator picked up the phone a friend of Stu's ran in, saw me with him and began shouting, demanding that I moved and let him take over because I wasn't doing enough. At this point Stu was still on his side with his face against the wall. All the while, the 999-operator trying to tell me to ignore Stu's friend and explain what I could see.

I gave a brief description while trying to roll Stu on to his back. For some reason I just couldn't make him budge so I told his friend to help me roll him over but neither of us were prepared for what was to come…

As we got him on his back and saw his face, the penny dropped - he was dead. The reason we'd struggled to budge him was because he'd dead for so long, rigour mortis had set in. His face had been almost glued to the floor thanks to the blood that had now dried from his head injury. His friend backed off crying knowing there was no coming back from this - Stu was gone. I told the operator to cancel the ambulance and to just send the police.

"What do you mean, what's happening!?" I told her Stu was dead and there nothing we could do.

"Ok, is the patient breathing?"

"No, he's bloody dead! I just told you this!"

"Ok, you need to start CPR immediately" the phone was on speaker so his friend heard what was being said."

"Matt, No, don't"

I snapped back "He's fucking dead. I've just told you this" only to get the response.

"If you're not a doctor, you can't declare somebody dead" from the operator.

"If the patient is not breathing you need to start CPR now"

I gave in, knowing that I couldn't do anything to help but thinking that I would be in legal trouble if I didn't follow the instructions I was being given. I looked down at Stu.

"I'm sorry mate" I muttered before starting CPR with the medic counting me on- all the while, I could hear his ribs cracking. After about thirty seconds I heard what sound like a gasp come from Stu, for a second I thought the CPR was working but I quickly realised it was just the remaining air being forced out of his lungs. The paramedics soon walked in, looked at me and just said.

"I think you can stop now mate"

Thank fuck! I told the dispatcher that paramedics had arrived and she ended the call "you've done really well, well done and take care"

I cut the call before I could say what I was really thinking. I could tell just by the way she said that, she had known he was already dead but I was still forced into a position I would never wish on anybody. Neither I nor Stu should have been put through that. I don't blame the dispatcher or hold ill will, I know she was doing her job and the situation was probably extremely difficult for her too. Legally nobody can declare a death unless they're medically trained to do so therefore some random guy trying to declare a death had to be ignored. It was just an awful situation for everyone to be in.

Once I had stopped CPR the paramedics asked to be left alone in the room with Stu while they did what they needed to do.

After spending some time with Stu's friend I went to sit in the office, I knew I was in shock and I was struggling to process what had just happened. I knew that I needed to call it in to the on-call manager so I decided to start with that. When he answered the phone I explained briefly what had happened. This guy lived and worked in Doncaster (2/3 hours away) but he offered to get to Hull in double time to let me go home which I refused. I just didn't see the point, this guy had never been to our hostel and was hours away and ultimately I guess a part of me wanted to stay and make sure everything was done properly. Plus I wanted a chance to see Stu off too.

After around an hour the police arrived to take my statement, as soon as they left I decided to call Rachel. I called from the work phone and she picked up sounding pissed off that work was calling her on a Sunday afternoon, I guess thinking somebody had called in sick and she was being asked to cover. The second she picked up though I froze - I couldn't speak. After a few seconds of Rachel asking if anyone was actually there, I finally managed to say something.

"Rach, he's dead. Its Stu he's fucking dead." I didn't even need to say another word, she told me to stay in the office and do nothing until she got there. I put the phone down and just cried. It suddenly caught up with me and hit me hard. I'd only seen Stu the day before and he was fine -what the hell had happened!?

Rachel soon turned up and thank fuck she did. I'd told the on call that I could and would stay and finish the shift but it soon became obvious I couldn't, Rachel wouldn't let me go home though because she knew that the first thing I'd do was grab a beer, that one beer would lead to two then three and so on.

However bad the day had been an incident report had to be completed - thankfully Rachel offered to do it for me because I'm not sure I could have, just talking her through how it had all unfolded was hard enough.

Her coming in the way she did that day, that's something I'll be forever grateful for and will always remember.

The funeral was a few weeks later, myself and one resident went along from the hostel. It was a fairly simple funeral and went as well as you can expect a funeral to go. There was a wake planned after in a local bar which I had no intentions of going to. I'd been to the funeral, paid my respects, said my goodbyes and had a brief chat with the family which is what I went there to do.

Any form of socializing with residents was against the rules at the hostel for obvious reasons. I'd had to gain consent from management just to attend the funeral but to then go to a bar with another resident would be a step too far and potentially cause me to face disciplinary action. But the family refused to accept that I wouldn't go and after some persuasion I gave in and said I'd stay for just one pint.

Stu's family though, just kept buying me drinks, we all got on really well and eventually it just seemed rude to walk away. In all honesty, I'm glad I stayed in the end and I knew it's what Stu would have wanted.

Although, I never did find out the official cause of death I was told that weed or Valium had been found in his system. Eventually I put the pieces together and figured out that it was more than likely he using weed and Valium as a substitute for heroin. When I got to him that day I noticed a severe head injury that had caused him to bleed badly. It looked as though while under the influence, he'd tripped or lost his balance before falling and hitting the side of his head on the corner of his desk. It's most likely the blow to the head is what killed him and I doubt he knew what was happening – at least I hope he didn't.

To this day, I have a huge amount of respect for Stu, he had suffered with his demons for almost his entire life but chose to do something that most of us could never do. He chose to break free from the chains of a god-awful addiction like heroin and that takes more strength than I could ever imagine.

Thanks for reminding me just why I love helping people Stu; RIP my friend!

CHAPTER 9

2017
The build up to shit hitting the fan.

This is a chapter in my life I like to refer to as "the build-up" because that is exactly what it is. *THE* build up.

Things had already started to change with me mentally and physically in the early parts of 2017. At the time I put it down to being overworked and stressed. Looking back, it's hard to understand how I couldn't see the signs that something was very seriously wrong but I had so much going on, it was hard to see anything clearly.

I had been working between seventy and ninety hours across two separate hostels and getting ready for my first trip to America.

The beginning of 2017 started quite well. We had a new manager at work who decided to put me on a secondment - working days as a "project assistant" to help me get experience working day shifts. I'd worked enough days to know exactly what I was doing but was ready for a change so figured this would help get my foot in the door for a promotion.

During one of my first days on the secondment, I got a call from a volunteer who was part of a charity named Hull Homeless Community Project (HHCP) who explained that they had found themselves with a large number of brand-new single mattress and wanted to distribute them between the hostels in Hull and asked if I thought we'd be interested. I said yes and left it at that and an hour or so later some volunteers from the charity turned up as promised. They explained that out of the three or four hostels that they had spoken to, we (I) were the only one to actually say yes to the free mattresses so instead of getting the two or three that I thought we getting they brought fifty which scored me a few brownie points.

After that I looked into HHCP and after a quick chat with one of the volunteers soon found myself volunteering with them.

Once or twice a week we'd head out in small teams looking for rough sleepers, the idea being to offer them a hot drink, someone to talk to and with any luck be able to signpost them to the right kinds of support to help them. I loved doing this and would spend a couple of hours in the evening doing outreach with the charity before I went to work my night shift and then be back at it again the next morning.

I preferred to head to the outskirts of town as I found that the people there were more likely to be genuine rough sleepers and not pretending they were happy. Every now and then, if you walked out of town into places like overgrown fields or demolition sites you'd find the rough sleepers that were going out of their way not to be seen, they didn't want to beg or be in a position where they didn't feel safe. It was rare that we'd find the people themselves though, sometimes we'd just find a tent and a make-shift campsite. In that instance I liked to leave a few bottles of water, a couple of chocolate bars and a leaflet with the charity details on in the hope somebody would see it and know that people did care and wanted to help.

I've always loved helping people; I don't know why but knowing that I was actually helping people and the thought of having some form of positive impact on somebody's day just made me happy.

I decided to try and do a little more to help the charity by doing some fundraising, more as a thank you for the mattress and other means of support they had thrown our way but also to raise a bit more awareness for people having to deal with the various forms of homelessness. Between doing the Hull

10k, my second Mudder, a coffee morning at work and a pie in the face raffle, I managed to raise around £300.

Around mid-2017 I was starting to really see things weren't quite right. I could never put my finger on what it was but something just didn't feel right to me in general. I would come home after a night shift and after a few hours' sleep I would wake up shaking, terrified, struggling to breathe and drenched in sweat. This always seemed to happen if I'd been working a lot or had been struggling to sleep.

I did what you should never do and googled the symptoms to find the most common hit was sleep paralysis and seizures. I didn't have epilepsy so figured it must have been sleep paralysis which to me made sense. Working long stressful hours and not getting a healthy amount of sleep clearly added up to that - or so I thought…

In July, after having already completed the Hull 10k for HHCP it was time for me to take on my next challenge. I was due to take part in my second Tough Mudder and just like before I was running solo. One of the volunteers from HHCP had come with me to spectate, offer moral support and take photos.

It was a great day and just as fun as the first. I can't really say there were any amazing moments that really stood out but getting my green finishers headband at the end, sure as hell left me hooked on Tough Mudder.

August of that year was a hard one for our family. My sister, Katy was pregnant and due that month. As there had been a few health issues detected with the baby the doctors decided a C-Section would be safer so she was taken to Leeds infirmary where the procedure was booked for the following morning.

Dan (Katy's partner and a friend I met way back at my petrol station job) called while I was at work to confirm that Katy had been booked in, all was well and she was getting ready for a night's sleep. Less than 10 minutes later though, he called back saying that Katy had been rushed to theatre and that I needed to call my parents and get them to rush back to hospital urgently and with that he hung up. I immediately called my mum, telling her what Dan had said and with that they rushed back through to the hospital leaving me to try and continue my shift at work.

The next couple of hours before Dan called back felt like forever but when he did it wasn't great news. Despite everyone's best efforts my niece [Serena Jane] hadn't made it and had passed away a couple of hours after birth.

The call only lasted a minute and I only got the bare basics as Dan was understandably too upset to go into detail. I decided to stay at work as there was nothing I could do to help them at that point in time. I was still in Hull but Katy, Dan and my parents were at the hospital in Leeds. Going home at 2am wouldn't achieve anything.

So I took myself up to the "roof garden" where no one could see or hear me and cried. I'd never felt anything like this before – ever! I felt like I'd been sucker punched but guilty for feeling like that knowing that Katy was sat in hospital after her daughter had passed away. Looking back, it's understandable to have been that upset.

Later that morning Mum & Dad came home to pick me up and take me through to the hospital. We didn't speak a word during the drive to hospital so I wasn't sure what to expect when I arrived.

As soon as I saw Katy I gave her a hug and told her how sorry I was; then we all sat silently in the hospital room not knowing what to say.

Eventually, Serena was bought in to us so that we could have a chance to hold her and say our goodbyes. As this happened a photographer walked in. It turns out, hospitals have them on hand to take final photos of families with their baby in the event they don't make it. After seeing this guy take shots of Dan, Katy and Serena my Mum passed her over to me so I could say my goodbyes. I looked at the photographer.

"No photos for me please, mate" but as I sat down with Serena there was a click and a flash; he'd taken a photo anyway. I looked up angry as I felt he had intruded on that moment even though I asked him not to. I gave him the "dagger glare" and he very quickly looked away, clearly knowing just how pissed off I was. A big part of me wanted to drag him out of the room for that. For me, that was a private moment and I was heartbroken. Death is something I'm more than capable of dealing with but a child, a baby, my niece. No. I was doing everything I could to hold it together for Katy and the last thing I wanted was some guy taking pictures of me at a moment like that. Katy decided she wanted a copy of said photo but to this day I have never been able to look at it.

A few seconds after the photographer took the photo I asked Mum to take Serena from me, stood up and got out of the room as fast as I could. I broke down as soon as the door closed behind me, dropped to floor and cried - I was a wreck. My mum came out almost straight away and gave me a much needed hug. There are not too many memories I'd like to forget but this is definitely one I struggle with to this day.

Our focus as a family over the coming months was to provide whatever support we could to my sister and Dan which meant I wasn't really paying much attention to my ever developing symptoms.

I still knew something wasn't right though and continued to try and find explanations. During a late shift at work in November, I found myself on the computer completing an autism test online through an autism charity website. It was a long test with around a hundred multiple choice questions. The end results suggested I had many tendencies of an autistic spectrum disorder. I wasn't too sure what to make of it to be completely honest but again it made sense and was another potential explanation for whatever didn't feel right even though I refused to do anything that would officially confirm if this was the case and obviously I know now there was likely a much more sinister cause.

A few days later a resident came to reception with a plastic bag in the early hours of the morning.

"Guys, can you tell me what the fuck this is please"

I reached over to grab the bag just as my colleague shouted "No! Matt look…"

As I examined the bag a little closer I realised that there were sharps (needles) poking out it. I therefore took the bag much more carefully than I had initially intended and asked the resident where she had found it. She explained that she had gone to the communal laundry room to do her washing and had seen it sat on top of one of the washing machines.

With that something in me just snapped and I instantly became so angry at the thought of someone placing what I assumed to be uncapped, used heroin needles in a plastic bag and dumping it in an area where anyone, (including me) could have been jabbed.

In general I had always been known for being laid back; sometimes too laid back but for whatever reason, this triggered me and I was furious.

I decided to go in to the CCTV room and look back through the previous day's footage to see who exactly had decided the safest place to leave a thin bag full of rubbish and dirty, used, uncapped needles would be in an area that lots of people use. Now, bear in mind it was seriously against company policy to just start going through CCTV as and when you felt like it. General staff were absolutely not authorised to plough through footage as and when they felt like it, in order for anyone to do so there needed to be a clear and valid reason and then only management were permitted to do so.

I could have and probably should have been sacked for that and I knew it but at the time I was far too angry to care.

After some time I eventually spotted who had done it, I watched the person in question stumble out of his room with the needle filled bag, stagger downstairs and walk into the laundry room, dump the bag and then just walk away. It was known amongst the staff that this guy carrying hepatitis, meaning if anyone had been jabbed with one of those needle there was a high likelihood of contracting it.

I was already angry but seeing this pushed me up another gear and I started shouting.

"Who the fuck does this guy think he is! This is wrong! He needs to go!"

My co-worker tried to calm me down and was clearly shocked as to why I was so angry about it. In my head I just kept thinking that any one of us could have been jabbed. I have kids, the last thing I wanted was to have to worry about the risks of passing hepatitis on to them.

Before I knew what I was doing I was making my way to his room while my colleague repeatedly tried to call me back on the radio. I ignored her; I was going to see this resident, demand an explanation and then kick him out.

When I arrived at his room I banged on his door only to get no answer so I tried again - still nothing. So I tried shouting him, again no answer. A couple of other residents were now starting to wake up and poke their heads out of their rooms to see what all the fuss was about.

After a few minutes of banging on the resident's door and not getting any form of answer, what I should have done is walk away, go downstairs and type up a warning to be issued to him when he woke up later or during a welfare check the next afternoon if he hadn't been seen beforehand.

In my angry state though that wasn't what I choose to do – instead I decided to use my key to gain entry, wake him up and demand an explanation. Of course this was a huge rule breaker as I had no valid reason to enter his room at that time so by this point I was well within the grounds of a sackable offence.

I poked my head though the door, shouted him but still got no answer.

"For fuck's sake!" I expressed, now getting more annoyed that it was pitch black in his room as his light was off and his blinds closed. I turned his light on so I could see where I was walking before going in to shake him awake but before I could get another word out I saw the scene in front of me and froze. This resident wasn't in bed at all and he hadn't been ignoring me. He was face down, on the floor amongst a pile of pill packs/boxes, some empty and some unopened as well as a few used needles. In a heartbeat, I went from being ready to have a big row to autopilot lifesaving mode.

I gave him a quick "top to toe" while trying to wake him but he was completely unresponsive. Discovering his breathing to be very slow and laboured I called for an ambulance. When the paramedics arrived they pumped him up with medication to counter any and all opiate drugs, like Valium or heroin which is used primarily when somebody has overdosed.

He soon woke up acting like nothing had happened. I told the medics that his next official check would have been in around twelve hours and asked what kind of outcome he'd have had if he was left in that state for that long. The response was that he was lucky to be alive now so a few more hours and he would have very likely been dead.

Of the fourteen lives I've saved over the years, this is definitely one of the most bizarre incidents. I should have been sacked or at least formally disciplined for what I'd done before I'd found him in that state but clearly, had I not snapped and broken the rules, we would have had a death on our hands. As a result the whole thing was pretty much brushed under the carpet.

When I look back at this now with the benefit of hindsight I firmly believe that the uncharacteristic anger I felt this day was in fact a symptom of what was to come. Of all the symptoms I ignored and the impacts they had though I would say that this one had the most positive outcome as in the end it undoubtedly helped to save a life.

CHAPTER 10

2017

An American Riverside Reunion

Like with 99% of what you've read up to now, this chapter will be filled with a seemingly never-ending number of stories that will either make you wander how I've made it this far in life without ending up dead or like I'm waffling on. Hell, it'll probably be both as one of my very few talents seems to be waffling on and on. -consider yourself warned.

In early 2017 I was having trouble sleeping more often than not and I was becoming more stressed and depressed as each days passed. One night, around 1am I gave up trying to sleep and in a foul mood walked to Hessle (8 miles away) to try and clear my head at the beach/foreshore and nearby woods. (Little Switz) After some soul searching and a lot of walking, I stumbled across an odd-looking rock that had been placed on a box, seemingly deliberately. I picked it up to take a look to see that it had a black leaf painted on one side and on the other a message that read "keep or hide, Beverley Rocks" Something about this rock just made me smile. I did some digging and it turned out that there's groups all over the country that are dedicated to painting rocks with nice images or nice messages and then leaving them in random places for people to find, keep or hide in a new location. I decided to not only keep the rock but to take it with me on my first ever trip to America that September, head out to the mountains in Colorado and leave it there.

I started that trip by heading to New York City for the typical tourist stuff then onto Denver Colorado to meet a good friend of mine Mary who'd I'd met while working at Riverside.

My flight out of UK was booked for 6am which meant I'd need to travel the night before. Thanks to being a cheapskate I decided to get to the airport for around 8pm the night before and just pull an all-nighter in the airport itself. I mean how hard could that be? I even took a coach to the airport rather than the train, just to save a few quid. I remember being at the last station before the airport at the back of the queue for the next coach when I noticed the guy in the front was being told he wasn't able to board as he only had a mobile ticket and his battery had died so couldn't produce it. Luckily for this guy, I had my power bank with me so I asked the driver to give him two minutes to get charge into his phone enough so that he could at least show his ticket. Thankfully, he agreed and the guy was able to board and make it to the airport.

It turned out that quite a lot of people had the same idea as me about spending the night in the airport so trying to find to find a nice quiet spot and chill was a task in itself. Even though I eventually managed to find a quiet corner that I could chill in I got no sleep that night.

Once on the plane and finally settled I decided to try and finally get some shut eye. I was sat on an aisle seat with a fairly chatty Irish couple sat next to me but after some brief chit chat with them, I got my head down.

Eventually I woke up in the same state I'd been waking up in after night shifts back home - struggling to breathe and making some kind of bizarre sound - like I was gasping for air and drawling. As always, it only lasted a few seconds (at least that's how it felt) and once it had passed I turned to look at the couple sat next to me, hoping they hadn't seen what had happened. Judging by the worried and confused look on their faces though they had.

I laughed it off saying something like, "what a weird dream that must have been" We didn't speak for the duration of the flight after that and given how embarrassed I was, I was pleased.

Just as we were preparing to land the flight attendants handed everybody a declaration card. I'd only ever been to South Africa before so had never needed to fill one out. It was quite straight forward though - are you carrying certain types of food, (meats & veg etc.) large amounts of cash and so on. I had a pack of sausage rolls that I'd brought to eat on the plane but never got around to eating them so figured I'd save them for later when I got to the hotel before I went exploring, as I definitely wanted to explore far more than I wanted to look for a place to eat. I marked on the card that I had a "meat product" just to be safe. (Thinking nothing of it of course).

As I came through customs, I was quizzed by one of the TSA guys who asked why I was in New York and what my plans were etc. After telling him I was heading to Denver in a few days, he began to grill me. I must have caught this guy on a bad day because he seemed snappy and annoyed and every answer I gave him seemed to annoy him even more.

After being grilled about why I was going to Denver after New York and having to explain how and why I knew an American, he decided to look at my declaration card. "

You've declared you have a meat product? What is it?" he asked.

I told him it was a pack of sausage rolls.

"A what!?" He snapped back and so I told him again and was met with the same confused look with the same question.

"What do you mean - "sausage roll?"

I was already nervous as it was so being quizzed by an angry TSA guy that could quite easily cancel my trip with a fair amount of ease didn't make me feel any better. But this is how I found myself standing in the airport having to give a very detailed description of what a sausage roll is, after which he told me to head over to another section of customs and explain what they are to his colleague.

"Ok, this guy's just an idiot that's never had a sausage roll before" I thought to myself but decided it would just be easier to bin them while heading over to the next desk. Clearly these sausage rolls were too much trouble!

So In the bin they went and to the next customs desk I headed. I tried to explain what the other TSA guy had told me and that he didn't understand what I meant by sausage rolls. Just like before though this guy had no idea what I was talking about.

"You've got a pack of what!?"

Turns out that sausage rolls don't exist in the States, hence the extremely confused looks when I tried to describe them.

"No, I HAD a pack of sausage rolls when I spoke to your colleague but I binned them before coming to you" I explained.

With that, he snapped at me and demanded I walk to the bin, pull the sausage rolls out and bring them back to him for inspection. By this point I was starting to think that this simple pack of pastries were going to ruin my trip or at least the first part anyway. But back to the bin I went, retrieved the "apparently hazardous to America" sausage rolls and handed them over, he had a quick look at the packet and said.

"You can't have these in the United States"

"Yes, no shit Sherlock!" I thought to myself.

He then said.

"We can fine you $1000 for this y'know. But I'll let you off with a warning"

With that, he let me go; never mind the "sleep paralysis" episode on the plane, this was mortifying but also pretty hilarious. When I got home, a few friends decided that particular story would be forever known as "sausage roll gate."

Visiting NYC had always been on my bucket list, I had three days to do the typical tourist stuff but the main goal was to visit the 9.11 museum. I was 11 at the time of the 9.11

attacks and will never forget it - it truly was a day that the world stood still.

Words alone will never describe just what the 9.11 memorial museum is like; the site itself is exactly where the Twin Towers stood and goes below the site. The vast majority of it is filled with an array silence. I remember being stood at an exhibit that was showing a transcript from a voicemail left from one of the first firefighters to enter the towers. It shows a timeline of calls/voicemails meant for this particular firefighter at home throughout the day. Essentially, the messages start off positive. The callers know said firefighter will be at the Twin Towers and ask him to be careful but over the course of the day you can see the mood has changed to desperation, with friends asking the firefighter to call and confirm he was safe. Eventually the messages coming though were full of sorrow; his friends were leaving messages telling him they knew he hadn't made it and they hope he finds peace.

There were two of these podiums side by side that were playing in sync together. There was a lady standing next to me reading from the other podium. By the time the messages were reaching their conclusion we were both in tears. It was the first time I'd ever cried in public around strangers. Even now looking back, thinking about that moment leaves me with a tear in my eye. I saw many sights in NYC after that before I left for Denver but none has stayed with me as much as that.

For my stay in Denver I had booked a room at a hostel (Hostel Fish) and thanks to a bit of looking around on google maps before I left the UK, I knew there was a bar within two minutes walking distance called View House. I walked in and a barman asked me what I'd like to drink. "I dunno, what do locals round here drink, mate?" He looked at me slightly confused and asked what I meant.

"I'm from the UK mate, this is my first time in the States. Recommend a drink and I'll have that please"

"Ahhh I see!" He said with a smile.

He poured me a pint of ale telling me that most bars in Denver brew their own beers and ales. I'd never tried ale before then and would never ask for it back home but figured it'd be as good a time as any to try it. It was beautiful! Although, the fact he let me have it for free probably did help.

Not long after arriving there I felt a tap from behind on my shoulder. I turned around to find it was Mary. After a few drinks and a much needed catch up we decided to head to a baseball game at the local stadium. It was about $12 for what turned out to be a fairly crappy seat. As we walked in Mary pointed out that if we were to sit in the "VIP" seats by the front, we'd have paid upwards of $150 a seat and to get to those seats you had to pass stewards/security staff.

By this point I was fairly drunk so told Mary to follow me as we snuck by the guards thinking we wouldn't be seen. We sat down and no sooner than our rear ends had touched the seat, a security guard came over and told us to move. He didn't even need to see our tickets to know that we shouldn't have been there. I just played the typical drunk tourist card.

"Ahhh. Sorry matey! My bad, not sure where we're meant to be!"

He watched to see that had gone back to where we should have been before heading off to do whatever it was he needed to do.

"Mary, follow me and play along" I said.

Drunk Me wasn't going to give up that easily!

I walked us around to the other side of the stadium, spotted a steward and walked towards her.

"Smile, nod and play along" I reminded Mary.

As we walked towards the woman, I said.

"Alright love, ow you doing? Good I hope!"

And just casually walked on by, she smiled and said nothing. I don't really remember much after that, I mean, to say I was wasted would be an understatement. I do remember getting a couple of cheesy selfies, seeing our faces pop up on the "kiss cam" (no kissing obviously) and then being at the stadium bar asking for a double vodka red bull only for Mary and the bar woman to tell me I wouldn't want that when I realised how much it would cost - Drunk Me disagreed - $20 later I had by far, THE most expensive single drink I'd ever had.

Me and Mary at the ball game

I woke up the next morning with zero memory of how I even made it back to my hostel, never mind the top bunk of my bed. I had a look at my phone and found a ton of pictures and videos that to this day, still make me laugh and cringe.

With the mother of all hangovers, at around 6am I decided to head out and find some food - I always seem to wake up stupidly early when I have hangovers.

I had no idea where I was going, I just wanted fresh air and food. I was stopped by a homeless guy who must have been in his mid to late twenties.

"Have you got a cigarette I can have please, sir?"

"Sorry mate, I don't smoke" I said.

With that, he said thanks anyway and started to walk away. I don't know why but for some reason I got an urge to stop him. I asked him if was homeless and he told me he was (it was a dumb question, you could tell just by looking at him that he didn't have a roof over his head) and we got talking about how he'd come to be homeless and what the support in Denver was like for people like him. We talked for about 10 minutes and as he turned to walk away, I called him back and gave him $20.

"Get yourself some breakfast and a drink mate". He seemed genuinely grateful, maybe a little confused but grateful all the same. I choose to work in a homeless hostel because unlike some people that you find working in that sector, I was there to help people. Getting paid to do it was just a bonus for me. That's why I choose to volunteer for the homeless outreach project too - I just like to help people. Random acts of kindness can and do go a long way.

The next day, I met up with Mary again and we checked out Red Rocks, went to a "dive bar" (a crappy bar) which actually seemed ok to me to be fair and then headed back into town for a few more drinks with her mum. Apparently, I'm more of a lightweight than I thought so ended up pretty pissed yet again. After that we all went our separate ways.

I ended meeting a couple of cool guys, Ambrose - from Washington and Deric from Canada. Ambrose, I met in my dorm and Deric, I met in the bar at the hostel. I was chatting away (drunk) to Ambrose when I realised Deric was sat filming us, a bit strange but after talking to him, he seemed pretty cool.

Me, Deric and Ambrose

The next day was my twenty-eighth birthday. Ambrose and I spent the morning shooting, then headed out to an aircraft museum - something Ambrose wanted to do which seemed fair considering I'd dragged him to a firing range.

There was a flight simulator in the museum that looked like something you'd find in a theme park - the thing was huge and encapsulated. You'd get in, be fastened down with a harness style belt system before being shut inside. You could choose whether to take on a passenger jet or a fighter jet. Ambrose took the passenger jet and me the fighter jet. Ambrose was up first and while he was in there I got talking to the woman in charge of the machine – there was a small bit of light flirting between us and some conversation about the differences between the US and UK. She had never left the States so was pretty keen to know about the UK. At one point, the machine did a barrow roll with Ambles shouting "whoahhhhh!" In excitement. Once Ambrose was finished and came out of the machine I looked inside. It really did look like a real cockpit. Just as I was about to step in, I stopped.

"Nah love" I think I'll give it a miss and let him [Ambrose] have my go."

Confused, they both asked why to which I just said I wasn't feeling it and so Ambrose jumped in, still confused but happy for a freebie. The worker stood there and asked.

"What happened?"

Again, I just said I wasn't feeling it, I hate fast rides, rollercoasters and the stuff that takes you upside down so realising that the simulator would do the whole upside-down thing, I had quickly changed my mind. The worker must have thought I was some kind of wuss and we didn't talk after that. Slightly embarrassing, I must say but looking back, I'm grateful for that last minute change of heart because at the time that simulator was reminding me far too much of the "strange turn" I'd had back on the plane and I couldn't shake the feeling that if I went in there I would have somehow been hospitalised.

Later that day I met up with Mary and a couple of her friends for a surprise birthday treat which turned out to be at a drag bar for a bingo/cabaret night. It was actually a lot more fun than it sounds although once again, I ended up wasted. It was such an amusing night, I vaguely remember being up on stage at one point having shots of tequila – I'm honestly not sure why but it's a fun memory!

My 28th birthday night out

So with another crappy hangover the next day I had an early start in order to head to an area called "Lookout Mountain." The plan was to explore the woods and open areas, check out the beautiful scenery and eventually, leave the rock I'd found back home somewhere.

After a few hours of wandering, I found a ridge that overlooked a valley. There was a guy sat on the edge of the ridge with a laptop, he looked over as I went a little below him.

Probably thinking I was going to jump he asked if I was ok and I told him I was just there to chill and with that he just left me to it.

I found what I thought was the perfect place to leave the rock, took a photo of it making sure my phone had logged the geo tag for the photo.

The "keep or hide" rock I left at Look Out mountain

I left a post on the Facebook page that was mentioned on the rock, explaining what I had done and why and posted the picture of where I'd left it with a screen shot of the geo tag - proving it really was on a mountain range in the USA. A woman reached out eventually, telling me that it was her and her 4-year-old son who had painted it and left it where I found it. Apparently, I'd made their day by letting them know about it; four years later I have no idea if it has been found or if those that may have found it understand its relevance but the thought of somebody finding it one day, always makes me smile.

I ended my trip by spending my last night heading out for a bit more exploring in the town, had a few drinks in a couple of nice bars then with a trip to the cinema to watch IT.

Overall, it was an amazing trip and one that I am pleased I was able to have before what was to come.......

CHAPTER 11

January 2018
"You still ok doing that for me, mate?"

If there was a time in my life I could describe as being when the shit really did hit the fan and get very, very real it would be everything you read from this point onwards. January 2018 is where life for me as I knew it was about to change...

Over the course of the year I'd started to notice things weren't quite right - I could never put my finger on what it was exactly but something just felt off with me both physically and mentally.

Early into January I spoke to my doctor about it explaining that I felt off, constantly fatigued and stressed. He asked what I did for work and how many hours a week I was working. So I told him I worked in a homeless hostel and although I was on a 40 hour per week contract I'd been hammering the overtime as much as I could, so was now working 70+ hours a week all on night shifts.

"Ah, I see. Matthew, you are working too much!"

He told me to cut back on the hours and recommended I take a break – I was in the room for all of around five minutes but I was happy with his diagnosis. I hate going to the doctors/ hospital and the only reason I had agreed to go in the first place is because I was fed up with people telling me how ill I looked.

As per the previous year I had decided to carry on with my fundraising challenges for HHCP and had elected to do two further Tough Mudders, The Hull 10k and Europe's Toughest Mudder (ETM).

The TMs didn't faze me too much, they were to be completed over the course of the same weekend but as hard as that seemed, I knew I could do it. ETM on the other hand; that was a on a completely different scale.

In short, ETM is a five mile Tough Mudder course with fifteen - twenty obstacles. Just completing that once though wouldn't really make it the Toughest in Europe so the idea is to complete as many laps as physically possible over the period of twelve hours – and just to make it a bit more fun...... It's held through the night.

Working full time night shifts made training at home quite hard. Luckily for me, we had a gym that I could use in the hostel before, during and after shifts. I'd go to work and providing there were no incidents to contend with, I'd be in the gym by 1am until at least 2am before taking a quick trip upstairs to use the staff shower (talk about perks of the job!).

I always made sure I had my radio with me just in case the other person on shift with me needed anything but none of the ever had an issue with me being in the gym, even if I stayed longer than an hour because they knew they'd also be able to take an extended break and catch some shut eye with no issues.

I started to become obsessed with the gym and fitness in general though and even bought a training mask that was designed to restrict your breathing while you train over four different levels in order to strengthen your lungs.

I got a heap of stick for using it though as nobody agreed that it was a healthy way to train. People who saw me training with it would always make a point of saying that it's too dangerous and that I'll get stupidly ill using it. Say what you like but getting my 5k run time down to 23 minutes with the mask on showed me that it was working, although finishing a 5k in that time with the mask on wasn't easy - I nearly passed out more than once directly after a run so maybe people had a point.

As well as training hard I was also working A LOT and soon found myself on my twenty third consecutive night shift without a day off. A couple of these shifts were doubles, meaning I'd go home after my night shift, get some sleep then be back at work for a 2pm – 10pm shift and then stay on for a night shift straight after. Technically speaking working that many hours is probably not legal but the company refused to allow agency staff to work days and would do what they could to avoid paying the higher rates to have them on nights, they were more than happy to have me work them instead.

On the 22nd of these shifts (my last night of that stint) I made a point of hammering the gym hard – my mask was on and a 90-minute session later, I felt incredible; even more so after a hot shower! I'd managed to get my 5k run time to less than twenty three minutes so was quite happy with myself. The rest of the shift continued as normal and I left slightly early at around 7am as I was due back in at 2pm for one more shift - after that though I'd have two weeks off.

My training session during the 23rd night shift

I went straight home and was in bed by 7:45am, no sooner had my head hit the pillow, and my neighbours began blasting music. No matter where I was in the house, I could hear what they were listening to word for word. This was fairly normal for them but I was normally crashed out before they'd play their music or I'd at least had a decent few hours' sleep first. I really didn't have the patience to go ask/tell them to turn it down so after spending an hour or trying and failing to sleep through it I gave in and decided that I'd either stay awake and go to work as planned (knowing that I was on shift with Rachel, who would be keen for an easy shift) or just call in sick, have a nice hot bath, tell the neighbours to shut the hell up, unwind and try to sleep later.

In a job like mine, where it was common to find yourself dealing with life & death situations, a job where being too fatigued makes you a danger to yourself and those around you, common sense dictated that I should call in sick. By 1pm I'd made my mind up, I wasn't going to lose out on a day's wages, especially when it was at the overtime rate!

I figured if I sank a few cans of Red Bull and found some odd jobs that needed to be done it would keep me going until 10pm and then I'd get a much needed two weeks off – easy, right? I got to work slightly early to find my best friend, Kris was there. He'd been out of the army for a couple of years by this point and was struggling to find work so was volunteering with us to help keep him busy and his mind occupied. I had a quick catch up with him before bumping into Rob, one of my co-workers from the previous shift who was just about to start clearing out a former resident's room. I stopped him and told him to leave it for me to do and get himself home early; obviously he was more than keen to take me up on the offer. For me, it meant I'd be able to go upstairs and keep myself busy in a quiet area out of the way for a good couple of hours.

At the start and end of every shift, there's always a "handover" a chance for staff that are starting the shift to hear what happened during the previous shift, get any updates and be informed about particular issues from the day. In this handover at the start of this shift there was me, Rach and one other staff member from the previous shift. I remember being stood up, leaning against a small set of draws. After a minute I was seriously struggling to focus on what was being said but as I was extremely tired I thought nothing of it. I needed to be in the handover so I decided to sit down and just chill out for ten minutes before I went to clear the room out for Rob. As I sat down, Rob poked his head though the door.

"Are you sure you don't mind doing that room for me mate?"

Before I had a chance to reply I realised that I was involuntary looking over my left shoulder and making the same kind of jarring noise that I'd make when I was suffering episodes of sleep paralysis except now I was paralysed and awake.

I couldn't move at all; I could hear but couldn't see. I instantly thought that I'd been so tired that I had fallen asleep during handover and now woken up in that state again.

For a few seconds I was quite embarrassed until I heard Rachel say.

"Matt, stop taking the piss and just answer him!"

I couldn't answer him. I couldn't move or speak. In that moment I thought I must be having a stroke and I couldn't do anything about it, not even ask for help.

This was a level of fear that I'd never felt before. Imagine being trapped in your own body, in a room with friends; you know that you're in a life-threatening situation but you can't get help because no one knows and you can't tell them. I was trying everything I could to move, to speak and beg for help but my body just wouldn't respond. After what felt like an eternity, I heard Rachel scream.

"What the fuck is going on!" I could hear the fear in her voice.

Suddenly, people knew I was in trouble. I remember thinking, "ok, this is it. I'm about to die" I heard someone shout.

"Matt!"

And then everything went dark...

The next thing I remember is being on the floor. I could feel somebody stroking my arm. I could just about make out that somebody had commented about me being red hot before I blacked out again.

After that I vaguely remember being stood up, feeling like I was losing my balance before hearing people shouting before everything else once again went dark.

The next thing I remember is being in the back of an ambulance that I have no recollection of getting into.

One minute I was in handover and the next I found myself arguing with a medic; I was trying to tell him that I needed to be back at work, I was fine and didn't need to be going to hospital. I felt like I was drunk – the whole ride to hospital was and still is a blur.

Once there I still felt like I was drunk, although over time this seemed to ease. I remember Mum and Dad coming to stay with me and eventually a doctor came by, he went through a few basic questions before shining a torch in my eyes. First the left then the right, then same again. He seemed to focus on one eye in particular and kept coming back to it.

I wasn't there too long before I was sent for a CT scan after which I was told I needed to be kept in overnight so I could have an MRI the next day. By this point, I was so dazed and tired that I just went along with whatever I was told, I didn't have the energy to argue or question them. In the back of my mind, I thought I knew exactly what had happened. To me everything seemed to point to a stroke and that's the signs doctors were looking for.

I called Rachel to let her know I was ok and that I was being kept in overnight and asked what had actually happened. She explained that as Rob had walked in to the office to ask if I was still ok to do the room for him, I'd put my thumb up and just froze, making a bizarre noise. Everyone thought I just messing about until I began to fall off the chair and started having a seizure, and an apparently violent one at that so they had lowered me to the floor.

Apparently the seizure went on for a few minutes before finally coming to an end after which I'd managed to stand up and taken a swing for one of the staff members in the room. I guess that when I remembered people shouting and me feeling like I'd lost my balance. As it happens, it's quite common for people that have just come out of a bad seizure to become aggressive and come across as if they are drunk. With Rach telling me this, the idea of stroke now sounded a bit odd. Maybe it was just a fit? Maybe I've just got epilepsy I thought.

The next day I had my MRI scan in the morning and in the afternoon an old friend of mine, Tam had heard that I was in hospital and decided to pop over to keep me company and have a little catch up. We had a good bit banter for an hour or so before a doctor came to my cubicle and introduced himself before asking if I'd like some privacy before he said anymore.

"Nah mate, it's fine, she's a good friend of mine. She can stay."

A part of me knew from the doctors tone of voice that this wasn't going be good news. But nothing could have prepared me for what was to come.

"Ok Matthew, the MRI has shown that you have a brain tumour"

At that I burst out laughing... It was probably the shock but the doctor looked more shocked by my reaction than I was.

I looked over to Tam who'd turned white, she was looking at me, almost in tears and there's me laughing.

I mean, what's the "normal" reaction to hearing that you have a brain tumour? There isn't one. There's no idiots guide on how to take life changing news – not one that I know of anyway. You just have to take it as it comes and hope that you're lucky enough not to be alone when the life changing shit rolls down the hill.

Of all of the reasons in the world I had thought of for what had happened the very last one was that there was something growing in my brain. The doctor couldn't or wouldn't give much more info other than a tumour had been found, it was somewhere on the right side of my brain and that I would have an appointment with a consultant to talk about it on Monday (in 3 days' time) and with that I was sent home to wait.

Surprisingly Monday rolled around quite fast. Dad and Rach both decided they wanted to come to the appointment which was fine with me.

Rach said she wanted to be there both to support me and also so that she could write up the notes of what was said, like we were in a formal meeting at work. She wanted a detailed description to help all of us know what was happening and to allow us to process it all afterwards. That was actually a really good shout on her part to be fair.

I remember getting in the car with the pair of them and opened up with the line.

"Don't worry guys, if it turns out to be a cancerous tumour, I promise I won't become the next Deadpool or Breaking Bad wannabe!" Neither of them found it funny Dad told me to shut the fuck up which I guess was a pretty fair comment.

When we arrived I was expecting to meet an average doctor that would run me though what had been found etc. Nope. This guy was a neurosurgeon (brain surgeon) and there was also a Macmillan nurse present. Her role was to make sure I could fully understand what was being said and to also explain how Macmillan could and would support me. Apparently, it's not just cancer patients they work with but any kind of tumour patient. After introducing himself and explaining what it was that he actually did, he brought up my MRI scan results. Seeing my skull, inside and out (including my brain) on a photo for the first time was definitely a shock to the system but seeing my brain tumour for the first time left me with a pit of dread in my stomach, in that instant all of the laughing and joking left me.

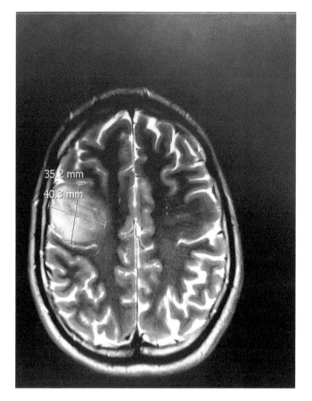

The first image I was shown of my brain tumour

The tumour itself was about the size of a Cadburys Cream Egg - 2018 sized Cream Egg that is.

"Can you tell me why you had a CT scan in 2010, Matthew?" The consultant asked.

Out of embarrassment I laughed and explained that I'd had a drunken reunion with a friend of mine that resulted in me falling over and having a nasty head injury but that it wasn't until the next morning that I went hospital.

"Ok, well this is your scan from 2010."

A CT scan isn't quite as in depth as an MRI but the brain was visible on it. He then pointed at the right side of by brain on the screen. "Matthew, that right there is your brain tumour in 2010"

He then explained that because I'd been taken to hospital for a head injury, nobody had any reason to suspect a tumour was there, regardless of the fact it could easily be seen on the scan results. I couldn't believe it. I'd been walking around with this tumour in my brain, getting bigger and bigger for eight fucking years? All because somebody didn't look at the scan results with a tiny bit more effort?

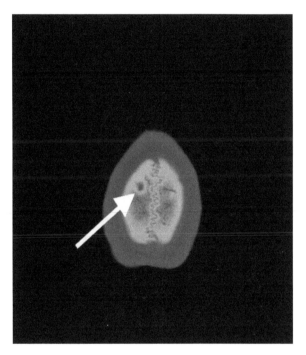

The 2010 CT scan of my missed tumour

The neurosurgeon then went on to explain his recommended plan of action. He explained that I would need "urgent surgery" to remove as much of the tumour as possible but of course, this was just a recommendation and I could refuse and leave it if I so wished.

Now I'm not sure why anybody would want to actually leave something of that size in their brain, knowing it would only get bigger so I obviously opted in for the surgery. The appointment ended with the neurosurgeon explaining that I'd need more scans to help him get a better picture to work with and more check-ups with him before the surgery date. The Macmillan nurse spent some time with me too, explaining that I could and maybe should start looking into the idea of leaving work with the knowledge that if I did, there would be a host of benefits and grants on hand if I needed them. I gave the smile and nod treatment, knowing that I wasn't going to be leaving work at all - brain tumour or not.

Just as we left the hospital, for whatever reason (to this day I still don't know why) I decided that instead of calling the tumour, a tumour, it would forever be referred to as "my little Hitchhiker" due to how long it had been "hitching" a ride with me.

After some thought, I realised that I couldn't or shouldn't be working with a brain tumour - especially one that was triggering serious and violent seizures. Officially, the company I worked for would allow me to take three months off on full pay (around £1200 a month) but in exceptional circumstances, that could be increased to six months but in order to get that you had to write a formal letter to one of the Managing Directors of the company. It was however, ridiculously rare for anybody to be granted the six months when they asked. Just a year before I'd been diagnosed, a co-worker who had just had major surgery to remove a malignant tumour in her breast had been turned down for it. With that in mind, I knew I wouldn't get it.

But before I even had a chance to write my letter, my boss called to let me know that the Managing Director had seen my request and granted me the six months off on full pay. I hadn't even written the letter yet so surly there's been a mistake? Confused, I just accepted the decision – I mean I certainly wasn't going to question it, six months to do whatever I liked, when I liked and still get paid? Go on then!

I later found out that Rachel had written a formal letter on my behalf explaining in detail how the tumour was affecting me and that I would need a long period of time to recover post-surgery. There was no questioning it. The time off had been granted with no fuss at all!

By February, I still hadn't come to terms with the diagnoses and hadn't really accepted it. I just couldn't get my head around the idea of there being an object growing in my brain - let alone the fact that it had been there for at least eight years!

I remember, around mid-February I'd arranged to meet Rachel at work for a quick catchup before heading to town for a bit of shopping and a Costa. I was wearing an Apple Watch at the time. After leaving work and walking to town, I could feel my heart racing even though we were walking quite slowly at that point. I looked at the heart rate monitor on my watch to see it was showing more than 150BPM. That's the kind of heart rate I'd expect to see during or after a hard run/sprint, not a slow walk!

"Not gonna lie, Rach, I think I'm going to have another fit today."

There wasn't much either of us could do at that point, and eventually my heart rate did slow down.

After a bit of shopping, we ended up in Costa where we could finally sit, chill and catch up, although the place was packed. Hungry, I ordered an extremely overpriced toasty and a smoothie (yes, a smoothie in winter!) After a couple of bites of the overpriced but bloody beautiful toasty, Rachel stood up.

"I'm just going to the toilet, I'll be back in a minute"

I had a mouth full as she said that, so I put my thumb up as if to say okie doke. Just as I tried to raise my thumb, my head locked back and I began making the same moaning noise that had occurred when I had the last big seizure.

"Fuck, not now!" I heard Rachel shout my name before hearing her shout for help and then just like before, everything went dark.

I came round to find I was mid conversation with a pair of paramedics. I was sat on the floor trying and failing to explain where I lived. Just like before I felt, looked and sounded like I was extremely drunk. I don't remember regaining consciousness at all or how the conversation started with them but there I was. I'd refused to go to hospital - I knew what had caused the seizure and knew that I'd be fine within in a few hours.

One of the paramedics told me that she recognised me as she explained that just a few months before she had attended the hostel on an emergency call.

I'd had a resident take a deliberate overdose but had then changed his mind about wanting to take his own life and asked me to help him. I called him an ambulance but when they arrived he had some form of breakdown and became violent and aggressive towards them. I was in the back of the ambulance with him as he'd tried to attack one of them which I put a stop to that. There's nothing worse than people who try to attack those in the emergency services. Especially those that are trying to help you!

It turned out that one of the medics with me was the one I'd stopped from being attacked. As random as that was, given the situation I was in, it was nice to see that my work was appreciated and remembered.

I noticed a mark on my top and asked what it was. Rachel explained that when I'd began to have the seizure, I obviously still had a mouth full of food. Her first reaction was to cram her fingers in my mouth and get everything that was in it; one of the things we were taught in first aid is that when somebody's having a seizure the last thing you should do is stick your fingers in their mouth as it's a fairly quick way to lose a finger or two! Knowing that I was going to choke on the food though Rach hadn't given a second thought for the risks and had only cared about making sure this seizure didn't kill me. I always have and always will respect that move. Had she not done that, I probably wouldn't be writing this book right now.

Knowing I was fairly ok and because I was refusing any further medical care, the paramedics soon left. After realising just how busy the place was and that a lot of the customers were having a good old nosey I decided it was time to leave as

I found the whole thing extremely embarrassing. The thought of me being like that in front of a room full of people that were all staring. Nope. We both left and went to my parents with Rachel insisting that I stayed there the night just to be safe, I agreed but after she left, I booked a cab and went home. I've always been quite stubborn and a "self-caring" kind of person. By self-caring I mean that no matter the problem, I prefer to deal with it myself. I've always hated asking for help or looking like I needed any form of help or support. I don't know why, maybe it was the idea of being a burden.

Obviously, I agreed to counselling but for me that was different, just being able to sit and rant about how the week had been to someone impartial who wouldn't start feeling sorry for me and would challenge me when needed. That was something I needed, any other kinds of help and support just wasn't for me.

It wouldn't be long before I'd slowly learn just how stupidly dangerous that kind of thought process is though...

CHAPTER 12

March - 2018

Brain surgery and the resulting cluster fucks

In February Katie once again decided to cut all contact between me and Billie after telling me that she couldn't and wouldn't trust me with her, knowing that I had a brain tumour. She told me that it was unfair to let Billie see me that way. To me though it felt as though she just wanted me out of the picture and me having a brain tumour just gave her the ammo she wanted to pull the trigger on getting me out of said picture so she could live her happy family life with her new partner. I was completely crushed but felt there was little I could do about it at the time – I certainly didn't have the energy to fight her as I had a fair amount of other shit on my plate.

I was attending the appointments and check-ups at the hospital as scheduled which I would always arrive at alone. I remember turning up to one such checkup and my consultant asked if I had anybody else with me.

"Nope it's just me today, mate".

He seemed quite pissed off by this, looked at my records and found my next of kin details before calling my Mum and having her on speaker phone while he conducted the appointment. This guy absolutely hated me turning up on my own and warned me that if I did so again, he would call my mum again. Grown man or not, this guy wasn't taking any shit from me.

After numerous appointments, check-ups and scans over January and February, in early March I received a letter from the hospital to confirm that a date had been set for my surgery. March 20th. I had barely two weeks' notice for what was to come.

My consultant had always said that I would need urgent surgery to remove the tumour/Hitchhiker (He never seemed to find the nickname as funny as I did) but by mid-February, I'd pushed the thought of having it to the back of my mind and obviously me being me still hadn't really accepted the severity of all that was happening.

The letter explained that I needed to be at the hospital the night before the surgery on March 19th – that was Jacks birthday. I knew Amy had planned a party for him that day, so I decided that whatever happened, I was going to be at that party, I absolutely wasn't going to miss out on seeing Jack on his birthday especially with the next day being what it was.

The days building up to the 19th flew by. I choose to spend the build up to the surgery focusing on seeing Jack as much as I could. I would have killed to get one cuddle from Billie before the surgery but I knew that wasn't going to happen.

Amy had called me on the 19th to say that rather than meeting her at her mums (where Jack's birthday party would be) I should wait at mine for her to come as they were passing anyway and could give me a lift. I thought nothing of it and agreed.

There was knock on the door early that afternoon, I opened the door to see that Jack, Amy and her partner were all there BUT Billie was also with them! It had been weeks since I last saw her and initially I couldn't quite believe my eyes!

Amy had gotten in touch with Katie asking if she would allow Billie to go to Jacks party. Katie was more than happy to agree on the condition I wasn't there. Obviously, Amy gave her the smile and nod treatment.

Amy knew just how serious the next day would be and what could go wrong and had no intentions of letting me go in for that kind of surgery without me being able to at least see both my kids and spend a few final hours with them. In the time that I've known Amy, she'd done more than a few things that I'll be never be able to forgive her for but that day... That day is day I'll never forget. For her it was a small but significant act but for me, it was huge. I might not be able to forgive a lot of what she's done but seeing Billie the day before I was due to have brain surgery and being able to get cuddles with both of my kids, together - words will never be able to describe my appreciation for that moment...

Being at the party was an odd feeling – I hadn't seen any of Amy's family for a couple of years by this point and yet there I was, at Amy's mum's house with all her family and friends. Obviously, they all knew that I was going for brain surgery the next day which just made me feel even more awkward.

Minus a quick nod and a polite hello, nobody really said anything and I was happy with that - I just wanted to spend a day with Billie and Jack, nobody and nothing else mattered to me.

The day went by far too fast and before I knew it, the party was over and it was time to get ready to leave. Amy and her partner both dropped me off before taking Billie back to her mum, without letting on that she'd just spent the afternoon with me of course. I got one last cuddle with Billie and Jack before walking away from the car and heading back to my house. Amy followed me to the door to say goodbye and good luck and we hugged before I walked through the door.

It was about 4pm by this point, I knew that I needed to be at hospital for around 9/10pm that night. I needed to be ready to go down to surgery by 7am latest the next morning - hence needing to be there the night before.

Since I received the letter telling me the surgery had been booked, there was one thing I knew I needed to do before I went in and it was something I'd put a lot of effort in to avoiding.

I'd been warned on more than a few occasions that this surgery could come with major side effects. I could suffer a bleed on the brain, a stroke, partial or full paralysis, severe brain damage or even death.

In preparation for a "worst case scenario" I needed to make video. An "if you're watching this, I obviously didn't make it" kind of video. Not only had I been warned that the risks were high for a surgery like this, Rachel had told me about a cousin of hers that had suffered a bleed on the brain during a similar kind of surgery and suffered an almost catastrophic stroke as a result. I had been struggling to accept the brain tumour thing since I'd been diagnosed but a part of me knew just how serious this was and could be.

I really didn't want to do the video because I knew just how emotionally hard it would be to do. Nevertheless, that evening, after I'd packed my bags for my stay in hospital, I turned the TV off, closed the blinds and set my camera up.

The plan was to do separate videos for Jack and Billie and then one for friends and another for family – I decided to start with Billie's video.

I never made it past the introduction. The "if you're watching this…" kind of intro, before starting to cry. So I tried doing the friends video instead and again, soon after I'd started the intro I began to cry. I ended up giving up in the end.

Honestly, I would never wish the thought of having to sit and make a goodbye video for your kids, friends and family on anybody. Trying to make those videos genuinely broke me.

It's a moment that even now, nearly four years later that still leaves me quite emotional.

Soon after, my friend Nikita called to check in and see how I was feeling and make sure I was ready for the next day.

"Yea I'm good, I'm ready for this but I'm really not liking the idea of having my belly cut open just to have a catheter shoved in the hole…" Confused, Nikita asked me to repeat what I'd just said. I thought she just didn't know what a catheter was, so went on to explain it to her like she was a bit daft for not knowing.

"Ermmm… Matt, that's not how a catheter works or where it goes…"

"Well, were the hell would a big tube go then?" Again, thinking she was being daft.

"Matt, it goes in your penis."

"Nah mate your wrong" I said.

She was certain she was right and I of course refused to believe that this would be an actual thing that could happen. She told me that she had a friend that was a nurse and that she was going to text her then and there to get a definite answer. The line went quiet for a few moments before Nikita was in hysterics laughing ridiculously hard which was all the answer I needed.

Suddenly it wasn't just the idea of having my head cut open and my brain chopped at. Nope the thought of having a large tube go somewhere no man should have anything go was almost at the top of my worry and cringe list.

I made sure I had at least a weeks' worth of kit packed up and ready to go before chilling for a couple of hours with a movie. My mum came and picked me up later that night and we took what felt like a fairly average drive to hospital with minimal conversation.

When we arrived at the hospital, Mum came to the ward with me while I got booked in which was almost like being booked into a hotel. We hugged and with that they left, there wasn't that much either of us could really say.

Strangely I managed to get straight to sleep that night and woke up around 5am. There wasn't much I could do as I wasn't allowed to eat or drink so I just sat and chilled. I'd packed "Monkey" in my kit bag; obviously I needed my lucky travel mascot with me. I took a quick photo of him sat on the window overlooking the hospital grounds and stuck it on Instagram. Soon after someone from the surgical team came over and started to go through what was actually going to happen that day, what to expect and to make sure I was 100% ok with going ahead.

Obviously, I agreed and gave him my version of what I expected to happen.

"You guys are going to open up my head, find this hitchhiker of mine and pluck it out!"

The look on his face showed he didn't find that as funny as it sounded in my head.

He then went on to give me a more detailed version of exactly how the surgery would go. I signed the paperwork - acknowledging what I'd been told and that I knew what I was letting myself in for.

Not long after he'd left, a nurse came over and introduced herself explaining that she was a student nurse. She wanted to know if I would be ok if she came to watch the surgery take place as she'd never seen neurosurgery (brain surgery) take place.

"Sure! Why not, if it's something that's going to help you with your learning then come with!"

I'm sure by now, reading this, you're starting to see just how serious I wasn't taking any of this. Sure, I had tried to make the 'just in case' video but that was it, for some reason it seemed normal for me at the time. The fact that I was about to be taken down to surgery, have my head split open and have my brain cut at with scalpels didn't seem to faze me at all. Looking back it is strange and worrying but that thought process was about to come crashing down. Hard.

Soon after the training nurse left it hit me. I might actually not make it out of surgery today. In the next few hours, I could die. Something I should have spent the last three months processing hit me in just a few seconds and I only had around half an hour to process it! There wasn't time to process anything by this point and before I knew it, I was being wheeled down to pre op.

The first room I started in was a large waiting room with several beds where I had to wait until the surgical team were ready for me. I was there for about twenty minutes but it felt like hours until I was wheeled down to a pre surgery room which was the last stage before going in, where I was to be pumped up with anesthetic. Take a moment to think about that – you're sat down while someone saws your head open and starts to chip away at your brain, all while you're still awake!

Just as I was being pumped up with whatever drugs were being used, one of the male nurses came and fitted the catheter. It's safe to say, that I was pretty grateful the drugs were kicking in by this point but it still didn't take me long to pass out.

The next thing I remember is being sat up right, in theatre. Everything felt normal, all be it with me feeling slightly spaced out. I remember feeling an immense amount of pressure on the sides of my head. I'd been told to expect some discomfort but this, this really hurt - almost unbearable. I remember biting my tongue and thinking to myself that I needed to stay quiet, I couldn't or wouldn't risk the surgery being called off. I discovered after that this was the clamp being screwed into my skull (literally!) to help keep me very firmly still -that tumour was leaving my brain one way or another!

I then remember hearing a saw cutting away at something which was of course, my skull! I was almost certain I could feel dust falling onto my back but given the fact I was slightly spaced out; I could have just been imagining it.

The pain didn't last too long, that or the meds kicked in. I must have passed out at some point because I remember hearing.

"Matthew, can you hear me?"

It was expected that I would occasionally drift off so that wasn't an issue but I needed to be awake as long as possible so the nurse sat with me could maintain conversation and check my responses. The idea being that if anything was to go wrong or if an area of my brain had been cut at that should be avoided, it would become apparent instantly - through changes in my speech or ability to answer certain basic questions. I remember being asked what my plans for the rest of the year were. I told the nurse that I was meant to be doing two Tough Mudder's and the Hull 10k in just a few months. She laughed.

"You won't be able to do all that! You'll be too busy recovering!"

"You'll be surprised" I replied.

She then asked about holidays I'd been on recently so I told her about America and then moved on to talk about South Africa and Riverside. I told her that in 2016, I'd been to South Africa to work with baboons and others animals. At this point she stopped me and asked where exactly this place was to which I replied, Limpopo.

"I think I know exactly where you mean. Was there an orange factory on the same road as where you were?"

"Yes!" I said in excitement.

She then explained that she had actually spent time there herself, not at Riverside but nearby. For the life of me, I can't remember what it was she told me she was doing but she described the area in detail and knew exactly where I was talking about. I don't know why, but I found this hilarious and began laughing quite hard. I remember saying.

"Fuck me, it's a small world isn't it!?"

No sooner had I said that, I noticed my arm rising with my thumb pointing down. My face felt incredibly strange and I couldn't speak. It almost felt like the last two seizures I'd had but at the same time, different. I could hear the nurse,

"Matthew, Matthew! Can you hear me!? Ok, we need to stop now!"

I then felt a wet trickling sensation going down my neck/back - the surgical team had poured water/saline on my exposed brain as a means to counter/stop the seizure. Before I had time to think and understand what was happening, I was out cold.

Just like after the last two seizures I'd had I don't remember waking up but the first thing I remember is being mid conversation. Well, mid argument this time. I was in a bed, shouting and swearing. I don't remember much but I remember the nurse that had been sat with me in the surgery telling me that I should wait and come back in six weeks to re-try the surgery. I don't remember my reply to that, I just remember the main surgeon (my consultant) asking.

"Matthew, what do you actually want?"

Again, I don't remember the reply, although it wasn't too long before I found out what it actually reply actually was...

Before I had a chance to think, I was lying down in a bed drifting in and out of consciousness and something felt very different. I couldn't open my eyes but I could hear voices around me. One of said voices was Philip bloody Schofield! Of all the people in the world that could be with me there and then why was Philip Schofield there?! He was talking about polar bears and penguins for some reason. I was trying to figure out why a morning TV presenter was talking about animals while in a hospital. I then heard him talking to someone about patients having a habit of pretending to be asleep and I remember thinking that he was talking about me. I couldn't move, talk or even open my eyes and was quite offended by that so tried my best to reply. Nope still nothing.

I must have crashed out again and the next thing I remember was waking up needing to pee. I was absolutely busting to go pee but I still couldn't move or talk, I then remembered I had a catheter fitted.

"Screw it, I'll just pee in the bag then!"

I peed so hard that the catheter blew out. I might still have been spaced out but knowing you've peed the bed in a room full of people is still pretty fucking embarrassing. Hilarious now, (I'm actually sat laughing at the moment as I write this!) but at the time, it was definitely embarrassing!

I managed to open my eyes just enough to make out that there were two nurses still stood by my bed.

"Excuse me, I think I need some help" while trying to lift my sheets to show what had happened.

One of the nurses changed the sheets as if it was such a normal thing but I remember being stupidly embarrassed and continuously apologising like an idiot.

I was starting to come round by this point and I very quickly realised that Philip Schofield was in-fact NOT by my side, at the hospital (shocker I know). It was, instead a nurse that just happened to sound a lot like him. I remember telling him that I heard him talking about patients pretending to sleep and told him that I hadn't been pretending to asleep at all. He laughed and told me he knew I was asleep and was just talking about patients in general, not me. I'm glad he saw the funny side in that!

As I was sat there, trying to work out where I was exactly and what had actually happened, I could feel an immense amount of pressure/pain building up on my head. I thought it was the clamp that had been screwed to my skull. Clearly the surgery had indeed been abandoned after my seizure and the clamp hadn't been removed yet. I asked one of the nurses if they could remove it as it was starting to hurt my head. She looked at me and told me that there was nothing on my head at all. Nothing other than bandages.

"Wait, have I had the surgery? Is the tumour gone!?"

The nurse explained that after the seizure, I'd been pulled out of surgery to evaluate whether I could handle going back in to finish off or not. The nurse then told me that I had made her day when the surgeon asked me what I wanted to happen after being pulled out and had replied with.

"Get me back in that fucking room and get this fucking thing out of my brain now!"

Apparently, they all found this quite hilarious even though it's also apparently quite a normal reaction for someone that's just been though brain surgery (or half at that point for me) - even the main surgeon found it amusing.

The Philip Schofield sound-alike then asked me if I'd like morphine to help with the pain in my head, I'd never had morphine before but was happy to take it if it stopped my head hurting the way it was. Needless to say, the pain soon disappeared.

Once it had, I had just started thinking that I needed to text everyone and let them know I'd come out of surgery ok when I looked up and saw both my mum and friend Nikita standing at a desk. I asked one of the nurses to get them to go and grab my phone for me so I could contact others. The nurse looked at me and said that the two people I thought were Mum and Nikita, were in fact two nurses. I didn't believe her at first, genuinely believing they were Mum & Nikita. The morphine and freshly injured brain appeared to have left me in a slightly baffled state. Obviously "Baffled" being a major understatement!

Anyway, I was soon taken upstairs to Ward 40 where I could be closely monitored for the night before being taken to ward 4 for my recovery. Waiting for me there were Mum, my sister Katy, Rachel and Nikita. I was meant to be out of surgery by around 1pm but thanks to my seizure during the surgery it was actually closer to 7pm when everything was finished. I'd been down there for around 11 hours; needless to say, people had started to panic. The morphine had well and truly started to kick in by the time I was on the ward.

Luckily, I'd prepared for such an instance. I'd seen videos of people who were on morphine and the hilarious crap they came out with while on it. So before going in to hospital the day before, I made sure that those who were coming to see me right after, would film me if I'd had morphine to which they were all more than happy to oblige!

As you can imagine, there were some interesting moments while I was on the morphine. One of which being me telling Rachel that if this is what it feels like to be high on opiate drugs, then I'll be going back to work and having a word with the boss about relaxing the rules on drug use! I was very firm and serious on this point while everybody found it hilarious!

Also caught on camera was a ridiculously hilarious "attempt" of mine to do the "Big fish, Little fish" song and dance. Re watching said video for the purpose of this book, well, let's just say that whatever I was doing, was definitely not any form of dance I've ever seen!

After a while, a nurse came over and told everyone that it was time for them to leave. They were only allowed to see me because I'd just come out of surgery. Given the fact I'd just had brain surgery and was high as a kite on morphine it's fair to say that I don't really remember too much of that night. What I do remember though is something that has forever been referred to as the "squirter story…"

So, there I am in bed post brain surgery, my friends and family have all left and the lights on the ward have been turned off for the night. The only light left on was at the nurse's station.

I've always hated being in hospital. Hell, I can't even stand waiting around in a doctor's waiting room for more than a few minutes. I'd somehow come to the conclusion that I didn't need to be in hospital anymore and that I'd be better off just going home, to my own bed, where I'd be a lot more comfortable and a lot happier. The problem with this was, I knew the nurses wouldn't let me out. I knew from past visits to floor 4 that floor had a secure "mag lock door" to get in and out of the ward. Floor 4 was for those that had suffered head and brain injuries, had any kind of neurosurgery or suffered with things like dementia etc. The mag lock door was to prevent patients from deciding they were going to up and leave -people like me. The only way through said door was with a key fob that only staff had access to however, at work in the homeless hostel, we also used the exact same mag lock system. I knew that next to the door there was a little green button, an emergency door release that could be pressed to open the door without sounding an alarm.

All I had to do, was get out of bed, walk as confidently as I possibly could, in such a way that it looked like I was just heading to the toilet -if I looked nervous the game would be up and the nurses would know I shouldn't be up and about.

There were four steps to this plan of mine; get out of bed without being seen, walk out of the ward and into the corridor, get to the main door and release the mag lock, then make my way out of the hospital and finally grab a taxi and get home. Easy!

Remember, I was high as a kite at this point so had no idea just how ridiculously stupid this sounded. To me, this was a master escape plan! Ok, Step one - get out of bed without being seen. Something that I'd not thought about was that I couldn't move any of the left side of my body. At all! I didn't understand why at the time and thanks to being high, didn't appreciate how much not being able to move a leg and arm could affect this master plan of mine!

As I tried to get my legs out of the bed, I suddenly realised I couldn't move my left side. Ok, no drama, I'll just shuffle out of bed then. As I tried exactly this instead of creeping stealthily out I fell on to the floor in heap. Not only had I not accounted for being unable to move any of my left side but I'd also completely forgotten that I was still attached to all the cables linked to the machines (including the catheter!) So, there I am, on the floor, in the dark and tangled up in all these cables. I looked over to the nurse's station and realised that nobody had actually seen me. My plan was still salvageable. Plan B was to just crawl along the floor, hoping I wouldn't be seen. I tried but as you can imagine, being half paralysed, high as a kite and still hooked up to a few machines - It's quite hard to crawl. No scratch that -it's impossible to crawl. Lying on the floor, I began to feel extremely cold which was the point where I gave up -clearly, I wasn't going anywhere. I tried to get the attention of the nurses without shouting in an attempt not to wake the other patients so instead, I tried whispering loudly. That failed. I tried waving with my good arm. That failed too! I gave up, realising that I was going to have to get myself back in to bed without being seen. Turns out, this was an even more complicated task than getting out of bed.

Imagine not being able to move your left arm and left leg at all, then imagine you're attached to various different cables and that one of these cables is in a rather awkward place. Between your legs. Then, imagine having to try and climb up in to a bed that's about 3ft high. Not forgetting that you're high of course. It must have been quite the sight to see.

"Matthew! What's going on here?" A nurse had spotted me.

She came over, helped me get up before asking how and why I was out of bed in the first place. "I'm just going out for some fresh air"

I've no idea how she replied to that but she must have thought I was losing the plot. As she turned on the light for my cubicle, she suddenly shrieked.

"Oh my god, what's happened here!?"

My nice white bed sheets were now soaked red in blood. The hospital gown I was wearing and the area I'd be lying in were also covered in blood. It turned out that I'd managed to rip out one of the cannulas in my hand while trying to leave. Being on blood thinners, meant that I was able to bleed more than enough to make an ugly mess.

"Well, it looks like we have quite the squirter on our hands doesn't it!" The nurse said.

After a quick bed sheet and gown change, and a new cannula fitted, the nurse helped me back in to bed, telling me that under no circumstances was I to try and "get some fresh air" again for the remainder of the night.

I must have slept like a baby after that because I have zero memories between being helped back in to bed and waking up the next morning.

CHAPTER 13

March 2018
"The Road to Recovery" begins

Before I'd gone in for the surgery, I'd been told that there would be a recovery time and that I would need to allow time for my brain to heal. I was told that it would be at least six months but I set myself a goal of three. Three months would be all the time I needed to be out of recovery, back at work and back to my normal routine.

The morning after the surgery I woke to find that I still couldn't move my left arm, my left leg was just about movable but still bad and my face, well the left side of my face was "drooping" meaning I couldn't talk or eat properly and I couldn't drink without a straw. I'd been warned that I could end up with partial paralysis on one side of my body so began to wander if that's what had happened.

"Am I now paralysed?" I asked a doctor.

"I can't answer that right now, we'll need a few days to know for sure".

Ok, I thought. I really am paralysed! My first thought was that I'd never be able to cuddle my kids properly. No sooner than that thought hit me, I was sat there crying my eyes out. The idea of not being able to hug my kids crushed me.

<u>Day one:</u>

After a scan to see what the damage looked like and how things were post-surgery, I managed to get a visit from the family. Other than that I don't really remember too much of day 1; I guess that's fairly normal.

I remember waking up during the night to a man in the bed opposite me. He was shouting and swearing at the nurses. They'd come over to see what he wanted but no sooner than they'd left, he'd be shouting again. The patient was quite old and suffering with dementia. Clearly the outbursts weren't his fault but it felt like I'd gotten no sleep that night.

Day two:

Things started to feel slightly more "normal" I remember being fed up and frustrated, I just wanted to get out and get home. Christ, I'd have settled for just being able to get some fresh air but I was still banned from leaving the ward. During the morning, my consultant/surgeon came over to check on me. I asked him about my left side. Although I could now move my leg better, my left arm and the left side of my face were still quite bad. The consultant explained what was happening in the simplest of ways. "Matthew, after the brain suffers a trauma, it will go into a kind of rest mode like a computer. Essentially, the right half of your brain is being lazy for a temporary basis."

Basically, what he was telling me was that I would have full motor movement in time, my brain just needed time to deal with being cut at.

Late that afternoon, a physiotherapist came over and placed a board game on my table. It was Connect 4. She explained that my recovery didn't just involve being sat in bed all day and that the best thing to do was start physio to regain the movement in my arm and face. Connect 4 is an easy game. But imagine trying to play with an arm that you can barely move. I'm right-handed but I wasn't allowed to use my right arm at all. We played about three or four games and the physio kicked my arse each time. It turns out they don't "let you win" to be nice, the idea is to challenge you. Those four games exhausted me. It was so mentally draining but I realised I could beat this. I could smash this recovery in no time, I just needed to focus on physio and fitness. To me, that was the key to my success. Looking back, I can't help but think how stupid I was. That thought process would later come back to bite me.

That night, I woke to hear the patient opposite me, snoring. Snoring so loud. I tried putting my headphones in but even that couldn't drown out the sound of his snoring. It was driving me nuts. I then needed a pee but still had the catheter in which I hated. It had been bugging me all day. I couldn't get used to peeing in it. It's like trying to forcefully wet yourself. Your body won't naturally let you. Between the stress of no sleep and the catheter bugging me, I just couldn't cope. Around 2am, I got a nurse to come over and asked her to remove the catheter. She refused, telling me I'd need to wait a day or two. That was the point where I broke down. I told her this was the second night in a row I'd had no sleep and that the catheter was part of the problem. I was in uncontrollable tears. I didn't even know why, maybe it was just the stress. The poor nurse didn't know what to say or do but eventually agreed to take it out for me. She disappeared for a minute before coming back with a couple of tablets which she told me would help me sleep. After taking them, I don't really remember much. I did however, have the best night's sleep I'd ever had!

Day three:

It was this day onwards that I made a point of wearing my 2x TM headband over my bandages. It felt like I was giving this little hitchhiker of mine, the two fingered salute. My sister Katy also came to see me.

This was a good day. Not just because of a surprise visit from my little sister but because for the first time since entering the hospital, I was allowed outside! I wasn't allowed to leave the hospital grounds of course and Katy wasn't going to break me out - I was just grateful for the fresh air and company.

Me and Katy in my first moments out of the ward

The first priority for me when we got out was to get into a shop and grab a can of RedBull. I'd been caffeine free for three days too long now, I needed my sugar/caffeine fix. Katy tried telling me I shouldn't bother and just stick to water but nope, I needed that fix!

My bank card however, agreed with Katy and was rejected three times when I tried to pay for said RedBull. I'd forgotten that I'd moved all my money into my savings before the surgery. Once I'd sorted that out, I got my first RedBull of the week. What I hadn't thought about at all, was that my face was still "drooping" (paralysed on one side) so I spilt most of the first mouthful down my top. I wasn't even capable of drinking without a straw. I was pissed off, embarrassed and humiliated.

After making sure I got back to the ward ok, Katy soon left. Minutes later, Amy & Jack turned up. I knew she was coming but for some reason it still came as a surprise. Amy looked almost shocked/horrified when she saw me with the bandages all round my head and just how much of a state I actually looked. I could have cried seeing Jack for the first time that week; what a rollercoaster that week had been. Just four days ago, I was making a "just in case the worst has happened" video, then thought I'd never be able to give either of my kids a cuddle again.

We took Jack out to the hospital gardens and I took full advantage of getting all the cuddles I could. Amy stuck around which was fine, I understood why. After an hour with Jack, it was time for him to go. They both came back to the ward with me. I got one last cuddle with Jack before he left. Caught up in the moment, I didn't notice Amy taking a picture of the two of us, cuddling. After a long cuddle, I said.

"Bye cheeky chops, remember Daddy loves you!"

As they both walked out of the door, Jack cried his little eyes out. That moment broke my heart. I walked back to my bed, closed the curtains around my bed and broke down. I cried my eyes out for a good half hour or so. Even now, thinking about that moment leaves me with tears in my eyes, it's still a very raw moment.

Day four:

Four days in to recovery and things seemed to feel never-ending. I still didn't have full movement back in my arm and face and I was bored out of my bloody mind. Although I was allowed to leave the ward now, I still couldn't leave on my own. I was beginning to feel like I was being treated like an idiot, like a child in day care.

I'd been given some play dough and a 1kg weight to use in my own time, to help with the recovery but that doesn't take a full day and I was getting boring by this point.

I was sleeping most days. I'd spend half hour with the weight and playdough before needing to rest. I'd gone from being at the peak of my fitness level to being a dweeb that couldn't handle a few reps of a 1kg weight - I hated this.

After spending the morning doing my physio, feeling sorry for myself and sleeping I woke up to hearing a nurse say.

"Matthew? He's in that cubicle over there"

I looked up knowing that somebody was coming to see me. I waited for a few seconds before seeing someone in a fucking monkey mask poke their head though the curtain and shout.

"Hello, Mr. Matthew!"

Kris with his monkey mask

For a second, I had no idea who it was but I soon realised it was Kris! He'd decided to come and see me and obviously cheer me up which I really needed. I found the whole mask thing hilarious but I don't think most of the other patients found it quite as funny. He'd walked all the way through the ward with that monkey mask on, on a ward for people with dementia and serious head injuries. The poor bastards probably thought they were hallucinating! Needless to say, that was a visit that really helped pick my spirits up. That's the thing with a friend like Kris -he has always had my back at the right times. Three years later, I actually still have the mask that he turned up in!

Later that afternoon, my physio came over and told me that we were doing something different today. No board games this time. Nope, we were using a Nintendo Wii. Wii Sports to be specific. The idea was for me to work on my hand eye coordination and getting my left arm moving again. Over an hour I was let loose on boxing, tennis and bowling. I found this really bloody tough and realised that my hand eye coordination was pretty bad but I could see how and why this helped so was pretty grateful for a go on it.

Day five:

This was the day that it hit me that this journey I was now on was a "Road to Recovery" I was starting to realise that this wasn't going to be a quick and easy two to three week job.

As a result not much really happened that day other than plenty of sleep and feeling sorry for myself. That afternoon, the physio came over with yet another board game. This time it was Jenga.

Attempting to keep my cool while "playing" Jenga

Once again, the idea was to play only using my left arm. After a few failed attempts, I began to lose my patience,

"I can't fucking do this" I said.

I told the physio that I'd had enough but no, she wouldn't just let me quit and made me carry on for about an hour. Every time I tried to pick out one of the pieces, I'd knock the whole tower over. Again, and again, I'd knock it over and have to rebuild and restart. I soon realised that this wasn't about winning and losing. It was about forcing my brain to start using both arms. Essentially, this was about strengthening not only my arm but my brain. Something about the constant losing and knocking the tower over made me realise that this road to recovery wasn't about winning or even losing. It was just about getting through it. Unfortunately, that thought process wouldn't last.

Day six:

I decided that I needed something to focus on. Something that would help me focus on my physio. I decided that I wasn't going to just consider doing my upcoming fundraising challenges anymore… I WAS doing them. I was going to do my Tough Mudders in a weekend even if I had to crawl my way through the entire course. The Hull 10k? Same thing. Nothing was going to stop me. Not even the current situation. Obviously none of my friends or family wanted me to even consider it and when I'd mentioned it during the surgery, the nurse found it funny.

Deep down I think a part of me knew I wouldn't be able to do it but it was a positive thought that I needed. So now, now I knew I was going to do all three events and that I had to train for my Tough Mudders at every possible chance I got. No more slacking and feeling sorry for myself!

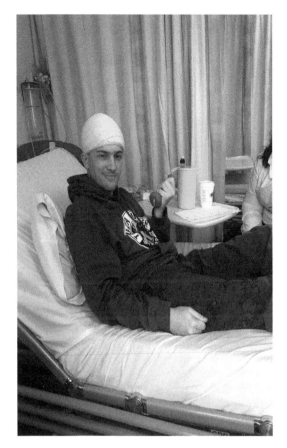

Having a crack at a 1kg weight during a Physio session

Day seven:

By now, you can probably tell that most days at the hospital were pretty much the same. Day seven was just an average day except I had my bandages removed and could finally see just how bad my head actually looked. I'd been shaved from my right ear to the top of my head, close to the top of my left ear. The area shaved was just the width of a razor- maybe a bit wider, meaning it looked like I had an odd looking "sideway mohawk." Filling this "sideway Mohawk" were about thirty staples that had been used to fasten my skull back together.

Looking back at the photos now, it's hard to believe that my head, my skull had actually been sawed open in such a way. It's a hard feeling to describe but seeing that someone has cut into your head and brain and what's left behind is such a bizarre thing to see and think about.

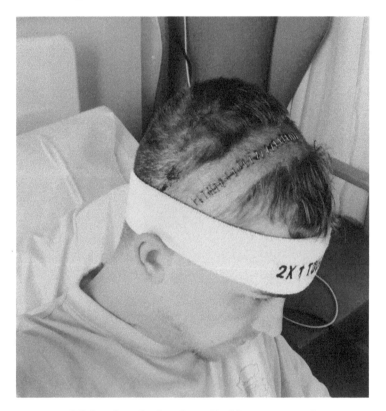

Right after the bandages had been removed

Day eight:

I liked day eight. It started with me being told that if I could show the physios I was able to walk around unaided and them see me walk up and down stairs, I'd be able to go home that day. I already knew I could do that because I'd been doing it with ease for the last few days. I wasn't worried about anything going wrong. Hell, even if I was to be told I couldn't go home, I was going. Nothing was going to stop me leaving.

Although I felt constantly tired, my arm was back up to 70% efficiency. My face still drooped but that was manageable. Yep. I was leaving no matter what!

Later in the afternoon I met a pair of physios who would be in charge of checking to see if I really could use stairs safely and walk around unaided. Obviously, I passed their "tests" with no problems. The next step was the one I was least looking forward to. Having all thirty staples plucked out. One by one...

Soon after, Rachel turned up. She'd arranged for her and her partner to pick me up and drop me off at my parents. She knew that if she wasn't there, I'd just get a taxi and make my own way back home. The plan was for me to spend the next couple of weeks at my parents' house while I worked on the next stages of recovery so Mum and Dad could keep an eye on me. Around 5/6pm I'd packed my bag and was ready to go. I just needed to hold out for a doctor to come over, give me my meds, explain what to expect and give me my discharge paperwork.

Rachel and I were sat on the bed waiting when I turned to look at her said.

"Hey I've been thinking about the times we've had to give CPR at work. Y'know when you're in the moment, giving CPR, doing your thing and then suddenly realise you have idiots stood around filming you. Next time that happens, right at the moment you see your casualty start to show signs of life and is at a point where you can stop CPR - just look at them and say out loud "3.2.1... And you're back in the room!"

(Referencing the crappy hypnotist from Little Britten)

By this point I was crying with laughter. Rachel was laughing but more so because of just how funny I'd found it. Yes, I was laughing at my own bad joke! The laughter soon became uncontrollable, I was laughing so hard I couldn't breathe. Literally. Which was making Rachel laugh even more.

I tried to say I was struggling to breathe but couldn't because of this continuous laughter. After a couple of minutes, I started to make some kind of noise that can't really describe in words but it was enough for a nurse to come over and ask if I was ok. A minute or so later I managed to stop laughing. Fun fact, people have and still do actually die because they were unable to stop laughing. There's a technical term for it but essentially you laugh so much for so long that you're unable to breathe and eventually keel over and die. Death by laughter. What a way to go!

Soon after this I was discharged and I couldn't be happier to leave that place. I was and still am incredibly grateful for all that was done by the surgical team, nurses and staff but eight days stuck on a ward isn't for me regardless of the reason.

My parents were out working when I got there so I let myself in. They had a puppy at the time, Charlie. He was a little Cocker Spaniel and a complete nutter. Extremely hyperactive but very loveable and I loved seeing when I'd visit Mum and Dad. When I got in, he was there to greet me and of course, he went nuts when he saw me. I got down to his level to say hello. Mistake. He launched himself at me as fast and hard as he could, sending me to floor before licking me half to death.

After getting past the nut job pup, I went straight to bed and was out like a light.

I woke up around 5am the next day, pouring with sweat. I'd been having some incredibly weird and bizarre dreams that to an extent, had freaked me out. Enough for me to not be able to go back to sleep. I went downstairs wanting Weetabix for breakfast but there was none in. That meant waiting until 6am for the local shop to open. The problem with this was I not only had a huge cut across the side of my head but I also had an odd-looking bold streak. I couldn't wear a hat yet, not that I even had one to hand. The idea of going out and being seen like that terrified me. My anxiety was working me hard that morning. Obviously, nobody would have been that interested even if they did see it, they'd soon forget me but I didn't think of it like that.

My need for some decent breakie soon outweighed the anxiety though and I set off. Of the few people that were actually in the shop, no one so much as battered an eye lid at the state of my head. That was an hour of my life spent worrying and panicking over something so trivial.

By the time I'd gotten back, I realised there was no way I could stay two weeks at my parents. I'd just spent a week at hospital and now a night at my parents. I just wanted to get home, to my own bed and back to some form of normality. I knew mum wouldn't take that, she'd kick up a fuss (for the right reasons) and try to convince me to stay. I was right. Mum tried everything to convince me that I should stay for at least a week. After a small, brief argument she gave in. She wasn't happy about my decision at all but she had realised I wasn't going to budge. She only agreed on the condition I stayed a few more hours and waited for my gran to visit, before hitching a lift home with her. I agreed as it meant I got to see my gran before I went home.

It felt great to finally walk through my door and be home. Just the thought of being able to do my own thing was a great feeling!

This is where the true "Road to Recovery" would begin. I didn't know it at the time but shit really was just about to hit the fan...

CHAPTER 14

"When shit finally hits the fan"

It felt great to be back home. I knew that I just wouldn't have been able to settle if I'd stayed at my parents. I had my neighbour, Chloe on hand if I needed anything urgently.

My first and main priority when I got home was to wash, find something decent to wear then make my way to work to talk about coming back. Yes, barely ten days after having had major brain surgery to remove most of a brain tumour, my main concern was getting back to work. Remember, I still had three months left on full pay. I really didn't need to be at work but I was worried about how people would see me. I was genuinely worried that people would think I was just being lazy and that I was milking a bad situation. In my head, I thought that if I could walk and talk, I was able to work and thought that's how others viewed me. It sounds ridiculous, I know but that's just how I saw the situation at the time.

I still had some major anxiety about the soon to be scar on my head so managed to put a cap on. Of course, it had to be very loose fitting, but it at least covered most of the wound on my head.

Work was exactly a mile away from my house. I choose to walk there just to take advantage of the fresh air and to prove to myself that I wasn't really an invalid. What should have taken me twenty minutes to walk give or take, actually ended up taking me around an hour! Just to add insult to injury, I'd somehow managed to contract conjunctivitis. Imagine just how much of a state I must have looked walking into work that day. With my cap on, messed up face and eyes, nobody actually recognised me at first. The staff on shift must have thought I was a resident at first glance.

After a few quick hellos and a quick catch up, I went to talk to the boss. I was expecting her to see me, hear that I was feeling good and was ready to come back and just welcome me with open arms. Obviously, that was not what the outcome would be.

The boss looked at me as if I was stupid before saying, that regardless of what I said, I clearly wasn't ready to come back to work, I would need a "fit note" from my doctor to even be considered allowed back and even then, I would need to be cleared by Occupational Health. In short, the boss told me to leave, go home and rest for the next few months.

Being at home, I soon realised just how ridiculously boring things were. I had a PlayStation to keep me busy pre surgery but now that I'd had the surgery and still struggled to use my left arm, it was pointless trying to use it. For the first few days I would wake up, chill for a few hours before needing a power nap and that's how my days would run. I hated it but couldn't do anything about it. I remember waking up in the early hours one morning, I was wide awake so decided to try a bit of weight lifting with a couple of 10kg bars I had. As expected, I had no issue with doing multiple reps with my right arm but when it came to trying to use my left arm I barely managed three reps before I was wiped out. I was so angry. I was so fit at the point of being diagnosed with the tumour. Three months later, I was at my lowest fitness level yet.

After a week or so of being back at home I decided to start trying to use the PlayStation again, to help kill the boredom as there wasn't much else I could do really. A new Far Cry game had been released while I was in hospital so I downloaded that and gave it a go. I soon realised that not only was I struggling with my arm but my hand eye coordination was still quite bad and I struggled to even see the screen. I had a fairly big TV at the time but even then, I struggled to see what was on the screen and couldn't track anything with my eyes for more than a few seconds. After only half an hour of playing I needed a break. That first half an hour quite literally wiped me out!

Over the next few days, I continued to keep trying to use the PlayStation and it wasn't long before I noticed a slight improvement in my hand/arm movement. Hell, I was able to last longer and longer on the PlayStation the more I played. I soon realised that like the Wii the physios had me using while in hospital, using the PlayStation was aiding my physical recovery. I put it down to the constant use of my hands with the controller and the fact I was being challenged by the game which seemed to be stimulating my brain. Much like someone who is constantly working out. The more they train, the fitter they get and the more they can handle in a physical sense. Your brain works the same way, like a muscle. The more you use it, challenge and push it, the more efficient it becomes.

In a week or two of being at home, I'd heard that HHCP had rehoused a young family and needed to redecorate the house for them. The problem was that they only had one person willing to help out so I decided to jump in and help. It was an excuse to get out of the house and do something productive that came with the bonus of knowing I'd helped someone in need. Plus, it was another way of me proving that I was capable of working.

Me and another girl, Lucy spent an entire day at the house, painting and cleaning, I actually really enjoyed it. The couple that had moved in with their baby seemed so incredibly grateful. As hard and tiring as it was, it was a great day.

A few nights later, I was woken up to the sound of my neighbour screaming for help. (the one who had kept me awake after my night shift the day I had my seizure at work) This was fairly common, her boyfriend would often knock her around the house and I or my other neighbour, Chloe would call the police, help and support as best we could before she'd take him back in, telling us that it wasn't his fault and he really did love her etc. This particular night, she was a few months pregnant and I hadn't heard her scream like this before. I went outside to find Chloe already stood outside not knowing what to do. Normally, I'd have called the police but this time, for whatever reason I decided not to, instead grabbing my baseball bat. I knocked on the front door then realised they were in the kitchen. Both me and Chloe went to their back garden to see what was going on - after seeing him hit the girl and pin her up against the wall I let myself in, raised my bat before shouting his name. He looked at me and obviously realised he was fucked. He let his girlfriend go before doing a runner. I was angry and fully ready to have to hit him with the bat if needed. A part of me wanted to chase him and do so anyway. Luckily for us both, I didn't. What kind of person attacks their pregnant girlfriend in such a way? A lowlife coward of course. The worrying thing for me that night, wasn't that she would obviously take him back (she did) no, it was that I had put myself in to a position where I was comfortable to attack somebody with a weapon. The circumstances were irrelevant, that was not who I was. I might have defused the situation but bringing a weapon in to it and to be so willing to use it, just takes away any pride from that moment.

Just as the second week had ended, I decided to reach out to a local newspaper to try and promote my upcoming fundraisers as I was determined to raise as much money as possible for HHCP. They decided to write an article about my journey so far which was published the day they interviewed me with the headline "I was awake when doctors removed a brain tumour the size of a Creme Egg" I'm not sure where the Creme Egg nickname actually came from but just like the hitchhiker's name and the tumour itself, it stuck. Thanks to that article, more donations started to come in.

There was another reason behind me going to the paper of course. I wanted "the powers that be" at work to see it and see that I really was ready to come back to work. Spoiler alert. It didn't work and I wasn't called back into work.

By the end of week three, I had finally made it to a point where I felt able to start training properly for my fundraising challenges so I decided that I was going to go back to the gym. Because I was constantly sleeping during the day, had a completely messed up sleeping pattern and was still incredibly anxious about the scaring/bald patch on my head, I decided to use a 24/7 gym and go later at night instead of during the day. As I made my way to the gym on the first night, I was stopped by a young-looking homeless guy who explained that he hadn't eaten all day and needed something that could go towards him getting some grub. Before I could tell him that I didn't have any cash on me, he piped up.

"Fuck, I know you! You're that guy that's had a brain tumour!" He'd obviously seen my article in the paper.

He went on to tell me that he remembered me from a presentation I'd given about mental health in the young person's hostel a few years prior, back when I was working for the Princes Trust. I had no idea who he was but he clearly remembered me. Seeing and speaking to this guy and hearing that he remembered everything I'd said in my presentation years back made my day. I couldn't give him money but what I could do, was walk into the takeaway nearby and get him a pizza and a drink, it was no biggie for me. He got something to eat and I got a nice feel-good moment.

I made it to the gym soon after, I only wanted to use the treadmill to get a feel of what I could actually handle and set a bar from where to start. I managed a 10-minute run and covered 1.27km - not even a bloody mile! I'd gone from 23-minute 5km runs with a training mask on to almost being wiped out over less than a mile. I was pissed off but knew that I could and would do better!

Around April, I had my first appointment with my oncologist. My tumour wasn't cancerous but I learnt during this process that oncologist's don't just deal with the cancerous stuff. Three years after said appointment I still find myself having to explain this to people. I don't mind as its part of my journey and my story but it always feels odd knowing that people assume I had cancer because I had a tumour.

The appointment was very basic, just a quick check up and a look back over my last MRI. I told the oncologist that although I felt 100% ok, the area around where I had the surgery felt "odd". I would find that there were days I would feel a "tingling" sensation in said area of my head. He told me that it was perfectly normal considering I'd had brain surgery last month. Makes sense, I thought to myself.

My first of the three fundraising challenges, The Hull 10k was set for June 11th, I should have been excited for this but instead I was pissed off. It had been almost exactly three months since I'd had the brain surgery and as far as I was concerned, I had fully recovered. At least, I thought I had...

I'd spent the last few weeks begging different doctors to give me a fit note to go back to work, I'd begged work to let me back but without a signed fit note from a doctor, work wouldn't touch me with a barge pole. A part of me actually hoped management would see that I had done the Hull 10k while on sick leave and would call me in to discipline me. At least then, I'd be able to prove I was able to work.

I only managed to run about half of the route but managed to finish in just under 58 minutes. I was actually really happy with that!

Originally, I only wanted to go back to work so people wouldn't think I was being lazy and for me to prove I had in fact beaten the tumour but by June I had been on sick leave for six months, which meant I would go from full pay to SSP (statutory sick pay) which was less than half of my normal wage. This meant I'd only have enough money for rent and a couple of weeks' worth of food. I wouldn't be able to pay for anything else like gas & electric, phone bill, internet and sky etc. Not forgetting the fact that I wouldn't have enough to buy a full months' worth of food shopping. Obviously, this was a stress that I really didn't need but I felt like nobody would listen to me when I tried to explain just how urgently I needed to be back at work. Looking back, it's obvious that everyone else could see what I couldn't, that I was definitely not ready to go back to work.

Payday was always on the 15th of every month - on June 14th, I stayed up until midnight just to see what I would be paid. I was hoping and praying that payroll would make a mistake and just pay me my normal wage but as we know, people in payroll departments aren't known for being daft when it comes to numbers and dates. I was paid my SSP. Seeing just how little I had in my account left me with a pit in my stomach. I hadn't told my landlady about any of this situation, not the tumour, being on sick or the surgery. None of it. She seemed like a nice person and had re-mortgaged the house when I moved in so the last thing I wanted to do was make her worry for nothing. Remember - I thought this would all be over and done with within a few months.

Sitting there and realising just how fucked I was and how ridiculously underprepared I actually was for this, well, my mind went into overdrive. The how's, the what's and the ifs all ran through my mind - I was panicking. I couldn't cope with what felt at the time, like an immense amount of pressure. My instant reaction was to think that everything was bad and would only get worse from here onwards. I thought about heading out to kill myself. I just couldn't cope with the stress and pressure anymore.

In my anger, I decided to vent on Facebook. I won't go in to what I actually wrote but it wasn't the nicest looking status. Essentially, I made it clear how much I hated the people in charge of my company and how much I hated them for not letting me back to work, costing me money and forcing me back into depression. I even mentioned the company by name and ended this little rant by saying "you may as well sack me now, I'd be better off" I knew that as soon as I clicked post, I probably wouldn't have a job waiting for me for much longer. It didn't really matter to me though as I had already decided that I was going to kill myself.

I didn't do anything after posting though, deciding to at least sleep on it. Looking back at moments like this, it's like looking at a completely different person. My head was so much of a mess and I couldn't see it for myself. The next morning, I woke up with a clearer mindset. It's amazing what a good night's sleep can do. It was the weekend so I knew other than paying my rent and getting a small food shop in, there wasn't much I could actually do.

I remembered that I had an appointment with my oncologist at Castle Hill on the Monday so I just had to keep my cool and chill until then. I knew that this would be the perfect time to get my fit note - I wasn't going to leave the hospital without one.

The appointment was a simple check-up, nothing too interesting. Just like before, the oncologist asked me how I was, how I was feeling etc. I told him that I felt great, was back at my fitness again and had recently completed the Hull 10k. I went on to tell him that I wanted to go back to work to help me back to some form of normality.

Without any hesitation, he said no. He wanted me to stay off work until September at the very earliest (three more months) not a bloody chance. Not only could I not afford that, I was genuinely fed up of not working. I needed to be back. I told him that the stress of not being able to work and being stuck at home most days was making my life a misery. He sympathised but reminded me that I was still in recovery. Before I could hit back with a reply, the nurse that was in the room with us - taking notes, suddenly waded in.

"I think what Matthew is trying to say, is that not working is effecting his mental health" for the first time in three months, somebody was actually on my side!

Listening to what the nurse said about my mental health being affected by not working, the oncologist agreed to give me a fit note. This is fucking great, I thought! I might have only been paid SSP that month but at least I had the security of knowing I would be back at work and on my normal wage in just a matter of days! Before I left the appointment, I mentioned that I still had an odd feeling around the area of my head that had been operated on. Just like before, I was told that it was normal to feel discomfort, even three months after surgery. I thought nothing of it and moved on.

As soon as I left the room I called my boss and told her I had a legit fit note, that I could bring it in that day and would happily start working that week. It was obviously quite expensive covering all of my shifts for that amount of time so providing I could prove that I really had been declared fit to work, I'd be back that weekend. After a quick meeting with the boss and handing over the fit note I'd worked so bloody hard to get, she stuck me back on the rota for a phased return. Instead of my normal eight nights on and six days off, she put me on four on, four off. As much as I just wanted to be back doing my normal shifts I had no say in the matter. Plus, I'd still get my normal wage and it would only be for a couple of weeks, so I just accepted what I could get. I was willing to do anything that I could do to prove I had finished my recovery.

I was back at work a few days later for the Friday night shift. This was my first shift back at work in just over six months! I was so excited. The shift was actually fairly boring, the emails I had, were irrelevant. I had nothing I needed to catch up on so the majority of the shift was spent gabbing to the person I was on shift with and catching up.

At around 6am the next morning, we could hear somebody shouting out of their window above reception. It was a resident; she was screaming for staff. We both knew that something was wrong so both abandoned reception, heading up to see what was happening, expecting the worst. This was still my first shift back so I was supposed to be hands off and wait at reception while my co-worker dealt with the possible incident but I was still the most experienced first aider in that place regardless of time off and I wasn't going to just leave somebody to deal with a possible incident on their own because I'd had some time off work.

When we entered the room, we found an all too familiar sight. A woman had overdosed on heroine, passed out and become unresponsive. Luckily, she had a friend with her to alert us. There wasn't much either of us could do though - other than monitor her and make sure her breathing was stable until paramedics arrived. If her breathing suddenly became too slow or stopped I was there ready to start CPR.

Within minutes, paramedics arrived and after a shot of Naloxone, she was back with us. She was taken to hospital but was soon back at the hostel acting as if nothing had happened. What a way to end my first shift back!

My second shift back wasn't any better. Barely a couple of hours in to the shift, one of the residents had gotten himself completely wasted. I could see him on the CCTV staggering around by the river at the back of the building, where there was no railings. The Council refused to pay out for fencing regardless of the fact people had fallen in to the river while drunk on more than one occasion.

Concerned that he would end up falling in, I went out to try and talk him back in to the hostel. When I got to him, he was crying, he was an emotional wreck and threatening to jump into the river. I spent the next couple of hours trying to convince him not to jump in but to come inside and talk to me. The tide was in at this point and it was a very cold night. If he had jumped in, he would not have survived.

Eventually I managed to get him back in to the building before spending another hour or so trying to calm him down - not the easiest of tasks when somebody is that drunk.

You'd think after those two incidents things would only get better, right? Wrong. Friday and Saturday's shifts had both come with quite serious incidents but nothing I couldn't handle. On Monday morning, just as the Sunday night shift was coming to an end, my boss came in early to do my "back to work" meeting. Basically, just an informal chat about why I was off, was there any help I needed or wanted etc. That kind of thing is just a formality for HR.

Once the paperwork for that was out of the way, she then went on to give me a royal bollocking for the previous two incidents. She was angry that I had spent so long with a resident by the river while he was in such a state and for getting involved with the overdose incident and reminded me that I was on phased return so had absolutely no right to jump in. She had a point, maybe but my actions saved at least one life that weekend.

The meeting ended with the boss telling me that we needed to talk about a complaint that had been made against me.

She handed me a piece of paper that had a screenshot on it of my Facebook. The screenshot was of course my little rant earlier that month about how pissed off I was about not being allowed back to work and how it was making me feel. The person that had taken the screenshot hadn't bothered to crop their photo so I could see what time it had been taken. Whoever this person was, had taken it within less than an hour of me posting it. My Facebook was private which meant the only people who had seen that status were my friends and because the complaint was made directly to the boss, it meant that the person who took the screenshot was a "friend" from work. Instead of dropping me a message when they saw the post of mine to see what was up, they choose to take screenshot and complain.

I knew just how serious this was, people had been sacked for a lot less. I'd blatantly called the people that ran the company, a set of pricks and declared just how much I hated them so I knew my days would be numbered.

I asked who it was that hated me so much that they would rather see me sacked than offer to talk to me, their "friend" about what was wrong. It was clear, she couldn't and wouldn't tell me.

I wasn't suspended or sacked straight away like I thought I would be so was still expected to work.

Not knowing who it was who actually hated me enough to try and get me sacked soon started to take an effect on me.

I was going to work and expected to continue as if everything was ok. I knew that one of my co-workers, the very people who would often ask how I was doing and offer support if I ever needed it could in fact be the same person who hated me and wanted me out. The issue I had, was not knowing who it was. If I had known, I would have just made a point of avoiding them in a professional manner.

Between the constant paranoia and the thought of being sacked at any point because of the status was wreaking havoc on my mind. I had gotten into such a state that I was quite literally circling the gutter. I was walking to work with a small bottle of vodka and a razor blade in my bag. As I would approach work, I could turn right on to the main road leading to work or I could continue straight on through town and make my way to a small forest by Hessle. The plan then would be to get pissed and then kill myself. I'd use the walk to work as a chance to think it though. I'd have twenty minutes to decide if I would turn right to work or continue straight on and kill myself. This was a huge problem, more so because of the job I was doing and the kinds of people I was working with.

I remember being at work and talking to Rachel one day, I wanted to talk to her about the state I was actually in. I might have a smile on my face at work but it was fake. I started by talking about how stressed I was about not knowing who it was that had actually taken the screenshot of my FB post. She interrupted by saying.

"People are getting fed up of hearing you constantly moaning about this y'know"

I left it there and stopped talking - if one of my best friends didn't care, clearly, nobody did. I'd put so much time and effort into being allowed back to work but was now in a position where I could lose said job.

Part of the problem was that I had an ABI (acquired brain injury) because of the surgery. That wasn't the biggest problem though, the main problem here was that I was refusing to admit that I had a brain injury and refused to accept that I was still in recovery. I may have been recovered physically - on the outside but as far as my actual brain went, I hadn't given myself any time to recover.

I was soon informed that my investigation had started. I always held my hands up to what I had done so I admitted I wrote the status but I explained why and how I felt at the time. After one formal meeting, I'd then have to wait until July for yet another formal meeting to find out if I still had a job or not.

CHAPTER 15

July - November 2018
You Matter

At the back end of June I got a call out of the blue from Dad.

"Matt, do you know anybody that would want a dog?"

A little smirk appeared on my face as just with the way he asked, I knew that this was a subtle hint.

He explained that with both him and mum always working, it wasn't fair for Charlie to be left at home for such long periods of time. Mum and Dad both knew that I was struggling more than I was letting on and figured that I would benefit from having a dog, just as much as he would benefit from having someone that had more free time to spend with him than they did. I already had a solid bond with Charlie so it was a win win for the all of us, including Charlie.

I'll be honest, the first few weeks of having my furry friend now living with me were far from easy. There were days that I found myself questioning why I'd taken him.

Obviously, he was in a new environment that he didn't know which stressed him out. I'd leave to get shopping in and come home to find he'd trashed the house. He'd destroy his toys, piss and shit everywhere, seemingly purposely avoiding his toilet pads.

But over time, with some patience and a lot of stubbornness we both got into a routine that seemed to work for us.

I was still having the odd seizure, every time I did I would come round to Charlie sat with me, refusing to leave me alone. As much of a dick as could be, he really did show his love and affection. This furry little guy was definitely my new best friend.

In early July, I was told that I had a disciplinary hearing regarding my little Facebook rant which had been scheduled for the Friday 27th of that month. That just so happened to be the day I was heading over to Skipton for the weekend to do my two Tough Mudders in aid of HHCP. At least if I was going to be sacked, I had something to keep my mind busy after.

Because of everything that was going on, there was a horrible atmosphere at work. People would go out of their way not to talk to me if they didn't have to and I had stopped talking to Rachel, in fact, I'd completely cut her out of my life. The comment she had made about me constantly moaning and complaining had really hit a raw nerve. It hurt. I needed to talk to somebody and she made feel like a moaning prick.

Paranoia soon got the better of me and I soon started to feel like the entire team were against me. I felt like I was hated, like I wasn't wanted or needed anymore. Imagine going to work every day and feeling like you are more worthless than the shit on the bottom of your shoe. It's a fucking horrible feeling and it caused a metric fuck ton of stress, at home and at work.

I remember a couple of night shifts where I'd go for a break, I'd sit at a desk in the office and before I knew anything I'd be on the floor struggling to get up. Being on my own, I can only guess that I'd had a seizure and fallen to the floor.

The couple of times this happened I must have been gone for well over an hour, the staff that I was on shift with at the time must have assumed that I had gone for a nap because they never questioned me as to why I had been gone so long. Night staff had an unwritten rule that we would always turn a blind eye to taking extended breaks if we were extremely tired, just as long as the favour was repaid, that you pulled you weight and any work that needed to be completed was shared equally.

I knew I couldn't tell anyone that I knew I had a seizure because that would mean I'd be signed off work again. I thought that if I so much as tried to ask for help or support, I'd risk being back in financial difficulties. No matter how bad things got, I was not going to prove everybody right by admitting defeat.

In July I'd spoken to my first TM team mate and utter legend Elizabeth, about teaming up for Sunday's TM but she was signed up for Saturday's TM. I knew I could do it on my own but I knew I would need somebody to help me just in case. I wasn't 100% sure that my left arm was back to its pre-brain surgery strength and wasn't sure if it would let me down so I reached out on one of the Tough Mudder Facebook pages, asking if anybody was running solo and if they'd fancy making a team. I didn't mention that I'd had brain surgery just few months prior as I didn't want to scare anybody off.

I obviously didn't realise just what kind of community the Tough Mudder crowd were at this point! I got a reply almost straight away, a guy named Lee reached out and offered to join me. After adding me on Facebook, he spotted my fundraising page which mentioned the whole tumour thing and my mental health struggles from the past. Lee ended up making a fairly large donation and leaving an amazing message on the page to go with it.

I was a complete stranger to this guy; he didn't have to do that but he did anyway, I'd not even met him yet and already I liked and respected him.

The only thing that made the rest of July bearable was being able to see my son, Jack. For a short while, Amy would drop him off at my house and let me have a couple of hours with him. I loved moments like this. I'd take Jack and Charlie to a nearby park and let the pair run about playing with each other. Charlie absolutely love's kids, Jack loves dogs and I loved seeing them play together.

Eventually, Amy spotted a photo of Jack sat with my parents on my Facebook, she called me not long after it had been posted to demand it was taken down. She always seemed to hate my family and I never did work out why. It apparently wasn't the photo that upset her, it was that I had allowed Jack to see his grandparents.

Soon after, Amy made a point of only allowing me to have supervised contact at random times and different places, normally once a month. I didn't see the obvious, she had been and still was controlling me but just like when we were together, my mind was focused on other things, leaving me blind to the obvious.

July 27th came around quickly, my disciplinary hearing was scheduled for 10am at one of our other sites leaving me a few hours after before I needed to start making my way down to Skipton for my Tough Mudder weekend.

Given how I felt being at work over the past month, you'd think I would have been terrified going in to this hearing but that wasn't the case. I'd accepted that I was going to be sacked and had come to terms with it; it was my own fault anyway. There's an old saying "If you make your bed, you lie in it" essentially, it means you should take responsibility for your own actions. That's exactly what I was doing here. I'd done wrong (regardless of the reasons) and now I needed to face the music.

In all honesty, I was more focused on getting to Skipton, having an incredible weekend, meeting new friends and catching up with Elizabeth. That was my main focus and priority. If I wasn't doing Tough Mudder, I probably would have broken down as I'd have only had this hearing to focus on.

There were two area managers conducting the hearing. One to do all the talking and the other to take notes. One of them Andy, I already knew from when he had worked at my hostel. He was a great guy that I liked and respected. From the beginning, he made it clear this wasn't a hearing that would see me sacked, it was a hearing to decide how we could move forwards.

It was Andy that would be doing the talking for the hearing. Just like the last meeting, I was asked to explain myself, why I posted the status about the company and if I was sorry etc, I was just confused as to how or why I wasn't being sacked.

I explained everything the same way as before, both Andy and the other area manager seemed genuinely sympathetic. They asked more than once if I needed to take a break or get some air which I was quite taken back by. I was in the wrong, why were they being nice? I wasn't complaining, I was just grateful for the pair of them making me feel at ease.

The hearing lasted just over an hour, I was given a first written warning by the end of it. I'd gone in, expecting to lose my job. I'd mentally prepared myself for the worst and somehow, was only given the bare minimum "punishment" - I was lucky to say the least. Obviously, I was grateful for the second chance too. As soon as I left, it was time to head home and get ready for my dirty weekend!

The plan for the weekend was to campout at Tough Mudder on my own on Friday through Sunday, meet Lee on the Saturday and then Elizabeth on the Sunday. I'd never been camping on my own before so was quite literally winging it. I had a cheap flimsy £10 tent from Asda, a camping chair, my kit for two days and of course, Monkey! I'd even bought a GoPro just for the weekend.

That night, I learnt two valuable lessons. One - don't pitch your tent in the corner of an open field on the top of a bloody hill and two - don't miss covering the hole in the roof of said tent because you think "it'll be fine" - of course there was a storm that night and I woke up to one side of tent caved in and a stream of water coming in through the hole in the roof. Eventually, the tent actually collapsed with me still in it!

The next morning - already cold and wet, I wolfed down a couple of breakfast bars before making my way over to the Mudder Village where I'd agreed to meet Lee by the bag drop area. After a while of waiting and thinking that we were going to miss each other, I finally found him and we hit it off straight away. He was just as cool as he seemed in the build up to the event.

This was his first Tough Mudder, during the course we were talking about our own stories and how and why we were doing a Tough Mudder. Lee explained that he had actually turned up the year before to do what should have been his first. He'd signed up to do it by himself and that he had made it to the car park but as soon as he saw other people heading over to the start line, people that looked like your typical athletes and all in big groups, anxiety got the better of him and he decided to bail.

Lee seemed so confident when I met him, I would never have thought that he would be hit by anxiety that hard but he was. He's human. Anxiety doesn't discriminate, nor does any kind of mental health issue.

The weather was terrible throughout the day. That wasn't so much of a bad thing though as it meant there was a lot more mud.

We ended up being pulled into a team from Newcastle area early on and went from a team of two to a team of eight in an instant.

I had always been told that if I did TM so soon after my surgery, I'd end up in hospital or dead. I'd had friends threaten to ditch me if I actually went through with it but in my stubbornness, I knew I had to. I knew that finishing both TM's would be a massive "fuck you" to this hitchhiker of mine.

I remember one obstacle in particular, named "Hydrophobia" which was a very basic obstacle compared to most. It's hard to explain exactly what it is but essentially it involves being in waist deep water and having to swim under two large tubes, now I can't swim to save my life but have no issues with water so thought I would be OK with this one – I was wrong. My problem started when I tried to get under the tube and back out on the other side. I, like a lot of other Mudder's kept getting stuck underneath said tubes and literally had to be dragged out.

I'd lost Lee and the rest of the team for a short while so was on my own but was refusing to give up on it - I would stay all day if I had to. I was not sacking of an obstacle that I should have been able to do. Luckily, three women realised I was struggling, came over and made a point and dragging me under and though both tubes. I was so bloody grateful!

Me, Lee and our newly acquired team all finished together. As we approached the finish line that day, I shouted LET'S ROLL! It was a different way of me saying let's go, let's sprint though the finish line. The team took what I said literally, so all got down and actually rolled across the finish line before being given our headbands, finisher beer and finisher t - shirt. I was so happy. I was aching all over but I didn't care! I'd had so many people tell me that I wouldn't be able to or be capable of doing a Tough Mudder so soon after brain surgery but here I was, at the finish line still alive and ok.

The finish line with my newly earned headband

I said my goodbyes to Lee and the rest of the team before heading back to the campsite. One of the perks of paying to camp at Tough Mudder is that you get to access to your own private, warm shower! If you've ever used the "showers" that were not in the campsite at a Tough Mudder, you'll understand what I mean when I say that they are like an obstacle of their own! I was definitely grateful not to be using them!

I'd survived Saturday's TM and earned my blue 3x headband but now I had Sundays TM to do. It was the same as the day before, the same obstacles, same route. Hell, even the weather was the same. My tent somehow stayed up this time but rain had still got in during the night.

I met Elizabeth that morning, we'd found a couple that had never done Tough Mudder before a few days earlier so we brought them into our little team. It was great to be doing another TM with Elizabeth, she had shown me why Tough Mudder is so great during my first one back in 2016 and here we were again, two years later.

Me and Elizabeth before we hit the start line

Everything went smoothly up until our second lap on Mud Mile. The idea of this obstacle is to scale a very large mud mound (about 10/15ft in height and very steep) then slide down the other side before landing in a muddy pool of water and then do this again over two more mounds. It's tough especially when the mud gets slippery, but if people jump in and help, it's not so bad – in fact it's actually one of my favourite obstacles.

While sliding down the last mound, I ended up completely submerged under the muddy water. Aside from a mouthful of mud and water, I also ended up with mud in one of my eyes. I just wiped it away, thinking nothing of it but ten minutes later, my eye was in constant pain. Just blinking left me in agony and we had about four miles left to go. I should have pulled out at this point but that was never going to happen. Instead, I cracked on.

By the time we made it to the last two obstacles before the finish line, I couldn't see anything out of my right eye and was in agony. I knew something was definitely wrong now. The last two obstacles were Pyramid Scheme and Everest, both of which I knew I would struggle to complete with my eye as it was.

When we arrived at Everest though we could see a lot of medical staff around someone who had clearly been injured. I'm not entire sure what had happened but they were crowing around the injured person at the bottom of the obstacle which meant it had been closed off to runners.

That left me with just Pyramid Scheme but I knew it would too risky to try and climb on others when I couldn't see. The rules of Tough Mudder state that you can skip any obstacle if you truly can't complete it without any penalty and I knew I couldn't do it. I could barely see with my one working eye and the other was in agony, it was the last obstacle on course and I had attempted every other one so I certainly didn't feel bad skipping it and heading straight to the med tent. A first aider came over, had a good look at my eye and realised I'd done quite the number on it. She couldn't see too much but she could see enough to know that my next stop needed to be a hospital.

I left the tent, grabbed my headband and t- shirt and found Elizabeth as she had agreed to drive me to the train station before heading home herself.

The train journey home was horrible, it was a three-hour journey split over two trains. Every time I blinked, it hurt. I was having to keep my hand on my eye just to help ease some of the pain. I didn't have time to get washed before leaving the event and only managed to get changed. My hair and face were a mess so I'm sure you can imagine the kind of looks I was getting on the train.

Once back in Hull, I dumped my stuff at home before heading over to A&E. It was quite busy when I got there so I used a "self-check in" kiosk to book in. With it being so busy, I expected to be there at least a couple of hours before being seen but I was called within five minutes of entering the waiting room. I assumed it was because I had an eye injury. The nurse who saw me brought me into a room and after hearing what kind of stupidity had left me with a messed-up eye, she pulled out of a piece of kit you would expect to see at an opticians. Basically, a giant magnifying glass that enables a nurse to see all of your eyeball. She took one look through the lens and shrieked.

"Oh my god!"

"Is it bad? I asked.

She drew an eyeball on a piece of paper.

"That's how your eyeball should look"

"OK…..And how does it look now?" I said.

She started to draw lines across most of the eye and explained that I had scratches that covered at least 90% of my cornea (the front of my eyeball) Long story short, when my head went under the muddy water, I'd managed to get a small piece of grit lodged under my eye lid. Every time I blinked, that grit would be dragged up and down my eyeball.

Thankfully, the nurse at the RedCross station back at Tough Mudder had washed my eye out. It might not have done much for the pain but it definitely prevented even more damage to my eye. I was given pain killers and a funky looking eye patch to go with my headband before being sent home.

An eye patch to go with my new headband

It wouldn't be long though before I'd learn that a scratched eyeball wasn't the most severe injury I was walking around with. I'd soon be back in hospital with a far worse issue...

In early August, during my six days off I'd arranged to meet an old friend for a catch up. The plan was to meet at Costa in town, have a couple of drinks, maybe some food and a good old catch up, nothing special. We'd planned to meet at around noon, I was running late though as I left my house - I was planning on catching a bus but after getting half way down my street, I realised I'd forgotten my wallet so walked back home to get it.

I quickly realised that I was going to be late so I text my friend saying I was going to be late and decided to skip the bus and just walk to town. Just outside of town, there's a bridge named "Myton Bridge" as I was getting closer to it, I could see a small crowd of work men gathered at the far end together looking at the middle of the bridge, I wasn't paying too much attention at this point until I turned to look at what they were looking at.

In the middle of the bridge there was a man standing talking to another man who happened to be stood on the other side of the railings. Shit! A jumper! Without thinking (without using common sense) I ran across the road without first making sure it was clear to do so. Knowing that someone was already talking to the guy I asked the workmen what was happening, how long had they been there and had the police been called. They told me that the man talking to the guy on the other side of the railings had been there for at least ten minutes and that the police had been called so I decided to walk over. I had plenty of hands-on experience talking people down from active suicide attempts thanks to my job. By "an active suicide attempt" I mean, where somebody is actively trying to take their own life and not just talking about how they want to.

I could see the guy wanting to jump was quite young, I was only twenty eight myself at the time and still looked quite young myself so I thought this would be something I could use as a potential ice breaker.

I started by getting as close as I could without causing any distress. I could see that the man trying to talk him down was being ignored so I quietly asked if he had gotten anything out of him like a name or age etc. I got myself close enough for the guy to be able to hear me clearly. I opened with something like,

"Hiya buddy, my names Matt, do you mind if I stand here for a bit?" He ignored me so I moved on.

"So what's made you want to be on the wrong side of the railings then, mate?"

I've always found being direct with someone in this situation is effective (obviously it's always worked for me but that doesn't mean its 100% reliable, in that kind of situation you need to use your own best judgement) It worked and he eventually gave me his name and told me he was nineteen. He spoke about how his ex had stopped him from seeing his child and that he just couldn't handle waking up in the morning knowing his life was so shit. He went on to explain that he was also homeless - the irony here, was that in many ways, I could relate to what he way saying. I'd tried and failed to take my own life on three separate occasions before this point. All attempts were when I was around his age. The irony had never hit me when I was in this position at work but this time, it did.

I managed to keep him engaged in conversation over the next twenty minutes or so, at one point I noticed a cyclist pull over to start taking photos or videos of us. As pissed off as I was in that moment, I had to ignore it - the kid was still on the wrong side of the railings.

By now, I'd managed to get close enough to be able to grab him if I needed to, if you've ever done a suicide awareness course, you'll know that trying to grab a potential jumper is a massive no go. I didn't care at that moment; I knew that the guy who had started talking to him was close enough to back me up if I needed it. If this kid made a wrong move, I was going to grab him. Thankfully, he decided to jump back on to the right side of the bridge just before the police arrived. I think he just got sick and tired of me waffling on really. The police came over and detained him.

While talking he'd mentioned that he was homeless, I asked the police what their plan was for him. They were going to take him to the local mental health unit to be assessed. I told them that he was homeless and that I worked in a homeless hostel, which happened to be less than a minutes' walk away from the bridge. Hell, you could actually see the hostel from the bridge. I asked them to wait around for a few minutes so I could pop in and check to see if we had any space available.

I asked the two staff that were on shift at the time who confirmed there was space but, as soon as I mentioned that the person I had in mind to fill that space had just been talked down from the bridge, they said no as he'd be too "high risk".

There was nothing I could do to change their minds. I had to go back to the officers and tell them we had no space after all because I wasn't going to say what had actually been said. Looking back, I wish I did. He absolutely should have been given a shot in that hostel.

The atmosphere at work still felt tense to say the least. Between all the incidents I found myself dealing with and defusing at work and the pressure that came with them (at work and at home) and the constant feeling of being hated by those around me, I was starting to feel like I was in free fall - trapped inside my own head. I was taking the stress from work home with me and not finding a way to offload - I felt like I had no one to talk to. Nobody would understand me even if I tried. I was stuck in a hole without a ladder.

Imagine being in a job where you feel like you're hated or at the very least disliked. A job where you know there are people in your own team that are bending over backwards to see that you are sacked. A job where people will go out of their way not to talk to you and a job where you often find yourself in positions where you're being verbally abused, dealing with people that need urgent medical care, seeing people overdose or threaten suicide and need to be talked down. Then imagine you've recently had brain surgery and have a brain injury that you refuse to accept is real. Well, that's the position I was in.

I was between night shifts one day in mid-September, I had only managed to get an hour or so sleep before waking up. I couldn't get back to sleep so went and sat on the sofa, it suddenly hit me that it wasn't going to be long before I ended up killing myself if things didn't change. A part of me was ready to call it quits there and then. I really couldn't cope and was struggling to find reasons not to do it, to the extent that I already had a plan in mind.

To this day, I don't why or where the thought came from but I suddenly thought "Riverside" I remembered just how much of an impact going to Riverside had on me back in 2016. Being there with people that I'd never met, the primates/other animals and of course, Bob, Lynne and Mias had a huge life changing impact on me.

Pre diagnoses, I'd always said that if I ever felt like I'd had enough, I should go back to Riverside for a break away and a reality check. What if I booked a trip back there ASAP, I thought to myself?

I had about £600 left - my bills had been paid, I had just enough food to last until my next payday if I was careful and made it last. "Fuck it!" I spent almost all of that money on a flight before letting Lynne at Riverside know that I had booked a flight and would soon be heading over.

Knowing that I still needed to book transport to Riverside from Jo'Burg and pay for my stay, I booked the trip for January 2019. I had two months and four paydays to cover the rest of the costs.

After I'd confirmed everything with Lynne, I went to work to book my annual leave for the trip although there was no guarantee I would actually be given the time off but to be honest I didn't really care at this point. I was going regardless of being authorised or not.

I quickly realised that the only way I could really afford to cover all the costs of getting back to Riverside without skipping on bills and basic essentials was to start taking shifts at our young person's hostel so I signed up for so much overtime between the two hostels that I would be working seven days a week for a solid month. Now, it might sound fairy easy but when you're doing night shifts it gets pretty exhausting pretty damn fast.

Kris soon realised what kind of hours I was working and unlike me, he knew just how stupid I was being. He asked me to pop over to his before work one night. After some food and a catch up, he told me how stupid I was being for working excessive hours. He could see I was getting ill and asked me how much I actually needed to pay off the rest of the Riverside trip. I told him roughly how much and roughly how much more overtime that would require me to do. There and then, he told me to forget the overtime and offered to lend me the money needed as a means of making sure I stopped feeling I needed to smash out the overtime. I was stumped. I tried telling him that it was too much and that I could handle the workload but no, Kris being Kris, he wanted to help. He's always had my back.

Thanks to him, I could finally work only what I needed to. What he did that night is something I'll never forget. It wasn't so much the fact he had lent me the money, it was that he recognised that I was doing more harm than good to myself and he wanted to help me.

There was one night in October - I'd turned up for a night shift. Within minutes of being at work, I spotted an ad on Facebook for "The Hull'timate Marathon", a 10k water themed obstacle course in town, the next morning. I instantly knew that I was doing it regardless of the fact I would be doing this directly after a night shift and that I would be back doing a night shift a few hours after. I remember calling my friend, Sophie and telling her about it. I knew she wouldn't be keen but tried to rope her in anyway. After ten minutes of bugging her about it, she hesitantly agreed.

The next morning, I came home to feed and walk Charlie before grabbing some brekkie and heading back to town to meet Sophie, buy our tickets and hit the start line!

I was shattered but also excited. Sophie on the other hand was not so excited, she'd never done anything like this before. Over 10km we would complete a dozen obstacles, including having to jump into and swim out of the marina around the local shopping centre. Not being able to swim made that bit slightly awkward.

After looking a twat debating whether I could or should jump in, I finally got it over and done with. I managed to make my way to some nets by the wall without actually drowning and get out, not without looking a twat of course!

The whole day was amazing. I was quite proud of myself for doing that kind of event post and pre night shift but more so of Sophie with it being her first event like that.

Me and Sophie with our medals at the finish line

In November I was at Castle Hill for a check-up and to get the results from my latest MRI scan. It was a crap day, I was in-between night shifts and running late so my anxiety was starting to take full effect. If I hadn't been so desperate to know what the results were for my scan I'd have just bailed to save stressing, but I needed to know what the results were so I choose to crack on and be late. I was obviously still stressing and becoming even more anxious but there wasn't much I could do.

As I was rushing towards the Queens Centre, I spotted something on a bench and stopped to take a closer look. It was a rock, a painted rock with the words "You Matter" written on it. I instantly realised that this was like the rock I had found in Hessle before taking it to Denver and leaving it on the mountains. I sat down for a couple of minutes to give myself a chance to relax and calm down. Why was I worrying about being a few minutes late I wondered? I'd never had a doctors or hospital appointment that had run on time anyway. "Just chill out and breathe" I thought to myself.

Suddenly, the panicking and stressing stopped. This rock literally stopped me in my tracks and helped me realise that I didn't need to worry and stress. I kept the rock and decided that I would bring it to Riverside with me in the hope of leaving it somewhere for another volunteer to find - hoping, like me, it would help make their day and remind them that they mattered.

I made it to the appointment a couple of minutes late but it didn't matter, they were of course running late anyway.

At the appointment, I mentioned that I had started to notice that the "tingling sensation" in my head was becoming more and more frequent. Just like before, I was told that this was normal for somebody that'd had brain surgery. With the all clear, I left in a much better mood than when I had started the day.

Over time, I started to notice that the area that had been operated on was starting to feel more and more "strange" - it never hurt but I started to notice that it had never actually healed properly. Over the past couple of months, I'd noticed that there was a scab covering a small section of the top of my head. Sometimes, I'd be at work and find that it was constantly itching or on the odd occasion, I'd notice that the area was wet, not with blood but a kind of yellow coloured water like substance. I mentioned that the area had been feeling "odd" to the oncologist and he told me this was normal, so surly this was just a slow healing wound, right?...

CHAPTER 16

I need this like I need a hole in the head

One of the main reason's I'd been so set on completing all three of my fundraising challenges and the Hull'timate Challenge was to prove to those around me that I was fine. I had become obsessed with proving everybody wrong by showing them that I had won. I had a brain tumour, most of it had been plucked out and I had won. Simple.

Funnily enough, it worked but not in the way you would think. I had been so set on showing everybody that I was physically ok, that I'd failed to see, understand or accept that I had a brain injury and that the more I refused to accept it, the worse it was getting. Over time I started to notice my short-term memory was getting worse and that fatigue was becoming a real issue, especially at work but I'd just make a stupid joke about it. For example, if I forgot to complete a particular task during a shift, I'd just say something like "oh, sorry. Must be the brain tumour fucking me around!" Obviously, I'd say it with complete and obvious sarcasm as I meant it as a joke. The problem was that people started to take my jokes seriously. Those I worked with soon started to call me out for being lazy and just blaming my tumour. The reality was, I had been living with a brain injury since at least 2010 (when the little sucker was missed during my first CT scan).

Looking back over the years after that botched CT scan, with the benefit of hindsight, I see there were a lot of signs pointing to something being wrong as far back as 2011. Be it pride, stubbornness or just plain ignorance, I never believed

I had a brain injury post-surgery. If I had taken the whole situation seriously from the day I was diagnosed, I might have kept a bit more respect and lost less friends but there I was, in complete denial and slowly falling apart.

I remember one day in November, while walking home from doing a food shop I spotted Katie with my daughter Billie stood at a bus stop. I walked over as fast I could and without acknowledging Katie went straight to Billie and gave her a huge, long cuddle. I hadn't seen Billie for eight months so I was taking full advantage of this moment. I knew Katie wouldn't like it but I really didn't care. I was giving my daughter a cuddle regardless of what Katie thought.

Katie knew that she had me by the balls as far as seeing Billie went. She knew that I couldn't and wouldn't be able to afford the legal fees if I dared to challenge her. All I could do, was continue to give her money for Billie each month.

After getting a much-needed cuddle from Billie and telling her I loved her, I stood up and asked Katie why she had banned me and Billie from seeing each other. There were a few people at the bus stop so I made a point of asking out loud. Her exact reply was.

"You have a brain tumour, it's not fair for Billie to be around you when you have it"

I saw a couple of heads shoot up as she said that - obviously, the people stood around waiting for their bus had overheard what she said. Katie went bright red when she realised that people were now looking at her. Good. It wasn't just me that thought that it was a pathetic excuse to keep me and Billie apart.

I gave Katie my number before leaving them, reminding her that Billie's birthday was coming up and that I would like it if I could give her presents directly. She agreed and took my number, telling me that she would call me to discuss details soon, but she never did.

Things had also gotten quite rocky with me and Amy, she was still set on only letting me see Jack once a month. Like

Katie, she knew that I couldn't do anything to challenge her in a legal sense. I made a point of paying more than what CSA would have demanded I pay. She'd never be able to call me out as a deadbeat dad if I was paying more than I was meant to be.

By mid-November I was back at breaking point. I'd been hammering the overtime again; easily bagging sixty - seventy hours a week (mostly night shifts) more often than not. I thought that constantly working would take my mind off the more negative thoughts and having access to the gym at work would also help. Spoiler alert. Overworking to get away from stress DOES NOT WORK. It makes it worse. Especially in the environment I was working in. I was constantly waking up depressed and going to bed depressed.

Between the constant working in a high stress environment with people I thought hated me, the brain injury I refused to believe I had and of course the minimal to none existent contact with both of my kids I was finding it harder and harder to find a reason not to finally be done with everything and kill myself. I'd already planned out to the letter exactly how I was going to do it. All I had to do was pick a day and say "fuck it!" Having Riverside to focus on though was a real help!

I should not have been at work at all by this point but I refused to see and believe just how fucked I was. There was one particular night shift that for my own good I probably shouldn't write about publicly. But what I can say is that I fucked up – my judgement of a situation was way off and as a result a near fatal incident started to occur, directly because of my actions. It was the kind of incident that the few people that do know about are either proud of me or like me, disappointed. Looking back at that shift, I'm almost ashamed of myself. Its moments like that where I realise just how shit hindsight is. Once the dust had settled, I was lucky to even have a job, let alone to not have been arrested.

Over time, I continued to notice that the scab on I'm my head was in fact covering what felt like a hole. Aside from the usual tingling sensation and itching, it never really bothered me – no pain just the odd tingling sensation. I never saw an issue with it though because I had been told on multiple occasions that it was normal so I just left it. I had bigger things on my mind at the time, like planning the details for my Riverside trip and trying to keep sane while at work.

I'd soon learn though that sometimes doctors get things wrong and that you should really always consider a second opinion. That and the fact common sense goes a long way.

December came and went - I worked all of Christmas and New Year, I wasn't permitted to see Jack at all over the festive period because Amy wanted "family time" and of course, Katie was still keeping Billie away from me. It was either stay at home and mope about or go to work and keep busy and keep my mind focused on other things. I just had to hold on for a few more weeks and then I'd be on a plane heading on over to South Africa once again for a much needed break away, or so I thought anyway...

I remember one day, going in to work for a day shift, as I walked in to reception I found that all the staff had locked themselves in reception behind the counter. They all looked worried and were watching the monitors, with one of them on the phone to the police. As soon as they saw me, one of the staff said"

"Matt, Get behind reception now!"

I asked why and was told me that a resident had armed himself with a knife while under the influence of drugs and was running around upstairs. Unlike the staff that were on shift, I wasn't remotely worried. I wasn't being brave, I just didn't see an issue so, I dumped my stuff behind reception and walked over to the office to dump my drinks in the fridge. I was more worried about having to have a warm energy drink while at work than I was about a drug fuelled resident running wild with a knife. Looking back, this wasn't the first time I had been in a situation like this and not felt worried or concerned in the slightest. No. This had happened a few times post-surgery. It's almost as if I just couldn't process danger the way a "normal" person would and should. I later learnt that this was just one of the many issues that came with a brain injury. Or in my case, a brain injury I refused to admit I had.

I received a letter in early January, a couple of weeks before I due to fly out to South Africa for an appointment with my oncologist for a check-up and to go over my latest scan results for late January. Obviously, I wasn't going to be in the UK at this point so I called the hospital to see if I could rearrange. I just wanted to know what the scan results were otherwise, I could have happily not bothered going in at all.

At first I was told there was no earlier appointments but after telling the receptionist that I didn't know how long I would be in South Africa for and that I needed my results before I left, an appointment was soon found for me -three days before I was due to fly.

I asked Kris to come to the appointment with me as I always seemed to get a lecture from the doctors if I turned up to an appointment on my own. Mum and Dad were both working so I asked Kris and he was happy to come along. The appointment was straight forward, there was no real change as far as the tumour was concerned. Feeling well and happy that the hitchhiker hadn't come back for round two, the appointment came to an end. Just before I got up to leave, I remembered the scab on my head and the tingling feeling it left me with so said to the oncologist.

"I know you've told me its normal but this hole in my head is still tingling and it's happening a lot more often now"

Just like the last two times I'd mentioned it, he began to say that the sensation was quite normal but before he could finish, the nurse that was sat in the room taking notes suddenly pipped up.

"Did you just say there's a hole in your head!?" She shot up and came to look at my head.

"Oh my god!" She shrieked.

She told the oncologist to have look and without saying another word, she went straight to the phone and called the

Neuro ward at Hull Royal telling them that I needed an urgent appointment that day.

I had no idea what was happening. After coming off the phone, she explained that this "small" hole wasn't just a small cut or something that I could just keep putting off - after cleaning it she said she could quite clearly see my skull below the hole. She sent me to get my bloods done and told me that I needed to get to Hull Royal ASAP.

I told Kris to go and do what he needed to do as I was probably going to be a while anyway. After having my bloods done, I made my way over to the Neuro ward at Hull Royal. I didn't have a clue what was actually happening at this point and thought this was a bit overkill. The nurse was just being overdramatic, surely.

One CT scan and an appointment with the consultant that had done my brain surgery later, I soon got a rough idea of just how bad the situation was. The consultant showed me the CT scan results before explaining that I had a "bone eating infection."

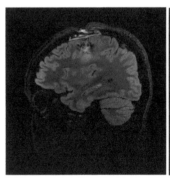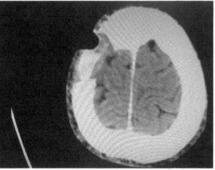

I had first noticed the tingling sensation in April, it's highly likely that I picked up the infection while in hospital. The consultant went on to explain that I would need to see another surgeon that day but I still hadn't grasped how serious the situation was at this point.

My sister, Katy came to meet me at the hospital while I waited to see the next surgeon. After an hour or so of waiting, the surgeon came to see me. After looking at the wound on my head, his first question was.

"Have you ever taken a picture of this so you could see what it looks like?"

I'd never thought to that, I'd already been told that it was nothing to worry about, so taking a picture to see how it looked was a thought that had never crossed my mind. The surgeon then asked if he could use my phone to take a picture and show me exactly what he was looking at.

It takes a lot to shock me, not much can make me cringe but when I saw what this wound actually looked like, I was nearly sick. You really could see my skull, well what was left of it anyway. The infection had eaten away at my skull from the inside out. The bit of skull that was left was paper thin, meaning just a minor knock to the head would be very likely to kill me.

He went on to explain that I needed urgent surgery to try and repair the damage so I told him that in three days' time I was flying out to South Africa to work in an animal sanctuary. "You're not, you NEED surgery"

Katy was just as direct but a lot less polite about how she said it - this was the last thing I needed. My bags were already packed, my annual leave had been authorized - I didn't have time to mess around with surgery.

I soon realised and accepted that I had no say in the matter and the surgery was booked in for the next day. I was allowed to go home but needed to be back the next day by 10am.

I came back the next day but was sent home within a couple hours as there had been some kind of emergency that took priority over the minor stuff like my newly discovered hole in the head. I came back the next day, for some stupid reason I genuinely thought that I would have the surgery and be sent home later that day so I didn't bring anything like a change of clothes or even phone charger.

I'd just been told that I had a hole in my head, that a slight bump to the head could send that small remaining paper-thin piece of skull in to my brain like shrapnel, killing me, yet my main worry was that I had lost my flight to South Africa.

If anything, this reinforced just how seriously I wasn't taking any of this situation, from the tumour diagnoses onwards. Again, that's the power of hindsight for you.

Just like the last surgery I had, a surgeon came to see me and explain the plan for the day which was for two separate surgeons to work on me (with their team).

The surgeon that had performed my brain surgery would be there to open up my skull and clean the area of my brain that had been exposed to the infection before handing over to a plastic surgeon who would then quite literally peel skin from the back of my head and bring it over the top of my head to cover the hole. There were points to all of this that I needed to question. Firstly, I asked if I would be awake for the surgery, like before. Thankfully the answer was no. Secondly, I had to ask if I had heard him right when he told me that my brain was going to be washed! Yes. Your brain has come into contact with a serious infection, so it will need to be cleaned before we close your head up, he said.

Well fuck me! I'm about to be brainwashed -literally! Yes, my main take away point from the pre surgery brief wasn't that I was just about to have a large chunk of skull permanently removed from my head it was that I was literally about to have a "brainwash"

The surgery went well with no issues and took around five - six hours. The first thing I actually remember is being sat in my bed talking to a doctor and a nurse, I have no idea what the conversation was about, they were probably checking up on me.

I remember throwing up all over the place a couple of times - I'd had a bad reaction to the anesthetic but nothing to worry about of course.

I remember later that night being sat there in my bed with the anesthetic starting to wear off. I felt a wet sensation on my neck so had a feel, not sure what it was. It was blood and lot of it too -my head was pouring with blood.

I shouted a nurse over who immediately took one quick look, gave my head a quick clean and then called the on-call surgeon up. The nurse was angry that my head hadn't been bandaged up at all -obviously, it had been stapled back together (again) but unlike after the brain surgery, there were no bandages this time.

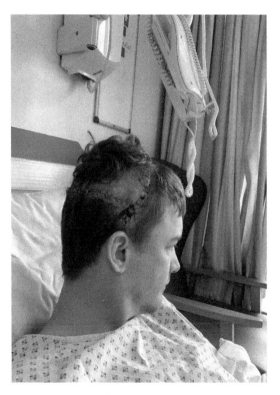

Post surgery

The on-call surgeon explained that this was necessary because of the infection that I'd had. They needed to be sure that they'd gotten rid of all of it and using bandages would just make it harder to see if the surgery had or hadn't worked.

Personally, I wasn't really worried but the nurse was still not impressed. She didn't agree with the decision but had no say in the matter.

The next day, my main priority was being discharged. I was meant to be flying out to South Africa that day - I knew that was definitely not happening but I at least wanted to be at home.

I waited for the doctors to start their "morning rounds" so I could ask the right people about what time I would actually be leaving. When I managed to speak to a doctor, I was told that there was no plan in place for me to be leaving at all, in fact I was meant to be there for a minimum of four or five days.

I tried to tell them that I didn't need to be in hospital at all - I was fine and minus the new horror movie look – I even looked fine. I was pissed off, although extremely grateful for the treatment I'd received I didn't want to be there at all.

Eventually I gave up arguing after being given an almighty bollocking by one of the nurses. "Matthew, you've come in with a serious, life threatening infection that's resulted in you losing a significant part of your skull!"

She went on to explain that I still wasn't in the clear, the risk of further infection was still very high and I pretty much agreed to stop complaining after that.

Mum came in and dropped off some supplies for me later that day. Nikita came by a couple of times over the next few days to make sure I had an endless supply of junk food and even got us both a takeaway one night - Nikita always was a little legend!

I remember seeing a guy a few beds down from me who had a huge wound that wrapped around the back of his head over to the top. It was fairly obvious that he'd had brain surgery.

I looked over, trying to be social and start a conversation; I introduced myself and asked what he'd been brought in for. He tried to tell me but couldn't remember and you could see the frustration in his face while he tried to remember. I interrupted by asking him if he'd had brain surgery.

"Ohhhh, yea that! That's what I had!"

Christ, I thought, at least I wasn't that bad after my surgery and I realised how lucky I actually had things.

Four days after the surgery, I was allowed to go home; I got myself a taxi and got home as fast as could. I got back quite late so got myself a takeaway before spending the night chilling out with a movie.

Although a part of me blames the oncologist for telling me that the tingling sensation in my head was "normal" I have to say, this could have been avoided if I had taken the situation more seriously from the start. I know my brain injury played a part but had I asked for a second opinion back when I was first told it was normal, I would never have been in that position. There's a saying "ignorance is bliss" well, I ignored symptoms that should have rang alarm bells before my tumour was found, I ignored a hole in my head because I believed it was "normal" even though nobody had actually looked at it. Ignorance is NOT bliss - it's lazy, dumb and just plain stupid.

CHAPTER 17

Ok, let's try again…

Once again, it was great to be home post-surgery. Unlike the last time, I was actually sent home with all the staples still in my head, about twenty five holding my head together which was a few less than last time. I was told that I just needed to keep my head clean, avoid any pressure on my head - so no hats and caps and to wait a week or so before going to my GP surgery to have them removed.

As I was meant to be at Riverside by now, I still had four weeks annual leave I could use to "recover" but I decided that ten days would be more than enough. I booked myself an appointment to have the staples removed seven days after being home and arranged to be back at work three days after that. I just wanted to get back to normal, whatever the hell normal actually was…

Although there was still an atmosphere at work, I'd started to care a lot less about it. I knew that sooner rather than later I'd be heading out to Riverside. It didn't matter how much shit came my way; I could handle it knowing that I'd soon be where I needed to be. My only real issue now, was that I would need to buy my airline ticket once again.

There was one night shift in February that started off like most shifts. Around 1am, I jumped in the gym for my normal workout. Part of the reason I was able to keep my cool in that place was because I had access to the gym as and when I needed while at work. I would always carry a radio with me in the gym, just in case there was an emergency. This particular night, I started off with a run on the treadmill. I'd been on it less than ten minutes before being called by Mike.

"Matt, Room 37 has just called to say he wants to kill himself."

I told him that I would sort it and that I would buzz him on the radio if I needed him. Still in my workout gear I ran up the three flights of stairs to the resident's room, gave myself a second to catch my breath and compose myself before letting myself into the room. The resident had opened his window as far as he could, technically he shouldn't have been able to open it that far but he did. I found him stood by the open window, ready to jump out. He was crying, telling me that he just couldn't cope anymore. Three floors up, it wouldn't have had a great outcome if he made it out the window and we both knew that this exact scenario had played out a month before. On that occasion, things did not end well and I wasn't going to let this guy be a repeat of that incident.

This resident was one of the more genuine people who we all really liked, after his wife died a few years previously, he turned to alcohol before his life slowly began to fall apart. I spent about twenty minutes talking to him before I was certain there was a degree of trust between us and that I was confident he wasn't going to immediately jump, I sat down on his bed and asked him to sit with me so we could talk properly. I stayed with him for a good hour or so before convincing him to come downstairs with me so I could make him a brew.

Of all the active suicide attempts I'd defused; this was the one that really hit me. Mike and I asked him to sleep downstairs in one of our emergency beds that night (for obvious reasons) once I was confident that he was ok, I went to the office and just cried. This was the first time I'd cried after dealing with this type of incident. I'm not sure why but it just hit me hard.

I soon realised it was time to start looking at dates to get to Riverside. I'd been told by the doctors before leaving hospital that I would need to wait around a year before I thought about going back but I had no intentions of waiting that long. I wasn't going for a holiday after all, I needed this trip.

Amy had started to go quiet and wouldn't answer the phone if I called, when I text to see how Jack was I'd get no reply. I'd get a random message once in a blue moon telling me when I could see him. Like always, the terms of me seeing him were set by her but she knew as well as I did that, I couldn't afford the thousands in legal fees to force her to let me and Jack spend real time together. By the end of February she was completely ignoring me, no replies to texts or calls, and no offer of seeing Jack at all.

Jack's birthday was on the March 19th, when the day came I knew that being stuck at home, not being able to so much as say happy birthday to him would only serve to make me worse mentally, so I booked my flight out to South Africa for March 17th. I'd stay in a B&B upon arrival in SA on the 18th and then fly out to Phalaborwa the next day. I'd have dropped everything in a heartbeat if Amy had just said I could a couple of hours with Jack but no. As hard as it was to know that I'd be out of the country for his birthday, I knew that I was doing the right thing.

On March 16th my friend Sophie arranged to come round for a catch up before I left for South Africa the next day. She came to my place for a couple of drinks and a movie. Nothing special just a chilled night before I left. She stayed the night as she was planning on coming to the train station with me in the morning. One chilled night out later and it was time to gear up and go.

I'd arranged for Charlie to stay at my Mum and Dads while I was away. Once I had gotten on the train, the plan was for Sophie to come back to my place, spend some time with Charlie before going home. My mum would then come and pick Charlie up soon after.

I made it to Manchester Airport about seven hours early so had plenty of time to chill out before check in. I always seem to panic when I know I have to be somewhere by a certain time. My anxiety always gets the better of me, meaning I always arrive stupidly early to meetings, appointments or in this case an airport. I'd bought a journal specifically for this trip, the idea was that in years to come, Jack & Billie could have read of it and get an idea as to why I was heading back out to Riverside. I started writing as soon as I found a quiet spot in the airport.

I remember, as I was going through security I put my hand luggage on the conveyer belt to be x-rayed. As I was stood waiting for my bag to come to me, one of the security officers came over, pointed to my bag and asked if it was mine, I confirmed it was. With a confused look on his face, he asked if I had a rock in my bag.

"I sure do mate."

It was the "You Matter" rock I'd found at Castle Hill back in November. He asked me to remove it and show him so I did just that. He took the rock from me for a closer look.

Monkey with the "you matter rock" at the airport

"I actually don't know what I can do with this to be honest…"

He still seemed confused as to why I had a rock in my hand luggage but rather than question me, he gave me the rock back before letting me make my way to departures.

My journey was slightly different to the last time. I flew to SA. I was flying with Ethiopian Airways and had two flights to get to Jo'Burg. The first would see me going to Addis - Ethiopia and then taking a connecting flight to Jo'Burg.

Both flights were fairly smooth and I spent most of my time looking back at pictures and videos of Jack & Billie.

I made it to Jo'Burg the next morning and all I had to do was get to my B&B. I remember trying to avoid the porters this time. I had quite a few porters trying to stop me, offering to help me but I wasn't interested. One Porter came over, telling me he was a driver before asking me where I was going. Fuck it I thought. I'll give him a go so I showed him my phone and where I needed to be, he offered to take me for around 300 Rand (about £15) The journey was only ten minutes away so I obviously paid too much but I didn't care, I just wanted to get to my B&B so I could get a shower and then chill. I remember being sat in the car with this guy and sending Nikita a live location through messenger with a message that said something like "If my marker stops moving, you know I've been kidnapped or killed. You can't do anything obviously but I thought I'd let you know!" Obviously, this was satire and said in jest - I knew I'd be ok and so did Nikita.

Once checked into to my room, I grabbed a shower, wrote another entry in my journal before chilling out with some TV that I'd downloaded before leaving the UK.

My flight to Phalaborwa was at 3pm the next day so I had more than enough time to relax before the next step in my little adventure.

The next morning, I was up bright and early. I had a fairly decent cooked breakfast before taking an early shuttle ride to the airport. I had more than enough time to kill before my

3pm flight, which meant I had plenty of time to mill about. I was slightly worried about my head; it had only been six or seven weeks since I'd had a chunk of skull removed - I literally had a hole in my head. The thought of a baboon jumping on my head and killing me was a very real concern. As nervous as I felt, I was actually quite excited. I needed to get back to Riverside, this really was my plan B and it was only hours away.

CHAPTER 18

Returning to Riverside

The flight to Phalaborwa was a bumpy one, we hit a lot turbulence around halfway there. Just like the last time, I clung on to my seat for dear life while looking around to see how the rest of the passengers were reacting. Unlike the last time though a few of the passengers seemed a little freaked out -at least it wasn't just me.

The flight was less than an hour and once at the airport I had a quick pee, grabbed my bag and then made my way to the exit. Almost immediately, I spotted a guy who looked around my age, holding a sign with my name on it. A big grin popped up on my face, as I looked at him and pointed at him with both hands. It's one of those moments you have to see to understand. Instantly, in return, without saying a word, he did the exact same thing. This was the moment I knew this guy was cool and would be on my kind of wave length. His name was Ben. The drive from the airport was the same as last time I was there, just over an hour which gave us both time to talk.

I took the chance to find out what I could about the place and what had changed (if anything) before I got there.

Learning from the last time was at Riverside, I wasn't dressed like a poor Steve Irwin impersonator this time. Remembering that the evenings were for drinking, I asked Ben if we could stop at one of the shops before we got to Riverside. I wanted to grab some drinks for when I got there. I ended up buying two big 24x creates of Stella which was more than enough to last me a good long while.

I'd put the two creates in to the back of the pickup truck, as we pulled in through the gates, some of the lads came over to introduce themselves and suss out the new guy, before quickly realising there were two creates of beer in the truck. It was safe to say, they approved. We'd turned up later than expected so after putting the beer away and grabbing a quick hello and a hug with Bob and Lynne, it was time for dinner.

Once dinner was out of the way, it was time for to get into The Hide and start socialising. Some of the lads invited me to join them for a drinking game which I was more than happy to jump in on. The game was simple, there were six of us lined up behind a table. We would have to down a pint of whatever alcohol we had with us as fast as we could before flipping a cup. First impressions count, so I knew that I was going to be judged on just how well I did or didn't do. Nothing like a smidge of pressure!

I couldn't even down my pint in one go! As I was very slowly drinking it, the lads suddenly started shouting "come on Matt Dog! Come on!" After a ridiculously long time spent with the pint, I finally finished it. Then came the cup flip. After a few shockingly terrible number of failed attempts to flip the cup, I ended up dropping it on the floor. I was too drunk by this point to actually remember if it even landed the right way. Luckily or embarrassingly - depending how you look at it, the whole thing was filmed beginning to end - I still have the video to this day. Looking back at it I actually find it quite entertaining, almost as much as I do cringe worthy.

After we'd all spent some time in The Hide we all made our way down to the dorms where we could sit by the fire and have some drinks. I ended up meeting two volunteers, Emma, who was from the UK and Karol, a guy from the Netherlands. We spent the rest of the night basically talking shit. I remember Emma trying to explain the differences between there, their and they're, in English to Karol. I don't know why but I ended up filming it. It must have seemed a funnier conversation at the time especially as we were all slightly pissed by this point.

The next morning, we were all up bright and early ready to crack on with the day's work.

It was a simple day and I managed to get some time in all three enclosures Monty, Georgie and Middles (Middles being the next step towards release for the baboons in Monty).

I noticed that a couple of the lads from the night before were calling me "Matt Dog" and I realised that for whatever reason that would now be my nickname in that place.

My main priority for that day, seemed to be finding a place to hide the "You Matter" rock so late that afternoon I decided to leave it just in front of a bench near the Georgie enclosure. I knew people liked to use that bench while they called home so the idea was that when somebody went to call home, they'd sit down on the bench before spotting this rock. I was hoping it would at least make them smile and that they would then find a new place to hide it or if it had actually had some form of significant impact on them, like it did for me, they would keep it and take it home.

I actually found the rock, in the food shed by food prep the next day. Somebody had found and then placed it on a crate of cabbages for someone else to find. I loved that someone had decided to play along and keep it going. I took the rock and decided to find a new home for it. I didn't know who had found/re hidden it but I definitely wanted to keep it going.

I remember on the third day, me and another girl were in a cage sifting through an enormous pile of bananas separating the ripe bananas from the non-ripe ones and we got talking about snakes. I asked her if she had ever seen one at Riverside or if she knew what kinds I could except to see. She said no but I had a rough idea that there would be some there, although I'd never actually seen a snake there before. I said that I'd heard stories about other volunteers that upon seeing a snake, would whip out their phone to get a photo of it. I told her how dumb that was and that doing something so stupid is a fast-track route to winning a Darwin Award. (A pretend award for those who end up dead because of an avoidable and stupid act they have performed) As I was explaining the variety of snakes that had been seen in Riverside, I said "this tarp (that we were sat on) this would be a perfect place for a snake to hide under for the shade" As I said that, I lifted a corner of the tarp only to find a small jet-black snake that had coiled itself up. I had been sat just a couple of inches away from this it. "Ermmm, Meg. There's a snake right here y'know"

As I said this, I quickly whipped out my phone to get a photo. I didn't know what type of snake it was but this was the first ever wild snake I'd seen so I wanted to take a shot. As I tried to get up close to get the shot, Meg grabbed me and dragged me out of the cage, telling me just how stupid I was. Just five minutes ago, I'd warned her about doing this exact same thing but there I was, trying to do exactly what I'd just warned her about.

Bob soon came over and upon seeing the snake, he very quickly removed its head... It turned out to be a stiletto snake that happen to be quite venomous. Killing it was the safest way to deal with it at the time. Trying to move it would have just put whoever tried to move it in danger. Good luck getting fast treatment for a venomous bite in the middle of Limpopo. Unless you have a good chunk of money readily available, you're not getting the treatment you need. Simple. I'd been sat barely a couple of inches away from this little guy. How I wasn't bitten, I'll never know.

Over the first few days, I spent a lot of time with Emma and she turned out to be pretty cool. I remember being out on a baboon walk and she found a Vervet monkey skull that looked as though it had been there for a fair few years. Karol went to take a picture of Emma with her new find and as she held the skull up, I managed to get a perfect photo of the pair of them right in the moment. It was one of those pictures that needed no editing at all. Something about it really stood out for me. I realised then, that I really like "moment shots" or "candid" photos. A photo of a moment. No-one posing for the camera or even acknowledging that a photo is about to be taken. Just a nice photo of a moment as it's happening.

From that point onwards, I made a point of taking as many photos as I could, not just for me but for everybody. If I saw a volunteer hugging one of the primates for example, I'd move in to a position to line them up for a photo without making it obvious what I was doing before taking a photo. The volunteer would then have a perfect photo of a moment between them and the primate they had with them. Sometimes I would capture some beautiful moments between volunteers and the baboons. What would often make them special, is that they had no idea the photo was being taken, meaning the photo really was a genuine moment shot.

I'd often end the day with around a thousand photos - the vast majority of them would be of the other volunteers. It was a ball ache, having to sift though and edit so many photos and to then have to find the people that they all belonged to so I could send them over, but it was worth it and people were grateful for it. I was starting to think that I may have just found a path that actually interested me.

At the end of the first week, a few of us went on the "panorama route" trip. A full day's road trip was just the kind of day out that I'd been needing for a long time now.

The weather was beautiful with clear blue skies - unlike back in 2016. There was me Emma, American Nikko or Jesus as he was known (extremely long hair and a huge beard to go with) and a few other volunteers and I'd brought Monkey with me.

I spent most of my day with Emma and Nikko, we had such a good time. I remember being at a the Bylde River Canyon, there were signs dotted around warning people not to go any further due to the risk of falling the 560meters to the ground below. I decided it would be a great idea to sit on the very edge of said canyon in some very awkward spots so I could have some nice-looking shots taken. The risk of death did seem worth it at the time but looking back, it was probably a bit of a dumb move.

**Taking a moment to appreciate the
views of Clyde Canyon**

I remember being at God's Window with Emma and Nikko, we were about 1000ft up and I decided to see if I could climb over a fence, again to bag a perfect shot. Emma had Monkey at this point and she dangled him over the edge, warning me that if I tried to climb another fence just for a photo, Monkey would be taking a little tumble. I didn't get to climb over the fence but I did grab a shot of her dangling my little travel mascot over the edge - it actually made a great photo!

Emma threatening to drop Monkey from God's Window

Overall, it was a great and much needed day out that left me with memories I will treasure forever.

I was starting to forget about all the problems I'd left behind at home and work, none of the crap at work mattered any more. It was so nice to be working in an environment that I was not only liked but also appreciated. Don't get me wrong, it was hard knowing that I couldn't see or even speak to Jack and Billie and I often had sleepless nights thinking about them and what, if anything I could do to convince their mums to let us see each other again.

The last time I was at Riverside, back in 2016, I'd met a girl named Mollie. I'd actually spoken to her online before either of us made our way there thanks to the overpriced booking agent we used to organise the trip. Mollie had come back in

January that year when I was also supposed to be there but obviously, a hole in the head changed that. She was staying at Riverside for six months with a two week break halfway though, I'd come back to Riverside about ten days before Mollie came back from her break.

When I left back in 2016 I hadn't been able to get an ink print of baby Darwin's paw, something I'd really wanted so I could get it tattooed and then frame the print. While I was in hospital in January, Darwin had been moved to main camp where he would stay until ready to be released. Seeing that was great news but I was absolutely gutted as I couldn't and wouldn't be bad to get an ink print of his paw.

I remember being sat in The Hide the afternoon Mollie had just come back from her break, she hadn't been through the gates long before she called me over. After giving me a hug she handed me a small piece of paper - it was Darwin's paw print!

She was part of the team that had moved Darwin and the other baboons from Middles at the time in to main camp. The baboons are put to sleep for this process for their own safety and that of the volunteers - while Darwin was asleep, Mollie had got his paw print inked on to paper for me! Honestly, this meant so much to me. Darwin had made the first trip to Riverside just that extra bit special for me which is why I had adopted him in the first place. I'll always be grateful to Mollie for doing that for me.

One evening, after a few drinks we were all heading down to dorms to get a fire going and continue drinking, listening to music and just talking shit. I went to The Hide to go and grab my day sack, I always had Monkey in my side pocket of my day sack, it was my mascot after all.

As I went to grab my bag, I noticed Monkey had been taken - that or he'd decided to go for an adventure of his own... I was so pissed off. Everybody knew that Monkey wasn't just some teddy that I liked to carry around - it was a symbolic, lucky mascot that came with a stack of memories for me.

I asked around but nobody knew what had happened to him – I was devastated and looked everywhere. Three days later I was walking up from the dorms after having had a shower, I'd forgotten about Monkey at this point, until that is I saw him sat on the fence by the office. Whoever had nabbed him had decided to leave him there for me. Looking back and writing this, I can't help but laugh. I genuinely hope that whoever took him, took pictures of him on his mini adventure! That's what I love about Monkey, once people hear the story behind why I have it/him, they embrace it just as much as I do.

I'll always remember constantly trying to play pranks on Emma but would always be out smarted - I'd grab the hose to spray her but she would see it coming and do a runner, if I tried to launch half a papaya at her (Yes, that's a thing at Riverside) she'd just see it coming and run. Apparently, my poker face sucks! She'd only have to see my face to know that I was up to something.

It wasn't long though before Emma had to go home, it was pretty crap to see her leave. In just a short space of time, she had had helped make that first couple of weeks so great. She was definitely one of those friends that I'll be forever grateful I met when I did.

After a couple of weeks, some of the lads asked if fancied taking a walk with them out into the scrubland by the river. We'd found hippo tracks by the dorms a few days earlier and realised that hippos would leave the river on a night while it was cooler and walk past our dorms to find a grazing spot. The plan was for us to follow these tracks to the river and see if we could track a pod of hippos.

"Fuck yea, I do!" I thought.

During an afternoon off, me and the rest of the lads all got ourselves a machete each, except Jona who opted for an axe for some reason. The machetes were for clearing the long grass and any bushes that got in the way.

Fun fact here: Hippos are THE most dangerous animal on the planet. They are responsible for more human deaths than ANY other animal, reptile or insect alive today. Hippos are dicks and they will kill anything or anyone that's stupid enough to get even remotely close to a patch of water that they happen to be in and good luck trying to out run one. Hippos are known to be extremely fast.

So along come the seven of us hoping to snag a cracking photo of said dicks of the animal kingdom. After a couple of hours of walking we came across an old fallen tree - this thing was huge. I decided that it would be the perfect place to get a cheesy group photo with us striking a ridiculously stupid pose. We opted for us all to have the machetes up in the air while all pulling a stupid face and then agreed that the photo would not be shared on social media because if Bob saw it, we'd be fucked.

The now infamous photo during our afternoon of Hippo tracking

Nobody was allowed to head out that far away from the sanctuary and nobody was allowed to take the machetes as and when they liked. To the surprise of nobody, we never did find any hippos that day or anything of any interest for that matter. We did have a good trek though and all enjoyed it.

The next morning, Mollie came over and asked me if I'd seen my Instagram - I hadn't. She told me that I needed to look at my last post there and then, I did and saw it just so happened to be the photo of me and the other lads on the tree the day before. I was a complete and utter idiot, I'd posted the photo without even thinking - Bob had seen it and was furious. We hadn't started the morning chores yet, so I went to the office to try and speak to Bob. It turned out that Bob had mistranslated the caption I'd added to the post. I'd mentioned that we had a great afternoon hippo tracking but Bob mistook it for a great day "hippo hunting" - combine that with the stupid pose with the machetes and the fact we were at an animal rehabilitation centre and you could see why he was so angry.

I apologised as much as I could in the few minutes I had before heading back out for work.

Later that morning at breakfast, Bob gave us all a speech about seven volunteers he was due to kick out that day but had changed his mind because of an apology he'd received earlier. Everyone knew who he was talking about. We were so lucky not to have been kicked out over that. It was obviously my own fault for posting the picture. I wish I could say I learnt a lesson that day but I'd be lying if I did. Events such as that would soon come back to bite me in the arse later that year...

After a while, we had a new baby baboon come to the sanctuary called Becca. Within a day or so, Becca became obsessed with me. She wouldn't go near anybody else except me.

When it came to girls in particular, she had true hatred towards them. If a girl came in to Becca's eyesight, she would freak out. She'd projectile shit everywhere (literally) before screaming and running away. You definitely did not want to be holding her if there were girls around!

Becca, grooming me while I slept

I remember one day, I was in baby Kitchen, giving Becca her morning bottle. I saw a girl heading towards us so I asked her to back off and tell me what she needed so I could get it for her. She ignored me and continued to walk over. Before I could say another word, Becca spotted her and freaked out. As expected, she shit, all down my top and my legs. (I was wearing shorts) while simultaneously screaming and trying her best to get away - scratching away at my belly at the same time! I ended up having to "scruff her" to put a stop to her little freak out.

Every morning, there would be two things that would happen and no matter what kind of mood I was in, I would always be smiling afterwards. Every time me and Nikko saw each other in a morning, we would point at each other, shout "morning bro hug!" before running towards each other and hugging the shit out of each other. It was dumb and just as stupid as it sounds but that's what made it so funny. Not one morning went by without a "morning bro hug"

The second daily occurrence would be a German girl named Lotta, she would normally pass me with a huge smile on her face and just say "smile, Matt!" There was just something about the way she said it that would always brighten up my morning.

I would then end most days after the work was completed by heading out for a run. I'd start at the dorms and make my way up to the main road and back again which worked out to be around 5k. I loved my Riverside runs.

One afternoon after the day's work had been completed, I was in the shower washing my hair when I noticed that the area of my head that I'd had the surgery on, felt different. The hole that the surgery had left now felt bigger and deeper. I panicked, left the shower and asked a couple of the lads that had already had a good nosey at it when they heard that I had a hole in the head to check it. Their jaws dropped and they agreed that it definitely felt different. I had no travel insurance but knew that I'd need to see a doctor so Bob took me to see a local one the next day.

After explaining how and why I had a hole in my head and showing the doctor my previous scans, he offered me two options. Pay what would be the equivalent to £1000 for a CT scan which would only serve to show if I was in danger or not - I'd still need to pay more if that was the case. Or I could just fly home and in his words "take advantage of the free health care the UK offers to see what was going on." Obviously, I didn't want to leave two weeks early and as worried as I was, I decided that as long as I was careful and put a bit more effort in to not banging my head while in the enclosures, I'd probably be ok.

So I decided to wait until I got home, before I'd book myself an appointment to check what was actually going on…

As the weeks went by, I was starting to think about how life was back home. Did I really want to go back to working in an environment where I wasn't liked and was under appropriated? Deep down, I knew I couldn't just leave though, I had to find a way of dealing with the issues at work. I realised my best course of action would be to just go back to work and work on trying to be the guy I was pre surgery.

With this in mind, I knew that I had a chance and I actually felt happy. It had been so long since I could genuinely smile without faking it. I felt like Riverside and the people I met there had all played a huge part in this. Its sounds ridiculously corny but I genuinely felt that these people had done so much for me. In fact, those I met at Riverside in 2019 actually did more for me in five weeks than those I worked with had done for me in the year post-brain surgery.

I decided the best way to thank everybody would be to stand up during dinner one night and talk about why I had actually come to Riverside. I'd not actually told anybody about the state I was in before I booked the fights back in November. I would rather have done it on my last night but some of those who this speech was aimed at were leaving in the next few days and I wanted them to hear how thankful I actually was.

So, one night after we'd all eaten, I got everybody's attention and went on to explain how life had actually been post brain surgery. How I'd been so fucking miserable and so set on killing myself before coming back. The speech went on for about ten minutes - everybody knew that I'd had brain surgery but nobody in that room actually knew what had been happening in the run up to me coming to Riverside. Most people sat there looked genuinely shocked, there were a few tears too. Reading this, you might think that it sounds incredibly corny or maybe even quite big headed doing something like that but to me, it needed to be said. Being able to offload like that and show just how thankful I was to have met each and every person in that room was an incredible feeling and a memory that I'll always be thankful for.

In my last few days there, a few of us had the chance to head out to Kruger National Park for a 24hr safari. Those of us that were going were all told that we would need to be up and ready to leave by 4am the morning of departure. Common sense would dictate that we didn't stay up drinking the night before so we could guarantee that we were up on time and clear headed for the trip ahead.

After dinner, the night before the trip, a couple of us were going to head down to the dorms and get the early night we needed but we noticed a group of people in the hide all playing drinking games. It'd be rude of us to not join in for a couple of drinks I said. We were only meant to stay for a couple of drinks and then be in bed by 9pm latest.

I very vaguely remember crawling in to my bed (trying not to wake the lads in my dorm) at 2am. I needed to be back up at 3am so I could get my bits ready and grab a quick wash before heading up to the mini bus. The whole staying for just a couple of drinks, clearly failed! I was still quite drunk when we set off. I remember grabbing breakfast at Mug & Bean with a couple of RedBull's on the way to Kruger. The breakfast and the caffeine fix definitely helped but for most of the first day on safari I was rough, I looked rough and felt rough. I just hid in the back of the bus and tried my best to grab the odd kip while I could without letting Bob notice. Once I'd had some lunch and sobered up, I started to really enjoy being out doing something different and by the end of the trip I'd seen hippos, crocs, lions and various other animals. It was definitely a worthwhile trip.

Our first morning at Kruger National Park

The morning I left Riverside was hard; I ended up having to hide away in The Hide at one point because I was crying. I really didn't want to go home but I knew I had to. I'd chosen to take the 8am coach into Jo'Burg rather than fly, just to save a few quid with the plan being to stay in the same B&B I'd used when I arrived, stay the night and then head to the Airport in the morning to get my main flight home.

After getting a few last cuddles with Becca and a few final goodbyes to the other volunteers, it was time to get moving to the coach.

The coach ended up taking eleven hours to get to Jo'Burg, by the time I'd made it to the B&B it was coming up to 9pm. I'd had issues booking my stay there, so I wasn't sure if they would even have a room for me. Luckily, they had one room left but I barely had enough to cover the cost. By this point I was ready for home and just wanted to get the next leg of the trip over and done with.

Leaving Riverside was hard but by now I felt confident and ready to take on the shit storm that I knew I had waiting for me back home. Looking back though I really didn't realise just how much of understatement "shit storm" would be. Things were about to turn very ugly, very quickly.

CHAPTER 19

The beginning of the end

I made it back home on April 23rd. Mum had dropped Charlie off at my place earlier that day. I felt crap having to leave Riverside but coming home to see Charlie waiting for me and to see just how happy he was to see me, well, my mood soon changed!

After unpacking my kit and getting a wash, I took Charlie out for some quality time then spent the rest of the day relaxing, knowing that the next day I had to start getting my shit in order.

The next day, my main priority was to head over to hospital to try and get an appointment to see why the hole in my head had seemingly gotten bigger.

I skipped A&E and went straight to Ward 4 where I was seen by my original consultant almost immediately which I definitely wasn't expecting.

After a quick chat and having had a look at my head the consultant explained that the hole hadn't grown at all. He explained that because I left for SA while still recovering my head was still swollen and that the swelling had clearly started to go down while I was at Riverside. I'd panicked over nothing, everything was as it should be.

My next job was to try and sort something out with Amy and Katie. I tried dropping them both a message only to find they had both blocked me. There was nothing I could do about Katie, not while I didn't have an address for her but with Amy, she hadn't counted on me reaching out to her partner. I sent him a message that day, asking him to explain to Amy that stopping Jack from seeing me would only serve to hurt Jack in the long run. I offered both Amy and her partner an opportunity to meet me that week, before I went back to work to sit down in a cafe and talk about why they had decided to ban me and Jack from seeing each other for almost nine months. After a couple of days, I was surprised to see that they agreed and we arranged to meet in a few days' time.

I met Amy and her partner as planned in a cafe in town. A part of me was ready to demand an apology, I was still so angry that she had stolen nine months of time from me and Jack but I knew that wouldn't achieve anything so I choose to sit there and allow her to feel comfortable.

Essentially the meeting was an hour of Amy giving me what I felt were poor excuses as to why she didn't want me having access. No real reasons, answers or even a real explanation - just excuses. To help move things forward I told the pair of them that I wanted to start again. I was willing to forgive and forget just so long as we could make a constructive plan that worked for everybody. The meeting ended with us all agreeing to work towards real access for me and Jack and not the once a month (if I'm lucky) rubbish that she had expected me to be grateful for in the past. It was starting to look like things were on the up.

Once I'd sorted access out for Jack at least, it was time to start working on me.

About a week after getting home, I was back at work and back to normal. For my first shift back, I turned up in my Riverside - "I survived Bob" t-shirt. Seeing that I was on shift with Mike, I asked one of the girls from the previous shift who was still working until handover had been finished, to take a photo of us both. She asked why I wanted a photo and I explained the significance of my t-shirt and being at work and that I was happy to be back and so she took the photo before we got handover out the way and could start the shift.

It actually felt good to be back at work, I knew there were those that didn't like me but I didn't care -as long as I was being paid, I was happy. I realised that before going back to Riverside, I'd been putting too much pressure on myself by caring about what others thought of me and look where that got me.

Over the next few weeks, things seemed to improve - life seemed just better in general. Amy had started letting me see Jack regularly, the atmosphere at work had completely gone and me and Rachel had started talking again. Life was good.

I soon realised that it was becoming harder to work though. I asked the boss for an informal meeting one day to talk about the possibilities of me being paid to leave the company. A "medical retirement" if you like. The company had already done this for another employee in similar circumstances, so I figured I'd give it a try. I'd worked out that I could end up with about £5000 if HR agreed.

I made a point of saying that there were only two ways I'd leave the job. Pay me off so I can have a shot at starting a photography business or drag me out kicking and screaming.

Within a week of asking HR the boss called me in to say that they had refused to pay me off as I was too young and hadn't been with the company long enough. Apparently, the person she had spoken to, laughed at her when she mentioned that I had asked.

Knowing that I wouldn't willingly leave without being paid off, she asked me if it was really fair of me to continue working there. She said that I reminded her of a three-year-old, I asked her to explain what she meant. She reminded me about the hippo tracking story I'd mentioned from Riverside and other dangerous situations I'd been involved with at work.

"You just don't see or seem to understand danger the way a normal person would" she said.

She went on to explain that she felt I was a danger to myself and to the people I worked with. I found that quite funny at the time but looking back, it was a cheap shot and quite unprofessional.

While still at Riverside, I'd managed to convince one of the volunteers to do a Tough Mudder with me when we were both back home. It'd be our very own Muddy Riverside reunion so we both bought our tickets for May's Tough Mudder, which would be in Grantham - Midlands on May 18th. Esther, the girl that had agreed to join me, had never done a TM before or anything like it for that matter but she was 100% up for it. Although we were both drunk when we bought the tickets.

For some reason when I got back I completely forgot to book annual leave for that day though. I was meant to be working night shifts before and after the TM so as the 18th fast approached, I was left with three options.

1. Book annual leave for the Friday and Saturday night, knowing that with only a weeks' notice, the request would most likely be rejected.
2. Work Friday night, leave work and go straight to TM and hope I could sleep on the train.
3. Call in sick for a couple of days and hope for the best.

I decided to go with option 3, I didn't want to, I hate lying just as much as I hate being lied to but a part of me was desperate to do this TM. It was for charity and I'd already raised more than £300. I couldn't just pull out because I forgot to book a couple of nights off.

I ended up sending my boss an email on the Thursday night, explaining that I was struggling with fatigue/tiredness which meant I wouldn't be able to make it in on Friday/ Saturday night. How I thought this would work, I'll never know. I turned my phone off when I left work that morning before going home and getting my kit ready for the next day.

While I was sorting bits out, I noticed an old bright pink gorilla costume that I'd used for a previous fundraiser back in 2015. I realised that I could probably get a few more donations in if I did TM wearing the pink gorilla costume.

That afternoon, Hull Daily Mail reached out to me over Facebook to ask if I'd be willing to do another interview to talk about how I was coping with life post brain surgery. Why not, I thought.

During the interview I spoke briefly about how I'd been struggling with my mental health and how I'd battled suicidal thoughts before going back to Riverside. I also mentioned that I had a Tough Mudder coming up in aid of PAUL for Brain Recovery, a local charity I had discovered earlier that year. I never mentioned when I'd be doing it, so I assumed my back was covered. The idea of the article was to help motivate and inspire others that may have been struggling with similar issues. The next day the article was posted on their Facebook page.

The next day I made my way down to Grantham. The plan was to not post anything on my own social media that would show I was out doing Tough Mudder when I was meant to be at home on sick.

I met Esther in Grantham before we both made our way to TM. After a quick catch up and a wonder though "Mudder Village" I put my gorilla costume on. The looks I was getting pretty much summed up just how ridiculous I looked but I didn't care. I was there to have fun and raise some cash for charity.

Me and Ester before we hit the start line

It was good fun running while dressed up; all the way up to the second obstacle - "Blockness Monster" I'd been wearing the mask to go with the costume. It turns out, wearing a loose mask in neck deep water while being weighed down is pretty hard, even more so when you can't swim! I ended up having to ditch the mask there and then but even then trying to climb onto and over the blocks with the costume on proved to be much harder than I thought. I was having to rely on Ester and other complete strangers to help drag me over, the bloody thing weighed a ton once it got wet!

Entering Blockness Monster

It was a good laugh running about in that costume though and the looks I kept getting made it all the more hilarious. I remember getting stuck in "Mud Mile" and literally having to be dragged out of the mud and up each slope because the costume (what was left of it anyway) was so heavy.

That Tough Mudder ended up being my favourite out of the five I'd done -we had so much fun. I don't know how but the costume actually survived all the way until the end – well, by survived, what I actually mean is that it was dangling from me and had been ripped apart but somehow got to the end.

I ended the day by posting a photo of me in the costume on the Tough Mudder Grantham page - thanking those who had gone out of their way to help get me over some of the obstacles that I'd been struggling to do while dressed up. It was a post that wasn't on my Facebook so I didn't need to worry about anybody I worked with seeing it, or so I thought.

I was back at work on Sunday night, to my relief, nobody mentioned Tough Mudder but they did mention my article in the paper. I remember being asked about the mental health side of it. I'd forgotten that I'd never actually spoken about the suicidal thoughts post-surgery before. I got the impression that staff were offended by finding out just how bad I'd been from the paper rather than from me.

On the Monday morning, I noticed the boss pulling up in the car park. I had a feeling it would be to do my back to work paperwork, just to make sure I was still ok to work etc.

She started by asking me to explain why I'd called in sick. I explained that I had been working a lot with minimal sleep and that fatigue had caught up with me.

"Ok, fair enough" she said before passing me a piece of paper.

"Can you explain this to me please" she asked. What was this piece of paper? It was a screenshot of me, dressed as a pink gorilla on Facebook. She'd read my article in the paper, spotted the quote from me about an upcoming Tough Mudder and put two and two together. She decided to google my name followed by Tough Mudder. Surprise, surprise, the photo I'd posted on the Grantham TM page, thanking everybody for their help was the first image to pop up.

I tried to stand my ground and say that I was still fatigued but had been dragged down there by a friend and as it was for charity, I felt I had no choice. I knew she wasn't buying it but I had to say something, even if it did sound ridiculous.

The boss warned me that she had already emailed the screenshot to head office and that an investigation would soon start.

"Fuck it then" I said with a raised voice before throwing the paperwork on the floor. With that I began to tear up and get emotional. Something began to happen at this point, the left side of my face began to spasm uncontrollably. So much so that I couldn't even talk. I didn't have time to think about it. I had no intentions of staying in the office with someone while I was looking emotional and with my face now in some kind of spasm - I had to get out. I left with the boss trying to call me back in - just ignored her, I had to leave. It was almost like I was having some kind of panic attack. I'd later go on to learn that the "spasm" was actually a type of seizure - a focal seizure that had been triggered because I was in a stressful situation.

It took me a while to calm down enough to accept that I was probably going to lose my job over this. I knew that it was my own fault, I was just pissed off that I'd worked so hard to get back to work and now through me being an idiot, I may have just fucked myself over. What a waste.

It took a while for the investigation to start and finish, just like before I was expected to continue working, knowing full well that I was more than likely about to lose my job at any moment. Eventually, I was called in for a meeting. I was 100% certain that I would be sacked that day but instead I was given a final warning and told to keep out of trouble for at least a year.

I didn't know it then but my days had already been marked as I would soon come to learn.

While I had still been in hospital back in January, I'd seen a few posters advertising a charity named PAUL for Brain Recovery. I'd actually been told about this charity by a friend when I was diagnosed with my little hitchhiker the year before but shunned the idea of reaching out because I refused to believe that a brain tumour counts as a brain injury. I was too focused on other things to have even considered checking them out post-surgery. They were based in town and only about twenty minutes away from me so eventually I decided to check them out.

Walking into the centre for the first time, I was nervous as hell, I had no idea what they did or how they could help me - hell, I didn't really think I needed help so was unsure if I even had a right to be there.

After a quick chat with the receptionist, a worker came over and introduced herself to me. Her name was Natalie and she was the Support Worker for the charity and was in charge of doing assessments for those who found themselves at the centre, possibly needing help. I was to be given an assessment to figure out how the charity could and would help and support me. I made it very clear that I didn't have a brain injury and that I was there more out of curiosity than anything.

After the assessment Natalie went on to explain that using the charity wasn't just about getting help, it was an opportunity to meet likeminded people. People who had suffered the same kind of experiences as me. If I ever needed anything, I'd know that the option was there. At the time, I just assumed that I'd maybe do some fundraising for them once in a while but I'd never actually use them. I therefore chose to support them for my Tough Mudder and other events that year but it was a while before I realised just how much of a vital role in my life they would end up being.

On June 2nd my next fundraising challenge came up which was the Hull 10k. I'd worked the night shift before the event and was due back for a night shift that night, pretty stupid I know but I was confident I'd be ok.

I went home that morning, stopping for a McDonald's brekkie on the way. I had about four hours to kill so, after getting changed I made my way back to work to chill for a while before hitting the start line.

I was quite confident about this run and was certain I'd be able to beat my previous 57 minute time. I hadn't done much training but it was more than the last event I'd trained for at least.

I managed to run the entire route without stopping this time, I was on a roll and pretty happy until I got close enough to the finish line to be able to see the timer there was sat at 62 minutes. 62 fucking minutes for me to complete a 10k, I was so angry. How the hell had I done so poorly?

I walked back to work to go and collect my bits before going home, I got myself so worked up that I ended up crying. It sounds ridiculous I know, but I just felt so lazy and so stupid - like a failure. I tried explaining why I was so pissed off when I got to work but the two people on shift they didn't understand. They told me to stop being stupid, telling me I was being ridiculous. After a few minutes of being at work, I got a text from the Hull 10k Organisation. It was a "congratulations on completing the Hull 10k" text with my finisher time on it. It stated that my run time was 55 minutes. It took me a minute to figure out what had happened. During big organised runs that have a couple of thousand people taking part, it takes time to get everyone passed to the start line. The time I read on the finisher board was for those who were at the very front at the start of the run, not for people nearer to the back like me.

I went from being so disappointed with myself to so bloody happy. It was only a two-minute improvement on the year before but it was better than the 62 minutes I thought it had taken me!

Although my fitness was improving again there were other parts of my recovery that wasn't going quite as good. During a routine check-up in June, I'd mentioned that I felt like my speech was starting to slur more and that I would often forget how to say certain words. The consultant mentioned that this could be a sign that the tumour had started to grow again. I always knew that this was a possibility as it's impossible to remove 100% of a brain tumour during surgery.

An MRI scan would later confirm that it had, in fact grown. There was 2cm of tumour in my brain meaning that the next course of action was radiotherapy and chemotherapy. I was set up with an appointment with my oncologist fairly quickly to talk though the options - the pros and cons of both treatments.

The oncologist explained that the plan would be for me to undergo six weeks of radiotherapy, five days a week. A month after that had been completed, I would need to start twelve months of chemotherapy.

I'd soon be sent to have a specialist mask molded to my face that would be used to hold my head in place during the radiotherapy sessions. I was walking into this entire situation blind. Just like the run up to the brain surgery, I assumed that this would be a cake walk. I even convinced myself that I could continue working through the entire treatment. As I write this, I'm rolling my eyes at the level of naivety and stupidity running through my mind that made me think I'd stand a chance at being able to work.

Just before I'd had the mask made, I'd gotten into a relationship with a girl named Jane, I fell for her pretty quickly. She seemed like the perfect woman and she ticked all the right boxes. Hell, even my friends liked her. We spoke every night, she stayed awake until 3-4am pretty much every morning, talking to me whilst I was on night shifts. She knew exactly what she was letting herself in for but was happy to stick by me and made that very clear from the start. Things were looking up once more!

I'd soon learn that not even a cracking girl can stop the shit show that was about to unfold. Things weren't going to stay perfect for much longer.

CHAPTER 20

Time to get radioactive.

Considering I knew I had just over a year of treatment coming up, I was quite chilled out. Things seemed to be going really well with Jane and I was confident that I'd be fine working throughout the treatment. If anything, I'd found myself someone who was willing to stand by me, no matter what. I needed that!

We used to go on random spontaneous dates where she would drive us to what seemed like the middle of nowhere. On one of these in particular we drove through a small village, literally an "in and out in a blink" kind of village where there were loads of handmade scarecrows on display in front of peoples' houses. I asked Jane to stop the car – photo opportunities galore!

We ended up at Stump Cross Caverns. Monkey came along for the ride, as always. It was a great day that ended with a double date with Kris and his new partner, Gemma for a night of drinks and bingo.

At the beginning of July, I was asked to pop into the PAUL for Brain Recovery centre to meet the founder of the charity so he could thank me for fundraising for them. I'd raised £310 doing the Tough Mudder and Hull 10k.

I met Paul - the founder of the charity after a night shift, I was expecting to pop in, and get a quick thank you and a photo of me handing over a giant check with the amount I'd raised written on it but that's not just what Paul had in mind.

Me handing Paul the giant cheque

Paul invited me out with him while he ran some errands so we could have a general chat and he could get to know me while explaining what exactly his charity was and why he created it. He asked me to explain my story. He knew that I had suffered a brain tumour and had most of it removed but that was it.

So I started from the beginning, I told him about how a drunken day/night out with an old friend had left me with a head injury and concussion the next day, resulting in me collapsing and that doctors had missed my brain tumour during a CT scan.

I explained that it wouldn't be until 2018 that the tumour was found and diagnosed properly and that I was told that missing a tumour is "just one of these things" according to hospital staff. I went on to explain the whole hole in the head saga and that whatever was left of the tumour had in fact started to grow again - meaning more treatment. Paul seemed genuinely shocked by all of this.

I've always hated telling this story; even though I've lived through it and documented the entire journey with photos and videos - I always feel like those that hear it don't believe me. I feel like it's a totally unbelievable story and that's exactly what people must think. Obviously, I've never met anybody that has actually thought I've made this whole tumour story up, why would anybody make up such a thing?

It has definitely made being open about the entire journey quite hard. The fear of what people would think of me was always a big issue for me.

I mentioned to Paul that I didn't think I had a brain injury although I was starting to see that some of what I was experiencing, was showing similar side effects to that of somebody with a brain injury. Small subtle things like a terrible short-term memory, the focal seizures, fatigue and my emotional responses to a lot of situations. Paul explained that I did in fact have a brain injury, an acquired brain injury (ABI) and that trying to convince myself otherwise was just going to make the side effects worse. You'd think that this would have been the wake-up moment I needed - a moment where I could appreciate just how much of a crappy situation I was in and that I could do something about it, but no, I left Paul after our meet and greet and continued to push the brain injury stuff to the back of my mind. If I admitted to myself that I had a brain injury, I would feel like a failure and that was not going to happen.

I carried on as normal, making jokes about the tumour and the side effects related to the brain injury that I still wouldn't admit I had. If I forgotten to do a set of tasks at work, I'd make a stupid joke about it being because of the tumour when in reality, I really had just forgotten or had been too fatigued.

Remember, I'd used fatigue as an excuse for my sickie when doing Tough Mudder. If I had been honest with myself and just accepted that I had a brain injury from the start, I would have had a much easier time at work although, I wouldn't have been able to stay from the point of admitting it. Looking back, that probably would have been for the best.

On one particular night at work, the person I was on shift with shouted me to come out to the courtyard telling me it was urgent. I got outside and found a resident being helped up by the staff member who had shouted me. The resident had apparently passed out and had a seizure. Another resident was the only one who actually saw it happen and said it had lasted for a few seconds. By the time I arrived though the resident who had suffered the seizure was already up and able to walk and talk with no issues. We both kept an eye on her for the rest of the night but she was fine and didn't want to be checked over by anyone else.

The next day I came to work to find an angry email from the boss, demanding to know why an ambulance hadn't been called the night before - let's just say, it wasn't the nicest of emails I've come across before and I instantly took offence to it. The short answer was that the resident didn't need one but I chose to fire back hard. I explained that I had a lot more experience in real life first aid situations than her, I was the only staff member who would pay out of my own pocket to complete annual first aid courses. I also reminded her that the resident in question was a known epileptic and that not only did I suffer with epilepsy, the person I was on shift with cared for somebody with epilepsy.

I went on to explain how ridiculously stupid and time wasting it would have been to call an ambulance because management wanted paperwork to look good. I got a short sharp reply telling me that if a resident has another seizure at any point, I was to call an ambulance.

I tried to explain that if you know someone is epileptic and their seizure lasts less than three minutes, you don't need to call an ambulance as long as they come around OK and added a copy of a first aid manual as a cheeky dig.

"That wasn't a request, it was an instruction..." she replied copying the area manager in the reply also.

I ignored her from that point onwards, attitudes like this were becoming normal for me, I didn't even notice the change though but I was starting to become a bit of a dick.

Mid July came which meant it was time for my first radiotherapy session. Much to my disappointment, the machine is not a giant gun that fires radiation lasers at you to kill the tumour, nope, it's quite like a CT scanner. You lie down and the machine will rotate around the area of the body that it's firing radiation at for around five minutes. In my case, I would have to lie down, a nurse would come over and place my pre made mesh mask over my face before bolting it to the table so that I couldn't move my head at all - not so much as a millimetre.

I remember heading out for my first session, still on my own as I liked to be able to enjoy my independence. I felt more comfortable doing all of this on my own if and when I could, plus there was the bonus that I could get some alone time to chill out with my music and relax.

The full years' worth of treatment would take place at Castle Hill Hospital. I couldn't drive at the time so I would often take the bus or Jane would drive me and/or pick me up if she wasn't at work that day.

Castle Hill Hospital, from my house was two buses away, on a good day, it would take about an hour to get there but generally it was always a three-hour round trip. While on the bus I decided to put headphones in, stick my music on shuffle and chill for a while. The first song to play just so happened to be Radioactive by Imagine Dragons. I found that quite funny and ironic.

I remember flicking through Facebook and seeing a Hull Daily Mail article pop up. It was about a girl that had been caught dealing heroin and been spared jail because she had good grades when she left school and was still young. I've always held a particular dislike towards those who choose to ruin lives by pushing heroin on people. As I've already mentioned, I've worked with enough people to see just how much dealers that sell that rubbish can and does ruin lives. I never read the full article but left a comment on it that read "drug dealer spared prison? The judge is pathetic"

Why mention this in a book about my little hitchhiker you ask? Don't worry - it will soon make sense.

I was due at work the night after my first treatment so was hoping I would be in, out and back home for some sleep before work later on. My appointment was at 1pm but I wasn't actually seen until around 3pm. I didn't know it before but it was common to have a radiotherapy appointment delayed because one or more of the machines had gone down, they are, after all left on all day and continuously used five days a week so a broken machine or two is to be expected I guess.

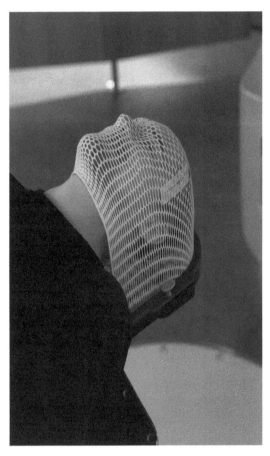

Me with my head bolted to the table before a treatment

The appointment itself was straight forward and only lasted around five minutes but I wouldn't get home until around 5pm, which meant I was lucky to get a couple of hours sleep before work. Determined (or obsessed) to prove that I was still ok, I was going to work one way or another.

Something that struck me throughout my treatment over the six weeks was that nobody seemed to mind when they were told there would be a big delay - me included. The nurses would always apologise and I'd usually reply by saying I didn't mind; I wasn't paying for the treatment so what right did I have to moan?

On day three of my treatment, I turned up wearing my latest Tough Mudder finisher t-shirt. One of the male nurses in charge of my treatment stopped me and asked if this was the new shirt for this season. It turned out he and most of the nurses on the radiotherapy ward were TM legionnaires too. Like all of the nurses I met while having my treatment, this guy was actually pretty cool. He always had a bit of banter with me and always helped make a crap day seem better.

After my third session had ended it hit me that I couldn't continue to work and have treatment at the same time. The treatment itself wasn't the issue, it was the fact that I was only able to get a few hours' sleep between night shifts because of the travel time and the delays faced while waiting for my treatment.

So I got myself a sick note that day, I was at the point in my rota where I had six days off so I wasn't going to be too much of an inconvenience as they would have time to find someone to cover for me.

Around the middle of week three, I remember being stood in front of the mirror while getting ready to go for my next treatment, brushing my hair to one side and seeing hair just falling from my head. Not just a few strands but a lot. In less than a minute almost all of my hair on the left side of my head fell from my head - I didn't know how to take it. I remember trying to explain to Jane over the phone and with photos, just how much had fallen out but I couldn't describe it. It was a "see it to believe it" kind of deal. I knew that this would happen eventually, but it still came as a shock. Unlike some forms of chemotherapy, with radiation treatment you generally only lose hair on and around the area that's being specifically targeted.

I knew at that point it was time to look at having my entire head shaved. I couldn't walk around with half a head of hair –not a chance. I was umming and arring about becoming bald but after speaking with Jane, I asked my dad to shave it all off later that day.

Jane came with me for that day's treatment and by then it was all starting to get a bit real. The plan was to get blasted with some radiation, head over to her parents' house to meet them for the first time before then going to my parents' house to have my head completely shaved. As if I wasn't nervous enough already at the idea of losing all my hair, I was also meeting the parents. Great, nothing like a bit of pressure!

We sat for what seemed like hours waiting for my name to be called for my blast of radiation. It was a really sunny day and the sun was beaming into the waiting area.

After being blasted and meeting Jane's parents for the first time, it was time for my head shave. I made jokes about it and made it seem like I wasn't bothered but in reality, I was actually quite nervous. Jane knew how big of a deal this was for me and kept reassuring me as my dad shaved every last hair off my head. I'd never been bald before and didn't know just how stupid I might look.

Looking back, one of my main worries was how Jane would see me. I was half worried that I'd get binned off once the hair had gone, how wrong was I? She stuck by me, and we became a lot closer than we'd been in recent months.

I looked in the mirror and straight away referred to myself as Walter White, from Breaking Bad. I was just missing the full beard and moustache, it wasn't as bad as I imagined.

I remember one night; Jane had come round for our weekly date night. I had a rock that I'd picked up from a beach the week before, while on one of our walks with Charlie. I'd picked the rock up with the intention of painting it at a later date, with some form of positive message and leaving at Castle Hill. The message we opted for was "Smile, I dare you!"

There was something about the quote/challenge that I just loved. Personally, I liked the idea of someone coming across said rock and actually smiling because of it.

Obviously, Sadie designed it and wrote the quote out on the rock, only because my writing is pretty atrocious and nobody would actually be able to read it! Sadie brought varnish and we got the crafty bits together to make it work.

The next day, I left the rock at the same bench at the hospital that I'd found the "You matter" rock. I'd recently started a photography page on Instagram, so we made sure that the Instagram account name was written on the back of the rock in the hope I'd be able to see how far it went.

The rock I left at Castle Hill Hospital to be found

It wasn't long at all before the rock was found and a message/photo appeared on my insta page!

Those six weeks on treatment flew by, the only way I can describe that time is it was like being constantly high. Essentially, I was on auto pilot for the majority of it. I was never ill like some people; I was just constantly in some form daze. What I seemed to forget, was that radiotherapy to the brain quite literally destroys brain cells. For those six weeks I was having brain cells destroyed every single day. I'd already had pieces of my brain removed during the brain surgery and now I was having my brain nuked. Literally.

During that time at the hospital it was common to hear a bell ring, I soon realised that people who had finished a round of radiotherapy, would ring a bell in the corridor to signify that they had made it through their treatment. I wasn't sure if I was even allowed to ring the bell, as I still had a year of chemotherapy to do after the radiotherapy, so I just put the bell to the back of my mind.

After I'd gotten into the swing of things, I'd often turn up an hour or two early go to the hospital café, buy an ice cream and a RedBull before finding a quiet spot outside to sit and chill. Little moments like that are what helped make the daily sessions that little bit more bearable.

In my last week of radiotherapy, completely ignoring the fact that I was still in treatment and still not understanding that my brain had been bombarded with radiation, I decided it was time to sort out getting back to work. Once again, I was told I'd only be allowed back if I could get a "fit note" and just like before this proved to be a tricky task.

It took me all of a minute to be given a sick note but when it came to getting a note that said I could go back to work - it was a hell of a challenge. It was almost like somebody was trying to tell me something. Again, just like before I became obsessed with getting back to work.

After being refused a fit note by one of the nurses in charge, my GP and my workplace healthcare team, I did what I did best and vented my anger on Facebook. Again. I wrote a fairly long rant that essentially called out the irony of it being so easy to get a sick note but it was seemingly impossible for me to get a fit note and how, since having the brain surgery, I'd saved more lives than most people ever would in a lifetime. Somewhere in the status I wrote that I felt like I had to lie and cheat my way back into work.

A few hours after I'd posted it, a friend called me and advised me to take the post down as it was a post that could get me in a heap of shit if the wrong people spotted it. I did as they requested all be it reluctantly. It'd be easy for me to sit here and blame my brain injury or the fact I was still being blasted with radiation for the post, but if I'm being honest I think I would have probably posted it regardless. Or maybe that's just a sly dig at myself - I guess I'll never know.

My last day of radiotherapy was on August 19th. Not only was I excited to finally be ending this daily routine of having my brain nuked, it was also the day Avengers - Endgame was released on DVD. I was in South Africa when it was realised in cinemas so had never got to watch it so I made a point of watching it before going to my appointment. Since being diagnosed with this hitchhiker of mine, I'd made a point of watching every single Marvel movie to see what all the fuss was about. I was not disappointed and not remotely embarrassed to admit that I cried watching Endgame that morning!

I'd decided I was going to ring the "end of treatment bell" that day and had my mum come with me. The appointment was about an hour behind, which as always, was fine by me.

A few days before my last session, I'd spoken to the nurse who had also completed a few Tough Mudders and asked him to join me in a photo for the last session with both of us in our TM gear with me holding my radiotherapy mask as a trophy which he was more than happy to do. After the last session had wrapped up, we both got a photo, both wearing our TM finisher t-shirts/headbands and with me holding my new trophy. It was actually quite a special moment for me!

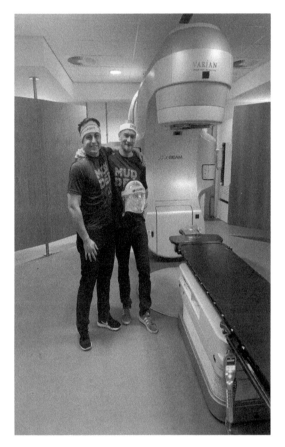

Me and one of the amazing radiotherapy nurses after my last treatment

Soon after we both took another photo next to the bell before I rang it. I wish I could say that ringing the bell was a special moment, like it is for so many others but it had no real meaning for me - I actually felt a bit of twat if I'm honest.

Obviously, everybody within ear shot starts to clap when you ring the bell and I really didn't like the all eyes on me thing but it was nice to know that I had a month away from treatment and that I wouldn't be getting nuked again.

Whilst I was having the treatment I lost interest in most things and became more and more agitated; things were changing but I couldn't see what or how.

Things with Jane also started to go downhill quite fast, I pushed her away without even realising it. She was a huge part of my life and I just let her slip away, through no fault of her own. It had gone from us talking and seeing each other every day possible to me not even wanting to answer my phone. I remember getting a text from her one day, asking me if we were ok as I'd been a little bit off with her recently. I replied by telling her we were over and to fuck off and do one. As far as I was concerned, I was single now. God knows why! Nothing bad had happened between us to make me want this, I just told her to leave me alone. She was oblivious to the reasoning behind it, as was I, but that night, I blocked her number and deleted her from every form of social media I had connected with her on. Again, I don't know why, she was everything I wanted and needed in my life, especially right now!

Before I'd started the radiotherapy, I thought she was perfect. Everybody loved her, even me, but within a couple of weeks of the treatment starting, I was fast becoming a completely different person. Had she asked me that same question before I started my radiotherapy, I'd have worked my arse off to find a solution to whatever the problem was. I got so much stick from those around me for binning her off, everybody knew that she was perfect for me and to hear that I just binned her off in such a way was just another sign that I was just as much of a prick as people thought I was at the time. Looking back now, it's scary to see the person I was becoming and I can definitely see why I wasn't allowed back to work so soon.

After a month-long break from treatment, it was time to start the next stage, my chemotherapy. There's a common misconception when it comes to chemotherapy. People (including me at one point) assume that chemo is only for cancer patients and involves hours of sitting on a ward having the poison pumped into you and that you'll soon lose all of your hair - well, that's not entirely true. There are three different ways to receive chemotherapy and a multitude of names for each type of treatment. You can have it injected, take it as a tablet or the way most people assume is the only way and have it pumped into a vein via an IV.

My treatment was named "PCV" this regime would last 12 months and consisted of six fairly complicated rounds;

Day 1 - Take five tiny blue pills named "Lomustine"
Day 7 - Go to hospital for a 20/30-minute IV treatment
Day 8 - Take two chemotherapy tablets a day for two weeks
Day 30 - Go to hospital for a 20/30-minute IV treatment

After all of that, I would have a month-long break before going back to start the next round. I really wasn't kidding when I said the rounds were complicated.

Just like every other aspect of this journey so far I expected this to be fairly simple. I was young and fairly healthy so the side effects wouldn't bother me – or so, I thought.

On day one, after an hour long briefing from the chemist who handed me the Lomustine, I went home and took them at around 5pm. I'd been told that I had to take anti sickness tablets beforehand but me being me decided I wouldn't need them. How wrong I was.

I went to bed just after taking the meds as fatigue was still an issue at this point. In just ten minutes though, I'd soon find out how stupid I was to think I'd be immune to the side effects. After the tenth time of running downstairs to throw up, I gave up trying to go back to bed and just stayed in the toilet for the next hour or so. The problem with being sick too much is that eventually, your body runs out of things to throw up. Have you ever been so ill that you can't be sick anymore?

It hurts. A lot. Eventually I was able to get back to bed and sleep the rest of the night away.

I felt ill for another day or so but it soon passed, which was ideal because I had my 30th birthday coming up just a few days after I'd started chemo.

It had been about a month since I last heard from Jane, she had reached out on my 30th birthday, deep down I had a feeling she would message me so I unblocked her number from my phone earlier that morning. Low and behold, I received a text message to say happy birthday. Neither of us had spoken since I'd binned her off in the shitty way that I had. I replied with a simple "thank you" before we both got into some basic chit chat.

She told me that she had actually got me a card and present whilst we were still together, but wasn't sure if I'd welcome her bringing it round. We ended up meeting later that day for a catch up, I had a much clearer head by this point. I knew that I was in the wrong to end things the way I did and obviously apologised. Rightly so. At the time, the pair of us didn't really understand that it was the radiotherapy on top of my brain injury that had made me so quick to lash out. If I'd told anybody that back then, I highly doubt I would have been believed, not because the people I knew were unsympathetic but because of the way I choose to deal with the entire tumour journey. I had never taken it seriously and always had some kind of sarcastic joke to make when the side effects were taking effect. How could I expect people to take me seriously when I couldn't even take my situation seriously?

Jane got me a card and a few special bits saying, "We are only 30 years old once"

She knew how much I wanted to kick off my photography venture and I really did want to get into it properly. I definitely classed it as my passion. She had designed a logo for me, for when I got myself fully set up and became a professional photographer, she had so much faith in me. This is just the kind of person she was and I still use the logo to this day. Jane and I never really got back what we had, again, my fault, I know. She is however, still, very much in my life and has even played a huge part in making this book a reality!

For my birthday, Mum and Dad had gotten me camera, something that I could use to get started with my photography venture. They decided to take me and my sister, Katy out for a family meal. It was nice to be able to take my mind off of the treatment, the stress of not being allowed back to work yet and just enjoy some quality family time.

Soon after my birthday, I reached out to a local boot camp ran by a Royal Marine veteran. I asked if he would allow me to come to some of his sessions as a photographer. I needed the practice when it came to photography and he was a veteran so I offered to do the sessions for free. I got practice and a chance to build up a portfolio while making a name for myself and he got free publicity. It might have been free but it was a win win for us both.

I soon found that I couldn't always use my own camera because of the rain and it wasn't made for sports photography. It wasn't a DSLR so there was no ability to change lens so I quite often had to resort to using my phone as it was waterproof and could capture moving subjects.

I'd soon be turning up most nights when the chemo wasn't kicking my arse to do the photography, it was nice to just feel wanted and appreciated for a change.

Not long after I'd had my surgery to remove the chunk of skull, I'd met a guy called Chris on one of the Tough Mudder Facebook pages. I was hoping to do Europe's Toughest Mudder (ETM) that year but had pulled out with me heading back to Riverside as it left me with no time to train. Although I never got to do ETM with him, we kept in contact. In early September he'd mentioned that he was doing the Yorkshire Three Peaks challenge (Y3P) Around 26 miles of walking through the Yorkshire Dales and up Yorkshires three highest peaks, the smallest being 694 meters high and the highest being 736 meters high. A small challenge for some but one week into chemotherapy? Even I knew this would be a tricky one.

Completing Y3P had been on my bucket list for a while so I asked Chris if he'd mind me joining him and his team, depending how I felt with the chemo. The date for the challenge was set for September 28th.

I warned Chris that I hadn't done any form of training and would potentially slow the entire team down, I was worried that I would end up ultimately ruining the day but Chris managed to put my mind at ease.

I knew that I shouldn't be doing anything like this, I was meant to be at home, taking it easy. I've never been good at taking it easy though so I decided I was doing the challenge no matter what.

— Smile, I dare you!

CHAPTER 21

Two months to go
The good, the bad and the fucking ridiculous

The plan for Yorkshire 3 Peaks was for everyone in the team to meet at the start point at around 7am. Obviously, not able to drive and unable to get a train that day, I was extremely limited as to how I could get there on time. Chris had offered to put me up for the night before and the night of the challenge, had he not done that I wouldn't have been able to take part. Remember, this guy had never met me before and yet here he was, willing to help somebody he only knew through Facebook. That's just the kind of guy Chris is though, the kind of guy that will bend over backwards to help anybody.

The plan was to meet Chris at his local church the night before, he actually worked there for the local youth group. I remember seeing Chris for the first time - it was like we already knew each other so well, you absolutely wouldn't have thought we'd never met before.

I'd turned up early so he gave me a little tour of the Church and spoke about what it was he actually did.

He mentioned that he had been working on a video application to be a Tough Mudder Ambassador. I'd heard of TM Ambassadors before but had no idea what the scheme was or what it actually involved. I wasn't going to have time to do a video application before the cut-off date so Chris put me in touch with one of the main guys in charge of TM called Giles and told me to mention that I was keen and that my video may be late. Giles (who turned out to be the Managing Director for TMUK) got back to me pretty quickly and gave me the nod. I didn't know much about TM Ambassadors but I did know that I wanted to be one, regardless.

After Chris had finished work, we headed to his house, we spent some time talking and getting to know each other while going through the plan for the next day. I was still on round one of my chemotherapy and at this point I had just started my two weeks of chemo tablets, I'd only been on them for a few days.

One of my main concerns for the challenge ahead was whether or not I'd be sick during the walk or if fatigue would catch me out and force me to have to bail during the walk. I knew that if I got ill, I'd have no choice in the matter of pulling out. It wouldn't have been fair on the team for me to stay and slow them down.

After a cracking night's sleep, it was time to start gearing up to go. Michelle, one of Chris's friends and a part of the day's team had arranged to meet us at Chris's place and drive the three of us down to the start line, where we'd meet the rest of the team where there would be seven of us in total.

As bad as my memory can be at times, I'll always remember the first ten minutes of the drive to the start point. It was around 4am, pitch black outside and the windows in the car had all steamed up. Chris decided to wait until the last minute to tell Michelle she was in the wrong lane on the roundabout, so she indicated and moved across into the correct lane. The next thing we knew the car behind suddenly had flashing blue lights on its roof, we realised it was a police car and we were pulled over. I guess we looked pretty dodgy at first glance - windows steamed up and a car full of people all wearing matching t-shirts (our latest TM finishers' tops). He asked what we were doing so Michelle told him that we were all going to climb the Yorkshire Three Peaks. He just looked at us all, giving us a confused look, he must have thought we were all nutters but clearly not the drunken nutters he had no doubt initially thought so as he couldn't say much more he just waved us on. We all found it hilarious of course.

Driving down we soon started to realise that the weather was far from ok. An hour away from where we were starting, it began to piss it down with rain and we were all starting to worry that the footpaths would be closed off, for safety.

We made it to the start line for about 7am. After quick meet and greet with the rest of the team and a team photo it was time to get moving. It was still raining extremely heavily when we made it to the start line but seeing other people making their way up soon convinced us that the route was open.

Not long after we started, the weather took a turn for the worse. I remember being at the top of the first peak when we were battered by heavy hail stone and gale-force winds, it was so bad that you couldn't talk to the person next to you without having to shout and the pain as the hail stones hit us was intense. At one point it was so bad that a few people started to be blown to the floor by the wind.

I think the winds must have been pushing the 30mph mark at the top of the peak, it really was intense. We soon made it to the bottom injury free but completely soaked and freezing. One peak down, two to go...

Thankfully, the weather soon changed after the first peak and we were hit with clear skies and a good amount of sun. Not enough to warm us up but it was better than the wind and rain we'd had for the first couple of hours, that's for sure!

During the day I'd overheard Michelle talking about parts of her past. She'd mentioned things that had happened in her life that made me realise we had quite in a bit in common. I would love to be able to share some of it but there are some things she likes to keep private, there was a lot that I could relate to though so I made a point of getting to know Michelle more that day.

Like Chris, she seemed like a genuinely cool person, the kind of person that, like me, has a story worth hearing – hell maybe one day she'll even write her own book!

By the end of second peak, two of our team had given in and headed back to the closest village - I don't think any of us were really prepared for just how intense the day was going to be, especially with the crazy weather.

The third peak was a fucker! It was the steepest by far. Hell, it almost seemed to be going vertical!

We managed to complete all three peaks and the 26 miles of hiking in 11 hours 40 minutes (ish) I think all of us were immensely proud of ourselves. I was amazed that I'd actually made it from start to finish while on chemotherapy! Hell, to this day I still am!

Meeting Chris and Michelle that day would soon prove to be one of my luckiest moments in this entire journey. I didn't know it back then but Chris and Michelle would soon become more than just friends, they would soon become family. This day carries so many memories for me, far more than I could write about but even this overview is an important part of the book because of these two people.

Not surprisingly, by the end of September work still hadn't let me go back. I was starting to wonder if I'd ever actually be allowed back and just how much fight I had left in me. I was half expecting work to call me in and sack me over seeing me do Y3P while on sick.

Earlier that year, Mollie (the Riverside friend who had hooked me up with Darwin's paw print) started to organise a Riverside "camp out reunion" for early October. It was an open invite for anyone that had ever volunteered at Riverside. Mollie's family owned a plot of woodland down south, so what better way to hold a reunion than a two-day, boozy camping reunion!

Emma, who I'd met during my second Riverside visit had offered to pick me up at a nearby train station and shared a tent while we were down there. It saved me having to mess about buying a new tent so why not.

Still on chemo, I was on a strict no alcohol regime so instead of bringing a couple of creates of beer, I opted for some non-alcoholic cider, which surprisingly, wasn't too bad.

The weekend was amazing, it was great to see old and new faces. Seeing people, I'd not seen since my first Riverside visit back in 2016 and the second visit was the kind of pick me up that I needed. It was so unbelievably great to be able to completely forget about all the shit that was happening, even if it was only two days. Just like with the paw print Mollie had gotten for me before she had outdone herself that weekend.

That reunion was one of my final highlights of that year. A highlight that I definitely needed and will never forget!

A group photo at Mollies Riverside reunion

In mid-October, I managed to get a fit note once again and finally be allowed back to work. Once again, I was actually quite happy to be going back, you could say I was excited. I'd soon come to learn that happy and excited were two words that wouldn't describe the shit show I was in for though...

My first shift back was set for October 16th. And went quite smoothly. The morning after my second shift back I was called in for a back to work meeting with my boss before I went home.

After the usual "is there anything we can do to help you feel better at work" routine, I was handed a stack of paper, telling me an investigation had been opened against me and asked to look at it and explain myself.

"Let me guess, I'm in trouble for doing Three Peaks" I said.

The boss just looked me as if I was stupid and said no.

There were four screenshots of my past Facebook posts.

"Just so you're aware, you're also being investigated for inappropriate relationships with residents" She said while I glanced at the paperwork.

I asked what she was referring to when she had mentioned "inappropriate relationships" and she told me that it was common knowledge that I had become friends with a former resident that had moved on two years prior. I snapped back by reminding her that there were two staff members that had openly admitted to being in relationships with former residents, why was befriending a former resident such an issue. She couldn't answer me and that allegation was never mentioned in any reports or "evidence" after that.

So, what had I actually done wrong this time? ...

If you've been paying attention up to this point, you'll already have a good idea what the answer is

1. A photo taken nearly six months prior of me and Mike on my first shift back from Riverside. I had mentioned the company name and if you zoomed in very closely you could see a man in the background, he wasn't identifiable because his face was out of focus but that was still a strike (apparently).
2. While on my way to my first radiotherapy session, I'd commented on a news article calling a judge pathetic for giving a heroin dealer a slap on the wrist. I hadn't seen, met or heard of the dealer before but it just so happened that she lived in a hostel owned by the company I worked for. I had no idea how I was meant to know this even now, but that was enough for strike two.

3. While on radiotherapy, I'd written a status on Facebook that had mentioned my willingness to lie and cheat my way back into work - strike 3.
4. Again while on radiotherapy, I and one other staff member had shared a news article about a former resident who we all loved. It transpired that he was a convicted paedophile and none of the team knew it but he had been busted by a paedophile hunting group. It just so happened to be that he was living in a property owned by my company. Again, I've no idea how or why I was expected to know this.

After seeing just how desperate somebody in that company was to get rid of me, I broke down. I knew people didn't like me and that was fine but whoever had taken the screenshots, had gone through six months' worth of posts to find anything they could use against me. Whoever did this, knew that I would have nothing as a result of being sacked. Everybody knew that I was already on a final warning and that just one more wrong doing from me would see me sacked.

At that moment I knew it was game over. I threw the paperwork on the floor shouting.

"Well that's it then isn't it? You've all got what you fucking wanted" I broke down again and started to cry before having another focal seizure.

Just like the last time I'd been in this position I left work, not knowing what to do. I was a wreck walking home so much so that I stopped off at shop to pick up a crate of beer. I was half tempted to off myself that morning, I couldn't understand why I was so hated by the people I worked with. I would never go out of my way to fuck somebody over in such a way. In my head I knew that if I lost my job, there would be issues with me getting benefits because I'd been sacked, I would lose my house, wouldn't be able to pay for my kids - making me look like a deadbeat. You must really hate and despise somebody to try so hard to go out of your way to ruin their life in such a way.

When I got home, I cracked open a beer and cried my eyes out. Literally. I knew there was absolutely nothing I could do to get out of this one. Technically, I could have fought my way out of it but why bother? The level of hatred for me in that place was far higher than I'd thought. I was meant to be back at work that night, a normal person would have called in sick. Remember, I was still on chemotherapy at this point, so I had every right to take a break but I choose to stick it out until I was eventually sacked - at least get some money behind me. I put the rest of my drinks away and went to bed.

That night, I came back to work and made a point of being as open as possible about what was happening. I wanted whoever had fucked me over to know what they had done. I made it very well known that I was still toying with the idea of killing myself, knowing I wouldn't cope without a job and that if I did go ahead and do it, the blame would lie in the hands of the venomous asshole that had worked so hard to screw me over. I didn't want attention or sympathy I wanted whoever that person was to feel the same kind of hurt as I was feeling and the thing is, I wasn't just saying it - I was extremely close.

I remember talking about what had happened that morning to one of my co-workers. I'd mentioned that one of the reasons I was being looked into was the "inappropriate relationship" and that I'd mentioned other staff had previously had actual relationships without any issues. I didn't know it at the time but that was the final nail in the coffin for me as it was looked at as me trying to drag other staff members down with me. It wasn't - very obviously it wasn't but it didn't matter. Staff made it perfectly clear that any friendship that existed before that moment, had just been pissed away by me.

As much as I had things going on at work there were still other things going on in my life too. In early November, I received a message from Billie's Auntie. She had been asked to start looking after Billie every weekend by Katie. She had never agreed with me and Billie being kept apart, so having been asked to look after Billie, she decided the best thing to do would be to reach out to me. She asked me if I wanted to take Billie for the duration of the weekend on the condition that Katie wouldn't find out.

The last time I had seen Billie properly, was the day before my brain surgery so an offer like this was something I never saw coming but I was absolutely taking it with both hands.

When the day came I could have cried seeing Billie again, it was a pretty emotional moment - words can't and won't ever be able to describe how happy I was. We spent the afternoon in town and got some lunch before heading to the arcade for a couple of fun filled hours. I was in between night shifts but I really didn't care, I could go to work with no sleep, we both had so much fun that not sleeping before work didn't matter. With all that was happening at work, this was a day that I really needed.

About a week after that day it was time to start round three of my chemotherapy. I turned up to Castle Hill on the Monday morning and was due back at work for my first of eight nights on later that night. While sat waiting for a pharmacist to bring me my first set of chemo pills, I noticed a van in the carpark with the PAUL for Brain Recovery logo on it. I recognised it straight away. While waiting for the pharmacist to bring me my meds over and brief me on the dos and don'ts while on chemo, I spotted Paul. After a quick hello and brief catch up, he offered to give me a lift into town. It'd save me having to wait for the bus so I took him up on the offer.

After collecting the chemo meds and getting the usual brief, I jumped in the van with Paul. I hadn't seen him since September so it was nice to be able to catch up.

After the usual pleasantries, we got talking about where I was in recovery and how I was doing etc. I opened up and told him that work had started to fall apart and that I had no idea what I was actually doing anymore. I explained that I didn't even know who I was anymore.

I still couldn't accept that I had a brain injury, I felt like if I said I had a brain injury, I'd be looked at as a liar. I'd only had brain surgery; how can I say I have a brain injury when there's people out there with traumatic brain injuries that had occurred in horrific ways. I was constantly comparing my "situation" to others. People like Paul had suffered a Traumatic Brain Injury of his own and had set up a charity - I just couldn't understand why I was struggling.

This was the first time I'd actually be open and honest about how I was and Paul seemed genuinely shocked. He went on to explain that every brain injury is different so comparing one brain injury to another doesn't work. Since I'd had my brain surgery, I had never allowed myself time to recover, I had forced myself back into work when I shouldn't have. Even when I was offered cash incentives to leave (charity grants) and more money in benefits than my actual wage I put my pride and ego before my health. As much as I didn't want to admit it, I really shouldn't have been at work. Whoever it was trying to get me sacked, was actually doing me a favour.

Paul never told me that I needed to leave but by the end of our conversation, I knew that I needed to consider it instead of staying and trying to fight again.

So with that in mind I sent a text to my boss the next morning after work saying that I was feeling ill and that I would be getting a sick note for a week. My plan was to keep getting one-month sick notes, knowing that I was only going to get basic sick pay, (about a quarter of my normal wage) my thinking was that I couldn't be sacked while on sick and that they would have to spend thousands on overtime and agency staff to cover me while I was away, not knowing how long I was actually gone for. I would do this every week until I had a new job lined up.

The boss replied with an "I hope you feel better soon" text with a smiley face at the end.

On Saturday, two days later, there was a knock on the door, it was the postman. He had a letter for me that had to be signed for. I had no idea what it could be and opened it up to find a report into my investigation with all the evidence that had been gathered. There was a letter with it from an area manager, I was being called in to a formal meeting with two area managers at one of our other sites and the date was for the following week. The game was up. Clearly, somebody had an idea of the kind of stunt I was pulling and I knew that meeting was to have me sacked.

After some thought over that day, I decided I wasn't going to be sacked, I was going out on my own terms. I decided to go to work the next day, knowing that it would be quiet with it being a Sunday – I decided that I'd go in the office, type up my resignation and leave, never to return.

The next day, I remember calling Jack's mum to warn her that I was about to be jobless and wouldn't be able to give her any money until I had sorted out benefits or another job. I had no idea how long that would take as quitting a job would probably leave me having to wait for a period of time before I could apply for benefits. She was pissed off but knew there wasn't much she could say or do about it.

When I got to work, I didn't tell anyone what I was actually there to do. Instead I made my way to the office and sat though the previous shifts handover while sat there typing up my resignation.

My formal resignation was less than two sentences and I ended it by telling the boss exactly how I felt at that moment.

"And just so you know boss, this genuinely breaks my heart"

Once the formal resignation had been sent, I typed up a farewell email to the rest of the team. I was going to be upfront, honest and completely truthful. I had absolutely loved my five years in that place, even when things got bad, I still loved the job. I wanted to tell everyone why I was leaving and what the ultimate cause was and I was pretty blunt. I made it clear that there were staff members in that building who were in a position of care that had managed to drive a fellow team member to the brink of suicide. I wanted them to see and understand the irony right there. I also made a point of emphasizing just how much a couple of people in that place had helped shape me in to man I had become (in a positive sense).

There was a lot I wanted to say and I wanted to be lot harsher in how I worded the email but what was the point? What would I achieve? So I made my point and said my goodbyes, which was enough.

I left after I'd sent it, there was no going back from that point - I blocked all numbers and emails that were related to that company and walked away for the last time.

When I got home, the reality of what I had just done hit me, I broke down and cried. I really did love that job and now it was gone. Permanently. After I'd settled, I realised that I needed to sort my next steps, I always said that I'd never go back on benefits - I'd worked so fucking hard to get into and stay in work. I'd fought tooth and nail to keep that job, even when I shouldn't have but now, now I had to suck up my pride and move on. I'd just been paid so had just enough to cover all the bills and get enough food in for me and Charlie but that was it.

The next day, I knew I had to try and apply for benefits to keep me going until I could jump into another job.

CHAPTER 22

November 2019 - February 2020

Onwards and upwards.
Apparently...

The day after I'd left work, I knew that I needed to start applying for benefits, I wasn't going to risk losing everything. Not now; not when I'd worked so hard to keep everything.

Losing my job was one thing, but to lose my house would just push me over the edge so I made an appointment for the next day to see if I could get anything at all.

I turned up to my appointment, expecting to be told that thanks to me quitting my job I wouldn't be entitled to any help. After going over some very basic questions and handing over some paperwork, the person I was sat talking to then told me that not only would I likely be entitled to benefits but I could have a cash advance of about £500 there and then which I snapped up with both hands.

He explained that if I was successful in my claim I would have to pay it back but would have a period of time of a year. Not a problem I thought. That money could get me a DSLR camera - the first step towards me starting a photography business.

Officially, that money was to cover me until I got my first benefits payment - if I got it. By the end of the appointment, I was confident I'd get the job seekers side of benefits with housing benefit and as far as I knew, I had my final wage and some holidays to come in December. What could possibly go wrong?

The first thing I did after that appointment was get online and buy a new camera, essentially an upgrade to something that I could use in a more professional sense.

I spent all of the £500 advance on a camera and the basic kit I'd need - no more using my phone for photography. Not now.

By the time December rolled around, I had just enough cash to get me though to my last wage in mid-December, not much but enough to cover trips to the arcade when I had Billie.

In my head, I'd worked out that my final wage would be around £1500 - £1800, made up of my normal wage of £1200 and the rest in holiday pay.

Over the next few weeks, things seemed to go quite smoothly; I had Billie every weekend and I was starting to get confident with my photography plus I was having more good days than bad with the chemo side effects.

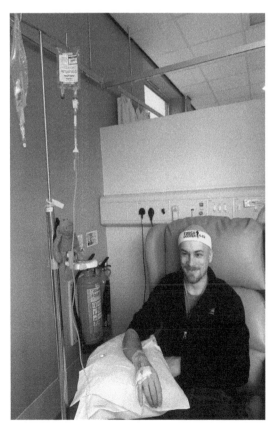

Me with Monkey during a chemo session

I remember turning up to bootcamp early one night, I'd just spent the afternoon on Hessle Foreshore trying to capture a time-lapse of the sunset and the lights being switched on on the Humber Bridge. One of the clients, Daz soon turned up, also early. He was so happy and impressed by some of the photos I'd taken for him during the last session that he'd decided to buy me a create of beer as a thank you and, just to sweeten the thank you, he'd brought in a camera to give me. It was almost as good as the new one I had bought!

He mentioned it was probably better to sell it if I needed the money and being in the position I was at the time - no job, no benefits and no money, I knew I would have to sell the camera.

It was soon time for me to end round two of my chemotherapy; the last stage of each round was always the IV treatment. Before you're given chemo via IV, you have to have a blood test as the doctors need to know you're actually healthy enough on that day to be pumped with poison.

About an hour after having my blood test, I was called in to see the Oncologist who told me that I wasn't allowed my chemo that day. He explained that my blood test had come back showing my liver enzyme count was through the roof. A normal enzyme count should be in the low double digit but mine had come back in the hundreds. I asked what would cause my liver to act up in such a way.

"You're drinking too much alcohol, Matthew"

I told him that in the time I had started my chemotherapy, I had only had half a can of beer and that was two months ago. He asked if, I was sure. Of course, I was sure, so he then asked about my diet and I told him it was pretty bad. Lots of caffeine and junk food when I actually had an appetite but I had been eating a lot of fruit - bananas in particular telling him that I liked to have one or two bananas a day. The guy's jaw dropped.

"Matthew, you cannot eat bananas!"

It seemed that during the brief I had at the start of each round of chemo I'd not paid much attention. One of the main foods you can't eat while on chemotherapy is bananas. Mixed with chemotherapy drugs, they become lethal.

Just my luck I thought! I try to be a little healthier and I end up making myself ill as a result.

The chemo was cancelled that day and I was told to go back a week later - if my enzyme count had improved, I'd be allowed to finish that round of chemo. If not, I'd have to skip it and move on to round three.

I remember turning up to the PAUL centre one day in December for the weekly group session. Paul took me to one side to tell me that he had booked me some one-to-one training with a photography tutor for the next six weeks. I was so bloody thankful, I finally had a chance to make something of myself with photography!

Mid December came by in no time - I had a friend staying with me for a while, so we both sat and chilled out with a movie for a while. Nervous and curious as to what my final wage would be, I stayed up until after midnight so I could see exactly what I was going to be paid.

I checked my balance just after midnight - £700. I had completely forgotten that I was on sick when I quit so I'd been paid less than £400 and my holiday pay.

My rent was £400, food, toiletries and dog food for the month was normally about £200 and then there was the kids, gas & electric, my phone bill, sky, internet etc. Not forgetting that Christmas was in just two weeks. I had exactly £700 to pay all of that. I'd been living well outside my means, even on a normal wage but this was another level of fucked.

I stared at the screen in shock and didn't say a word to my friend. I couldn't figure out how or why I had thought I'd get a normal wage. I didn't know what I was going to do. If I'd stayed at work and challenged the witch hunt, maybe I'd have been able to stay and not be in this mess. Maybe I shouldn't have bought the camera? At least then I'd have enough to clear some of the bills. I must have looked like a deer in the headlights just before its hit by a truck. The deer knows it's fucked but it can't move - knowing it's about to die. If there was ever a moment in my life where I thought I was truly fucked with no way out, this was it. Game over.

I went into the bathroom and grabbed one of my cheap razors - I wasn't thinking clearly, it was almost like I was on auto pilot. I made my way upstairs, to my room and closed the door behind me. I sat down and began to break the razor apart so I could get to the blade itself.

With that, Charlie came bouncing up the stairs and immediately started scratching away at my bedroom door. Normally, when there's company in the house, Charlie will leave me alone and stay with whoever is about. He always has but, on this occasion, he must have sensed something was off. My friend must have thought I was going to bed without saying anything and just being a bit rude but Charlie must have known that wasn't the case.

He wouldn't leave my door alone and kept scratching and whining, trying to get me to let him in. After a minute or so of trying to pull the razor apart with Charlie still scratching away at the door, I gave up. I opened the door to let him in. He was so excited to see me. It was like I'd been out for hours and just got back in through the front door.

What was I thinking? How the hell could I go and kill myself, leaving this furry little guy behind. Not to mention having a friend still in the house at the time.

After some time to chill out and think a little more clearly, I realised that I could push though this, I'd just need to hold out until I got my first benefit payment. I assumed that it would be in January but I'd soon find that not to be true...

Knowing that Christmas was just around the corner and just how broke I really was, I decided to sell my phone. I had an iPhone 10+ at the time so I knew I could get decent amount of cash to keep me going. I'd only had the phone for 6 months; I really didn't want to sell it but it was that or the camera. I knew the camera would be worth more in the long run but that was going nowhere.

The plan was to sell the phone for about £300, I'd then use as little of that money as possible to buy a cheap phone and use the rest to pay for the bills that I needed to cover there and then.

I ended up with a tiny, incredibly old iPhone SE. This thing was terrible! The battery couldn't handle half a day of usage and would constantly crash but times were tough and all that.

As a distraction from everything I decided to take part in the "Santa Run" with Paul For Brain Recovery that month. A few of us from the charity all joining in and dressed in Santa outfits. Obviously, I used this as a perfect opportunity to have a good and much needed laugh and of course, do some photography for the event. It turned out to be a great day and we all had so much fun.

When I got home, I had a voicemail from Hull Daily Mail, they wanted to do a follow up piece from my last article earlier in the year. I agreed to talk, they had no idea that my tumour had grown again and that I'd left work so as soon as I mentioned that, the reporter was even keener to get a story out of me and I was happy to talk.

It gave me some comfort to think that someone in a similar position may read it and see that they weren't alone.

In the beginning of January Chris had arranged for me, him, Michelle and another guy named Gaz to meet in Hull and do some bouldering and rock climbing before heading out for a meal later that night. I could barely afford it but needed to get out of the house and besides, a day out with these guys sounded great!

We all met at Rock City, Chris had offered to pay for my session, knowing just how skint I was. Still putting my pride and ego before anything else and not wanting to look rude by refusing his offer I quickly paid before anyone else.

I'd brought my camera, it seemed like the perfect excuse for a bit of photography and a good chance for us all to get some great shots together.

After spending the afternoon having a good laugh and making idiots of ourselves, we went out for dinner. I had about £20 left by the time we got to the restaurant, it was enough to cover a meal but I didn't know how long I'd need to make that money last. Chris jumped in and paid for the meal – now it might not seem like a big deal but to me that meant a lot then and still does now.

Around the 9th of January, expecting to be paid some form of benefits in the next few days, I logged into my online benefits account to try and find out how much I was due, if I had upcoming meetings etc.

I was supposed to be getting about £317 and another £300 to go towards my rent - not enough to cover all of my bills but at least I could cover the rent and food for me and Charlie.

The first line of the statement read something like "your payment this month is £0" I didn't panic because I thought this must have been a simple mistake; the statement explained that this was because my previous employer had reported that I had earned £1343 in December. I knew that I had bank statements and wage slips to show that wasn't the case so this would be an easy one to fix.

I went to the job centre later that day, ready to sort it out, I'd brought six months' worth of bank statements in with me.

Wage slips, proof that I had actually quit work and proof the company I worked for had accepted my resignation.

The staff member soon realised what the problem was - there had been no mistakes at all, well not on their part anyway. They had grouped parts of my November and December wage together. Essentially, they worked out my earnings from the beginning of each month, meaning they decided that between November 7th and December 7th I must have earned over £1300. To me that was a stupid way of working it out; even if I had used my advance on bills, I wouldn't be able to make that money cover all of my living expenses.

I asked the woman what I was meant to do and told her that I wouldn't even be able to pay my rent that month, let alone buy food.

"You need to learn how to budget better" she said.

She then handed me some leaflets that explained how to budget.

I had no idea how to take that, I had no money and no options. I still hadn't told my landlady about any of the situation, not the tumour, the treatments nor the leaving work. Nothing. I tried to call her but got no answer so I sent her a long text explaining everything and saying that I couldn't afford that month's rent. I ended the message by telling her that I understand that she had a mortgage on the house so would leave within the month if she wanted me out.

It seems ridiculous that I was worried about somebody who had nothing to do with me, I know, but that's just how my thought process was at the time.

I got a call back within an hour, to my surprise, my landlady was more concerned about me and my health than she was about the rent. She was obviously quite shocked that I had been through all of that and not mentioned it to her. She told me to forget about the rent for that month and to focus on me and my health. She explained that one way or the other, it would be sorted out and rent was the last thing I should be worrying about.

She had plenty of experience with the DWP so was fully aware of what kind of situation I was in - I could have cried. I was ready to have to give up my house, knowing that there was no room for me and Charlie at my parents and that the one and only homeless hostel in Hull that allowed pets, wouldn't allow me in because of a "conflict of interest"

To say I was grateful would be a huge understatement, not having to worry about the rent was a huge weight lifted from my shoulders!

I'd been working on some fundraising for Paul For Brain Recovery just before I had to stop working. By January, I had decided to roll with another pie in the face fundraiser - it's something that had brought in a good amount of money in the past, so I figured it'd be worth a shot.

I was chatting to Michelle about it and asked if she would be up for taking a pie in the face for charity. She got back to me almost straight away, telling me she'd be more than happy to take part! I wasn't planning anything big, just a quick live stream where people could donate a set amount to see her take a pie in the face.

In mid-January, Michelle was coming over to Hull for work so we decided to catch up while she was there and do the pies. The plan was to go for a walk through Hessle and then back to mine where we could set up the live stream. However, Michelle had a different plan in mind.

She just so happened to be a regional manager for DW gyms and had arranged for us to go to the gym in Hull and set up there, knowing that we would get even more people willing to either take part or donate. The staff didn't mind either, in fact they were more than happy to chuck a few pies at their regional manager!

Holding it at the gym worked out to be a much bigger success that I had expected and over a few hours on two separate days, we ended up raising £346. Michelle took all of the hits like a complete and utter legend! The event itself may have been my idea but Michelle definitely earned all the credit for that one!

It was a lot of fun and turned out to be a great way to take my mind off the shit storm I was in.

Michelle during the pie in the face fundraiser

In late January, Paul and Nathalie asked me if I would be willing to meet with a new service user, named Scott who had reached out for help from the charity. He was a young guy that had a rare brain disorder called AVM (essentially knotted veins in the brain) There was a chance that he would need brain surgery so I was asked to meet him during a walk with the three of them.

Paul and Nat both figured that with me having had brain surgery, I might be able to help him get an understanding of what to expect and show him that he wasn't alone.

It was nice to feel needed again, over the course of the walk, we got to know each other and I gave him a basic run down of what to expect if he did actually have brain surgery.

After the walk when Scott had left, Paul asked me how I was getting on, what was my diet like, how was I coping now that I wasn't working etc. I guess he could see I had been holding back a lot and was stuck playing the "I'm fine and don't need help" card.

After showing me that it was obvious that he knew I was holding back, I told him that I felt more like I was a worker at the charity than a service user as I still didn't believe that I needed help with my brain injury. I'd accepted that I had one now but I felt like I was fine and didn't want people thinking I needed help.

Both Paul and Nat were taken back, I explained that nobody had done anything to make me feel like that, I just felt more like I was there to help. They both had to drill it in to me that I really did need help and that I needed to accept that. I'd spent so long trying to help others, like forcing my way back into work instead of working on my recovery and working on fundraisers. Truth be told I was in no fit state to help anybody. I may have accepted that I had a brain injury but never accepted that I needed help. Once again, Paul had helped me take the next most important step in my recovery.

By February I'd still not had any money come though and was clutching at straws by this point. I'd already borrowed and spent what I could from friends and family. I had been keeping myself busy by doing the Boot camp photography, I refused to sell my camera because by that point, it was keeping me busy and sane.

To help me out, Shaine, the guy that ran Boot camp had offered to buy the flash for my camera; the idea being, it would stay at boot camp and belong to Shane until I could buy it back. Basically, lending me money with collateral. Little did I know, Shaine had been working on something behind the scene.

I turned up to Boot camp one night in early February, ready for another night of photography. It was a busy night and while we were all in the gym having a bit of a chin wag and a catch up as we always did before a session, Shaine asked me to go out to the shed and grab some bits for him. Thinking nothing of it, that's exactly what I did. When I came back to the gym it was just before 6pm. At 6pm on the dot Shaine would always shout at everyone to get moving and get out to the pitch. As I walked through the door, Shaine shouted for everyone's attention, he then went on to give a speech - a speech about me.

I'd be lying if I said he didn't knock me for six, I'd been doing the photography at Boot camp for free since September. I'd never asked for or would even consider wanting to be paid but the work I had done and the shit I was in had not gone unnoticed. Shaine had started a collection at boot camp, telling the clients just how fucked I was. Most of the clients didn't even know I was on chemotherapy or had a brain tumour so that obviously took a few of them by surprise. Everybody wanted to chip in to whatever extent they could. The whip round consisted of two huge food parcels, four big bags of dog food, a large amount of dog treats and a thank you card that contained £200!

Charlie with the donations from bootcamp

I was pretty close to tears by this point - nobody had ever done anything like this for me before. None of the clients really knew me but they all wanted to help me in one way or another - I was speechless and had no idea how I could even begin to show how thankful I was.

That night and what Shaine and all of those clients did for me is something I'll be forever grateful for and something I'll never forget!

I posted a photo of what had been given to me with Charlie sat behind it all on my Facebook and a Facebook page run by a Hull Daily Mail reporter. I was hoping the reporter would see it and do a piece about it, at least that way, I could show just how thankful I was and hopefully get a bit of publicity for the Boot camp.

A reporter spotted the post and got in touch the next day. She was extremely keen to know the ins and outs of how and why I was in such a desperate position.

I explained that minus the £500 advance in November, I'd not received a penny in benefits and the only other help DWP offered me was a leaflet about managing money. I told her that even with proof, DWP refused to believe that I had no money and that if it wasn't for Boot camp, I'd have no gas or electric and still be struggling to get food in. After a good half an hour of talking, the reporter asked about sending a photographer out to get a few shots of me, I agreed but asked for the shot to be done at boot camp - I even managed to get her to interview Shaine.

After I'd spoken to the reporter, she reached out again and asked for my consent to speak to DWP about me and my case with them. I obviously agreed but knew they would try to make me out to be lying, so I sent her the same proof I'd given them. Bank statements showing that I really had only been paid £700 in December.

A few hours after the reporter had asked for my consent, I received a message on my benefit account stating that my case had been reviewed and that I was owed around £150, which would be paid to me later that night. How convenient I thought.

When I told them, they had made a mistake, they told me I was wrong. When a reporter asked them about said mistake, DWP suddenly realised they did in fact make a mistake.

Something else I noticed was two more messages on the account that I hadn't seen before.

One, from the day before told me that I had been declared fit to work and would now need to meet a job coach and start looking for work (regardless of chemotherapy) and the other had been sent around the same time as the message telling me they had made a mistake and they had now declared me unfit to work.

Had the reporter not spoken to DWP, I would have been forced to get back into work and not receive any money, regardless of the fact I was still on chemotherapy.

A couple of days after the amazing gesture by boot camp, there was a Yorkshire Moors walk that Shaine had organised for some of us to do. It was a 16-mile walk. So I came along as a photographer.

Obviously, like with every other little trip and adventure I brought Monkey along with me - strapped to the side of my rucksack.

Minus some crap weather at the start, it was actually a great day. It was nice to be able to get out in to nature with some great people. During the day, I'd stop and get a couple of daft photos of Monkey posed in a way that made him look as though he was admiring the views or just a random posed shot with him. As always, a few people asked why I was carrying a PG Tips monkey around with me so I explained that it was my lucky travel companion. From my first trip to SA, America, to brain surgery, Tough Mudder and all the adventures in between it (he) tagged along with me on all my journeys.

Later that night, when I got home and started to unpack my kit, I realised that I didn't have Monkey. There was a lot of sentimental value that came with Monkey so I was pretty gutted that he was gone but understood he was likely still up on the Moors somewhere so there would be no getting him back.

I posted a status on Facebook that night, essentially taking the piss out of Monkey being lost and that he had fobbed me off to start his own little adventure. It wasn't long before people were commenting and saying they were gutted for me and how shit that must be. I made a joke out of losing Monkey because I thought people would find it funny or just take the piss out of me for having a teddy in the first place but no - people were actually gutted for me. One boot camper even went as far as to put a post-up on one of the village Facebook groups near to where we had walked, added Monkey's story to the post.

To my shock that post got a lot of attention, locals jumped up saying that they would be looking for Monkey while out walking over the next few days.

Another boot camper got in touch to say that she wanted to go back to the moors and retrace our steps in the hope we could find Monkey. I genuinely couldn't believe just how seriously people were taking this. Again, Monkey held A LOT of sentimental value but I never thought other people would share that value.

A few days after the Moors walk, a boot camper picked me up and drove us back up to the Moors, one of the local villagers had mentioned that they had a PG tips monkey that she was happy to hand over if we couldn't find Monkey. That would be plan B. If we couldn't find Monkey, we'd just take the new one from the local. After a full day of walking, we didn't find Monkey, I mean it was pretty obvious we wouldn't but the walk was nice.

The local that reached out to offer her monkey met us later that afternoon. When I thanked her for the gesture, she seemed confused and told us that she had thought it was a child who had lost their teddy which is why she was so keen to help. Nope just a grown arse man that lost his teddy monkey,

Named Monkey. She didn't seem to understand the story behind it but handed the monkey over anyway.

This monkey looked identical to the lost one, so I decided that this would be Monkey also. The same monkey, the same lucky mascot with its own unique story.

A couple of days later the Hull Daily Mail article ran with the headline mentioning that I was a cancer patient. I didn't need to read any more than that to know that I was going to be pissed off. I had never, ever said that I have cancer. Even now, I get annoyed when people assume that I must have had cancer when they hear I had a brain tumour or was on chemotherapy. It wasn't that much of a big deal, it was more that, thanks to the way my paranoia worked, I was worried those who knew me would assume that I was pretending to have cancer.

DWP had a small piece in the paper too, they tried to stand their ground by saying that I really was still earning money after leaving work. I had all the evidence that showed they were wrong and made it publicly available for others to see. DWP were wrong. It was that simple.

After seeing the article, Michelle reached out and advised that I apply for PIP (another form of disability benefit) I told her that I already had and actually had an assessment the next day.

I'd heard all kinds of horror stories about PIP assessments and how people rarely passed the assessment as the assessors were known to be brutal.

I was planning on going by myself to the appointment in Scunthorpe which was couple of hours away from me. Michelle didn't ask much more than what time the appointment was. It didn't matter what I said, she was coming with me.

I was grateful that I had somebody coming with to be fair and more so that it was somebody like Michelle - she has always been the kind of person you'd want in your corner, especially for an appointment like that.

I was pretty nervous walking into the assessment, I had a rough idea of what kind of questions to expect and assumed that they would all be about the tumour and the surgeries I'd had. The assessor introduced himself and told us that he was a serving paramedic but did PIP assessments on the side so at least I knew this guy actually had medical experience.

At one point during the assessment, I was asked about my mental health. I was prepared for any kind of questions except my mental health and I didn't know what to say. Michelle jumped in and answered for me, mentioning that you'd only need to look at my arms to get an idea of how I'd coped mentally in the past. She'd never mentioned the scars on my arms before so it wasn't until that moment that I realized she had even seen them.

After briefly explaining how shit things had been, (mentally) he asked if I'd want my doctor to be told so I could get more help and support. No sooner than he asked me that, I started to get emotional and with that I began to cry. Just like the times at work when I'd cried, my face began to spasm.

I tried to get up and walk out so I could look less of a tit but Michelle wrapped her arm around me, convincing me to stay sat down. Once I'd calmed down, the assessor said and acknowledged that I had indeed just had a focal seizure and mentioned that he would mark that down on his paperwork.

Afterwards, even though I'd had a seizure during the assessment, I was confident I didn't pass and would be left to do an appeal. At least I knew I'd have some money coming in March when I was due my first official benefit payment. All I had to do now, was play the waiting game.

CHAPTER 23

Well, look at that!
Things really do get better!

In the days after the Hull Daily Mail article had been published, a few people reached out to me though Facebook after they had seen it wanting to help however they could.

As I had just been shown so much generosity by the guys at boot camp I turned down the offers of help, asking that they forward that help to others who might benefit more than I would. I appreciated that people genuinely wanted to help but I had food and enough money to last a few weeks at least. There were others out there who didn't have the same luck as me.

One particular message I got though, stood out. It was from a chemo nurse at Castle Hill, named Clare.

Clare had read the article and was left disgusted by the shit state I'd been left in and couldn't understand why I'd been left in the shit while on chemotherapy. She asked me to go to Castle Hill that week and meet with her, telling me that there were options that she had for me that could help me. I'd already had my PIP assessment and thanks to the article about said situation, I knew that I'd soon get some benefits, including basic disability. I didn't think I was in a position to ask for or accept help at this point, even though I had minimal food in and was back on the emergency credit for gas & electric but, I was confident that I'd be ok in just three or four weeks' time. I told her this but she insisted I pop in for a chat at least.

Clare was a nurse in the children's chemo unit and was a part of the Teenage and Young Adult Unit (TYA). Although I was out of the age range covered by TYA, they said they could still support me.

Clare gave me a tour of the unit and showed me how younger people are treated when it came to chemo, it was a big eye opener to say the least. The rooms were fitted with big comfy recliner chairs as well as PlayStations and Xboxes hooked up to big TV's that had all been donated to the unit.

As nice as the set up looked I soon remembered what the purpose of the set up was. Kids on chemo. It's a horrible thought - kids having to spend hours at a time being pumped with poison.

I was still on chemo but I was an adult and quite resilient but seeing how it worked for children was a stark reminder that there is ALWAYS somebody worse off than you are.

Later that day, Clare and another nurse explained that I was eligible for two grants from two different charities which were the two grants I had been offered when I was initially diagnosed with the tumour if I chose to quit work. In my reluctance to ask for help, I'd completely forgotten that these grants existed.

After completing some paperwork Clare and another nurse told me to hang about as they had asked what my clothing situation was like. I guess they could tell just by looking at me and the kinds of clothes I had on that I hadn't been buying new clothes for a while. Scruffy trainers, scruffy jeans with tears in the bottom etc. etc. Buying new clothes hadn't been an option for a while and it was showing so they said they wanted to give me some gift cards to get new clothes and food etc. they even included a pair of cinema vouchers.

Once again, I'd been sucker punched by random acts of kindness by complete strangers. 99% of my friends from before the brain surgery had fucked me off not long after the surgery and had no intentions of helping me, especially not now. But since leaving work, I was finding people who either barely knew me or didn't know me at all were going out of their way to help me.

The gift cards were a massive help, I managed to get some decent food in and some much-needed new shoes.

A week later, the first grant came though and I spent every penny on new clothes; it was the first time in long time that I had actually been able to get new cloths and it was definitely needed!

By the end of February, I'd decided to quit my chemotherapy, I just couldn't handle the constant fatigue, not being able to eat and the constantly feeling ill. Aside from the brain surgery and the skull removal surgery, I'd had three full rounds of chemo on top of the radiotherapy, not to mention all the personal shit I had going on at the time. I'd just had enough.

Mid-March soon came which I knew would be the month I was due my first benefit payment. My first actual payment since December and the start of some stability. After the mess about I'd had over the last few months with DWP, I decided to stay up until midnight to see if I would actually be paid. I was half also expecting to be screwed over for some kind of imaginary problem that DWP made up or something crazy like that. When I finally checked to see if I really had been paid, I was shocked to see that not only had I passed my PIP assessment I had been paid my first payment for it too! Finally, things seemed to be back on track!

I quickly fired off a message to Michelle, thanking her for coming with me, I was and still am certain that had she not been with me the day of my PIP assessment I would have failed it.

This was the first time since leaving work that I actually felt confident I was going to be ok. I knew there would be no more worrying about how I was going to keep me and Charlie fed.

A couple of weeks after I realised life was on the up, the world started go to shit. Covid19 had now became a global issue.

By March, everybody knew what Covid was and there had been rumours that the UK were about to go into a form of lockdown, which is exactly what happened at the back end of that very month. No leaving the house unless you absolutely had to, all but essential shops closed, no gyms or places people could meet. Even supermarkets would make you queue to get in.

A month or so into lockdown, Nat, from PAUL reached out and offered to bring me food parcels once a week. Normally I would have turned an offer like that down but I was becoming so bored and lonely by this point. I missed being able to actually see and speak to someone in person and not just over the phone so getting food parcels dropped off meant I could stand in my house with Nat stood a few meters away and have a little catch up. In all honesty I wasn't so bothered about the food, I mean I really appreciated it but being able to just talk to somebody and have some form of routine is half the reason I was able to stay sane during lockdown, with Charlie being the other half.

The whole lockdown thing finally started to ease around July – at least enough for the team I was in, The Dream Team to do the Yorkshire Three Peaks once again. There was Chris, Michelle, Gaz and a few others who were part of the team. Unlike the year before, the weather was actually set to be perfect.

I met Michelle the day before, the plan was for me to stay at Michelle's and then travel together, whilst there she convinced me to sign up to a new version of Tough Mudder, called Tough Mudder Challenges. Obviously with Covid and lockdown, there couldn't be any TM events for 2020 so, every month there would be a new TM Challenge released with a theme that would be completed over a period of twenty-one days. Each challenge would come with a set of tasks or virtual "obstacles" that had to be completed with proof. These included a set distance and elevation, a set amount of specified bodyweight exercises and a variety of daft but fun challenges.

So we set to work there and then on some of the tasks that had been set for that month; the first of which was a two-minute plank over the top of six eggs. I'd soon learn that the TM challenges would be a highlight of 2020 for me.

Just like the previous year, we had a 7am start ahead of us which meant an early night. I didn't know it before that day but I soon realised I was extremely allergic to cats and Michelle had several. Because I was sleeping in the living room where the cats were I spent almost the entire night wide awake, scratching my eyes out, I only managed to get a couple of hours sleep before it was time to wake up as we needed to be on the road by 4am so we could meet the rest of the team and be ready to start walking by 7am.

The dream Team during the summer Yorkshire Three Peaks

I'd bought my camera with me with the intention of being the group photographer bur it turned out Gaz was also a photographer which meant I could actually be in some photos this time and know that they would be professional quality as like me, Gaz didn't mess about when it came to photography.

As a team, we managed to smash all three peaks and the full 26 miles in 11 hours 13 minutes. Just like the first time, it was a great day that was much needed and well worth the aches and pains!

Around late July though I had started to notice that I was having more trouble with my speech, I was having headaches and my memory seemed to be worse than normal and I started to become paranoid that my tumour was growing again.

The symptoms were exactly the same as they were the last time it was found to be growing so it wasn't long until the paranoia soon turned in to fear. I was struggling to sleep on a night, worrying about the what ifs. I knew another growth would likely mean more radiotherapy or even another go at brain surgery and I couldn't face more brain surgery, not knowing what the side effects could be.

I was beginning to think that I shouldn't have quit my chemo, if the tumour had been growing again, it would be my own fault. For the first time in this ridiculously crazy journey of mine, I was actively taking the situation seriously and it terrified me.

I booked an appointment with my oncologist and explained why I thought the tumour was growing again. I wanted him to tell me that I was being daft and that the symptoms didn't mean anything. He agreed that the symptoms did sound suspicious and warranted an MRI to see what was happening.

Thanks to Covid and the delays in just about everything it was causing, I would have to wait until late August for the scan and in the meantime, I'd have to try and keep my cool.

Luckily for me, I had my Dream Team to help keep me focused.

Around mid-August, was our second TM Challenge. One of the "obstacles" in this was named "Waterfall." The idea was to have someone pour cold water over you while you shout out a number of classic TM obstacles. Being the absolute set of nutters that we were in the Dream Team though, we opted to one up this particular challenge and improvise a little bit.

So we found a waterfall close to Malham Cove named Janet's Foss. The plan was for the six of us present to spend a day hiking though Malham Cove then hike back down to Janet's Foss and use the waterfall there for our challenge.

As we made our way to the waterfall, two things became clear, firstly there were a lot of people stood around taking pictures and admiring the scenery and secondly that the water was deeper than I was tall and I couldn't swim so this might be an embarrassingly stupid problem.

Luckily, my team knew that I couldn't swim so Michelle crouched close by on a rock she climbed out to at the edge of the falls, making sure I couldn't sink while another guy in the team jumped in with me also making sure I was ok. It was already embarrassing at this point, a grown man who can't swim trying to tread water underneath a waterfall makes no sense to a lot of people but knowing I had a challenge to finish, I didn't care.

Each of us had to scream the obstacle names as the waterfall was just so loud which obviously this just made it all the more hilarious. One by one, we all jumped in and completed our challenge while other visitors to the area stood by watching in disbelief.

A few days after the waterfall challenge, the day had arrived for the Dream Team to do Europe's Toughest Mudder - Virtual Edition. Thanks to Covid, everyone taking part in the event all across Europe had to do it in their own location in no more than groups of six. Michelle had offered to host the event for our team from her house as it meant we could safely run rural routes with minimal contact with others and remain outdoors at all times in order to comply with the regulations in place at the time.

The idea of the event was that over 12 hours (though the night, 8pm – 8am) the team would run as many 5-mile laps through and around the local village as possible completing an obstacle/challenge between each lap.

I had initially wanted to compete but at the last minute decided it was too much for me so told the guys I was bailing. But because they knew how worried I was about my upcoming hospital appointment they convinced me to at least come and do some photography so I could still be part of the event with them all.

I decided they were right and I could make sure everyone had nice shots of the event too.

The night went really well, I'd bought Charlie with me; he loved being out and doing something different to his normal routine and being able to spend time with new people was just the cherry on the top for him.

Once darkness fell, I ditched the photography to follow some of the team while riding a bike. The idea being, I could give them snacks and drinks but also help keep them motivated when the pain started to kick in.

The next day, with the event wrapped up, it was time to head home, grab a quick nap and then get to hospital for my MRI.

This was the first MRI that I'd had that actually left me worried, I knew I wouldn't get the results for a while but I was still worried that the outcome would be bad.

As always, the scan was straight forward - I'd actually watched a YouTube video that morning about situations where MRIs had gone wrong and left people dead. You'd think I would have learnt my lesson after the brain surgery video the day before I went under the knife but apparently not.

In the weeks after the scan, I managed to keep busy while waiting for the results, I was spending more time getting out for my photography and not just for Bootcamp either. I was managing to get some cracking moon shots and spent a good amount of time working on my animal photography. I was also lucky enough to get more time with Jack too.

One of the many highlights of that year came about in mid-September. At some Tough Mudder events, every year there are certain themes at the start of a wave designed to raise awareness for good causes and money for charities.

One of these annual waves is "Granny Wave" where anybody taking part in it would complete the event while dressed up as, you've guessed it – Grannies with the goal being to raise funds and awareness for The Alzheimer's Society.

It was started a couple a few years previously by two Mudders and had become so much of a success that when TM had been cancelled, the Community decided for Mudders across the country to do their own virtual version of the "Granny Wave" and "Take it to the Streets"

Our Dream Team though decided to Take it to the Hills and do a walk/hike though the Peak District while all dressed up as grannies.

The weather was absolutely perfect and there were people everywhere. You can imagine the kind of looks we were getting throughout the day…

The Dream Team before we started the Granny walk

As always, a day out with the Dream Team, was a great day and another where I didn't find myself stuck thinking about the upcoming appointment to discuss my results.

Said appointment was set for September 17th and Michelle had offered to come with me, knowing just how nervous I actually was and partly because she knew I probably wouldn't be able to take in most of what was said. Now I know I told you I'm not allowed to tell you any of her story but I am allowed to tell you that she has spent more time than she would like at Castle Hill too, so I knew it wouldn't be much fun for her but she insisted on coming to support me anyway.

Once we'd both sat down and got the pleasantries out the way, the oncologist brought my latest scan result up on his screen. Compared to all the other scan results I'd seen before, this one looked very different. There was a hole where the tumour had originally been and the area surrounding it was white which the oncologist explained was due to scaring from the radiotherapy.

He went on to explain that the tumour hadn't been growing and the mid-September feelings I had been experiencing were just part of the brain injury. He also went on to explain that although there was no visible evidence of a tumour anymore they couldn't yet guarantee that minute pieces of it weren't still in my brain.

He explained that a brain tumour like mine, a glioma, branches out a bit like the roots of tree would but in a very flat manner which made them harder to detect. He therefore advised I continued the chemotherapy to "mop up" any potentially remaining tumour cells if they were there.

There were still three more rounds of chemo to complete if I wanted it. I choose to re start the chemotherapy in the hope that it would finally nail whatever was left of this hitchhiker of mine and started round three the same day.

The routine was the same as before - a month on and a month off. This time though I wasn't dumb enough to skip the anti-sickness meds before I started my overly complicated chemo regime.

With my birthday coming up in the next couple of days, Mum and Dad wanted to have another family meal. Dad was working over my birthday, so we opted to have the meal on the 18th, two days before my birthday. As always, it was nice to be out with the family. It wasn't often that we all got together so it was a nice evening.

In mid-September, I'd signed up for the virtual Worlds Toughest Mudder in an attempt to raise money for Riverside. Thanks to Covid, South Africa had shut their borders meaning Riverside had no income and no new volunteers so if I could help in anyway, I would and it wasn't long before I hit the first £100 in donations.

That same night, a girl named Miek sent me a message on Instagram as she had seen that I was fundraising for Riverside and had hit the first £100 so wanted to say thank you.

After some quick chat, it was pretty obvious that there was a bit more to Miek reaching out than her just wanting to say thanks and I certainly wasn't complaining. She was good looking, seemed pretty cool and was a Riverside volunteer too. After a couple of hours of talking it seemed we had quite a lot in common.

It wasn't long before we started talking over WhatsApp and the more we spoke the more interesting she seemed to be and we soon progressed to talking over FaceTime. We clicked immediately with the first call lasting about four hours, it was crazy but neither of us were complaining.

For the day of my birthday, Chris and Michelle came over to Hull and we arranged to go Go-Karting for the afternoon. Nothing special but things were still limited and under restrictions plus it would be a laugh and the perfect opportunity for us to unleash our competitive sides.

Needless to say, Michelle ended up kicking both our arses but it was great fun and definitely an afternoon well spent.

Chris had actually brought cake too so it wasn't long before I found myself sitting and chilling on an old abandoned pier on Hessle Foreshore with two best friends, eating cake and talking shit. It might sound odd but that was actually one of my best birthdays in a long time.

Me, Michelle, Chris sat eating birthday cake

Although we were thousands of miles apart, things with Miek soon started to get quite serious. We were talking every single day without fail and not just a couple of messages. We would FaceTime for hours on end throughout the day and spam each other with videos and photos that described our day. We soon started to realise that there was a connection between the pair of us and started talking about meeting.

The South African borders had been shut when they went into lockdown but the UK, for whatever reason, had decided to keep the borders very much open and accessible. We decided that at some point soon, she would come to the UK, stay with me for a while and see what this connection we had was.

In late September, I was due to start college, I'd signed up to re-do my Maths and English so I could jump on to an access course that would enable me to start studying at Uni to become a paramedic. All I needed to do was complete about seventeen weeks of part time college and then I would be ready to start working towards becoming a paramedic. It should have been an easy ride, the college side at least.

I remember walking to college and talking to Miek the whole way there, telling her what the plan was and what the pay would be. At least she wouldn't think I was just some benefit bum that couldn't be bothered to work, I had goals and I was taking them with both hands.

I got to college early, I always liked to be early when it came to appointments or new jobs and courses etc. that way, if anything goes wrong I have time to sort it but then I realised I had absolutely no idea where I going.

I spent at least forty minutes wandering around the college trying to find the particular room I needed to be in. Eventually I found it and stood outside the classroom, in the corridor with all the other students.

There were quite a lot of people waiting to go in to different classes, all chatting away between themselves. Within just a couple of minutes of getting there, I could feel my heart racing and I felt like people were staring at me,

"I must have looked a twat, standing here on my own" I thought to myself.

I was starting to panic at the idea of walking into the room and the more I thought about it, the more I panicked. I knew that I was having an anxiety attack, I had to bail, and I just couldn't stay any longer. Even walking away, I was panicking that people would be looking at me thinking I must have been some idiot that had been waiting around the wrong area.

Once I got out and away from the college, I felt like I'd just fucked myself over. I knew that without the Maths and English being re done, I wouldn't be allowed to take the next steps towards studying for my paramedic course. I'd told so many people that I was going back to college. How was I meant to say that I couldn't even make it through the door? I felt like a complete and utter loser.

All I needed to do was drop an email to the tutor and let them know what had happened and I'd be fine. I would have been able to go back a different day and sort it, but nope. I couldn't even face doing that. I felt so stupid. I wasn't going back so I'd just have to suck up the fact that I would never get away from benefits and dead-end jobs.

In October I was taking part in my third Tough Mudder Challenge and the theme for this one was Marvel. One of the "obstacles" for this challenge was searching for Infinity Stones, the idea was to place five different pieces of fruit into a bucket of water and using only your mouth, remove all the fruit. The colour of each piece of fruit represented each of the Infinity Stones - a blueberry, a lemon, an orange, an apple and a grape. Once completed, you had to pour the water over your head.

I chose to tweak my challenge and make it that little bit more ridiculous so I used six different four litre bowls and used food colouring to make the water in each bowl match the colour of the fruit. After I'd removed the fruit from each bowl, I would pour the full bowl of water over my head.

The 6 bowls of water for the Infinity Stone challenge

Something that had completely slipped my mind though was that I was still on chemotherapy. My immune system was weak - leaving me extremely susceptible to getting ill. As fun and hilarious as the challenge was I became extremely ill a day or so later. I was so weak; I could barely get out of bed and couldn't even walk Charlie. I was stuck to the sofa for a couple of days and eating was out of the question.

Charlie could see I was ill and just kept cuddling up to me, not wanting to leave my side. I was waking up in the night, drenched in sweat. It was horrible.

I was due to end round three of my chemo that week, I knew I wasn't going to be allowed to have it but figured I should try and get to the hospital so I could at least have my blood test and see what was wrong. I looked a state and slept the entire bus ride there.

After I had the blood test, I was told that I was definitely too ill to be pumped with the chemo as my white blood cell count was far too low. I was given six injections that I would take home with me and take once daily.

On the second day of using these injections, I started to feel amazing and had even more energy day to day than I normally would. I'd gone from being too ill to move to suddenly not being able to stay still. This stuff was great!

After I had finished using all of the injections, I remember waking up in the middle of the night drenched in sweat again but groggy so I soon crashed back out. When I woke up, I felt great again. Whatever was in those injections, it had certainly done the trick!

**Monkey posed with one of the daily injections
I needed to take**

CHAPTER 24

No lessons learned.

I always found that talking to Miek would help make a crap day just that little bit more bearable. We soon started talking about an actual plan to get her here to Hull to see what we actually had, if anything at all.

Looking back now, I should have seen the signs. Talking to Miek definitely made my days feel and seem better but clearly there was more to the picture than I wanted to see.

Amy had stopped access between me and Jack again, Billie's aunt wasn't able to get Billie for me anymore and the whole not being able to handle a basic part time college course because of anxiety was still pulling me down. As perfect as Miek was and as great as she made me feel, she was merely a distraction. A welcome distraction but, a distraction that was making it easy for me to hide away from my problems - allowing them to fester and get worse.

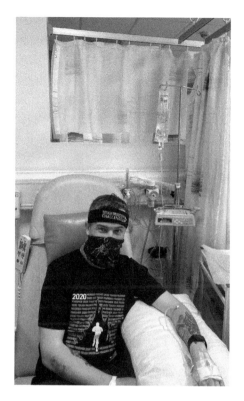

Septembers chemo session

In October, a few people from bootcamp had arranged a hike up Scafell Pike. It would be an all-day walk, covering about twelve miles - mostly uphill and over rough terrain. Should I have been doing something like this while on chemotherapy? Absolutely not but I didn't care, it was an excuse to get out and look less lazy with the bonus of being able to get some photography done. Win win I thought.

It was tough going at times, a few of us hadn't trained at all for a hike like this, including me but I was determined to get up that bloody hill and reach the peak!

As we got closer it became clear some of us weren't going to make it up to the top of the peak. Of the ten of us that started the day only four of us made it to the top –just getting to the base of the peaks was a challenge in itself. I remember trailing at the back of the group with a girl name Casey who I was trying to keep motivated by talking. As we approached the peak though she called it a day and no matter how much I tried to convince her to give it a shot, she was done. Hiking isn't for everyone and there's nothing wrong with that, hell, I'd be lying if I said I wasn't at least slightly nervous about scrambling to the top. Not only was it high but it was going to take all the effort I had just to not fall down.

I waited for the rest of the group that chose to abandon the attempt to link up with Casey before I moved on down to the base of the peak.

It took a while but I finally made it to the top and I felt amazing. I'd accomplished something tough and challenging while on chemo - it was another fuck you brain tumour moment.

Everything about the hike and that day was just perfect - the views, the company and the sense of accomplishment. It was a day I won't forget in a hurry!

Me at the top of Scarfell Pike

By mid-October a plan had come together - Miek had a package due to be delivered any day that had been sent by her Mum for her birthday. The plan was to wait until after her birthday and after her mum's package arrived then book the next available flight over.

On October 28th, her package arrived so she booked a Covid test and a flight the same day meaning she would be in the UK in just three days' time. We were both so freaking excited - sure, it would be a leap of faith but we both knew we had a solid connection. Whatever it was, we needed to find out for ourselves.

Miek started her journey to Hull at the end of October. In the short time we'd been talking, I'd fallen for her - it was crazy.

She finally made to Hull on November 1st; seeing her face to face, in person for the first time was one of those moments words can't justify!

In November, I was due to take part in Virtual World's Toughest Mudder - I'd raised more than £500 for Riverside, mapped out a five-mile route that I would use and brought the items required to take part. The plan was for Miek to stay at mine and act as my "pit crew" making sure I was good before and after each lap - things were looking good, in fact things seemed like they were perfect. I hadn't felt this happy for a long time.

I remember, we sat and binge watched "The Boys" in that first week and had takeout most days, for Miek, it must have been like a holiday. After all, she had just spent the last year working seven days a week at Riverside with nothing but a skeleton crew.

It didn't take long though for the cracks to start to show. After a day or two of being together, I remember realising that things weren't quite as perfect as I thought they were and I very quickly realised that we weren't going to work. I was starting to see that we were two very different people. Yes, there was a connection but the cracks only seemed to be getting bigger and I realised that I'd been kidding myself - things hadn't been perfect at all.

I was finally starting to understand that I'd been hiding from my problems - using Miek as an excuse not to have to acknowledge my issues rather than face them and tackle them and that was the point I started to go downhill again.

I decided I couldn't and wouldn't do World's Toughest Mudder, after all I shouldn't have been doing it anyway. I was still on chemotherapy, not that I cared.

I ended up binning everything related to the event, meaning that even if I changed my mind, I wouldn't be able to do it.

Exactly a week after Miek had arrived, I was just about to head out and get a drink but before I could leave, she stopped me to say that she didn't think we were working and that she wanted to break up. I took it quite hard, once again, I'd set myself up to fail and felt like I'd wasted the last couple of months.

I decided that instead of heading to grab a drink, I'd go and pick up a crate of beer and spend the day getting shit faced. I knew that if I had any alcohol, I wouldn't be allowed to start my next round of chemo, which was only a few days away but I didn't remotely care. Just like old times, I'd become self-destructive.

When I got back, I took myself upstairs and spent the day getting pissed while watching TV. I didn't want to be around Miek so figured keeping out that way would be best. It was pretty obvious I was going out of my way to avoid her.

Sat upstairs, on my own, I started to realise just how much of an idiot I was. I couldn't hold down a job, I couldn't handle college, my dating life was clearly shit and I couldn't even handle a relationship. My conclusion was that I was a loser, a loner and and a retard. That's clearly how my life was going to pan out. I hated myself and was starting to wish that I'd stayed home and had a bath the day I had the seizure that got my tumour diagnosed – at least then I'd have likely died and been none the wiser.

Later that night whilst completely shit faced, I decided to take a walk into town and head over to the marina, buying a few bottles of cider on the way.

I must have spent a good few hours, just sat at the marina getting even drunker. I remember toying with the idea of just jumping in and being done with the constant fuck ups but obviously, I never made it past the railings.

When I got home I tried to sneak back in without waking Miek but before I knew what was happening she was standing on the stairs having a go at me. She knew that I was pissed but had no idea where I had been and said she had sent me messages asking where I was but I'd ignored her so was worried as she had absolutely no way of knowing what I was doing or if I was even ok.

The next day, Miek told me that she had booked a flight back home to the Netherlands for the next day. I didn't blame her to be honest, in her position, I'd have done exactly the same thing.

The rest of the day I was hung over to hell but decided to be less of a dick and spend some time downstairs and at least try to be semi social.

She left the next day as planned, I helped her out to the taxi with her bags before we hugged goodbye. As soon as I got back in I broke down. I genuinely thought Miek and I had something and I'd managed to fuck it up and I knew that we'd never see each other again after that. I was pissed off, blamed myself and hated the idea that her final thought of me would be that I was a prick.

Loser, loner, retard... These words would haunt me over the next few weeks. A loser because I couldn't hold down a job or even college. A loner because I wasn't able to hold down a decant relationship. A retard because my short-term memory was terrible, I struggled with basic tasks at times and felt that most people around me viewed me as slow in some kind of way.

I'd soon cut Miek out of my life in every way I could, scrubbing any trace of her from my social media and deleted any pictures of us together - to say I was struggling would be an understatement.

By December, I was at rock bottom. I knew I wouldn't be allowed to see Jack or Billie over Christmas and thanks to the whole lockdown situation, I wouldn't even be able to spend it with my family. I couldn't cope with the idea of spending Christmas on my own, I was already in an extremely dark place and knew that if I didn't do something drastic, I would kill myself. It was really that simple - I couldn't handle life anymore.

I felt like my life had fallen apart post brain surgery - I lost my job, my pre surgery friends, two seemingly perfect relationships, my dignity and self-respect. I hated who I had become and felt I couldn't change that.

I decided that if I could just get back to Riverside, I might stand a chance. I'd be working everyday so I wouldn't have time to feel sorry for myself and I'd be around people who also wouldn't feel sorry for me so hopefully I'd be able to straighten myself out a little. I mean it had worked twice before, so why not now?

So In early December after checking flights and border restrictions, I dropped Lynne at Riverside a message to see if she was ok with me turning up with minimal notice. Thankfully she was fine with it but advised me that Miek had returned to Riverside. I knew it would be hard with her there but at that point I was too desperate to care, if I didn't get away soon, I'd be putting my makeshift rope to use.

I gave myself less than three weeks' notice to fly and only told my parents and Kris that I was leaving. My parents strongly disagreed with the decision but Kris seemed to understand. I soon told Chris about the plan and although he wasn't happy about it he did seem to understand.

I knew though that if I told anyone else I was leaving, I'd only piss them off because of the Covid situation and I didn't want to cause an argument so I decided the less people who knew the better.

CHAPTER 25

The Final Chapter...

I made it to Limpopo on Christmas Day, the plan was to stay for a minimum of six weeks or longer if I felt I needed it. Debbie, who had been at Riverside since I was last there came to meet me at the airport in Limpopo, after the long travel time it was certainly nice to see a familiar face.

She briefed me on what had changed, how they were managing with minimal volunteers and what the new routines were like then told me that Miek had returned and asked how I felt about it.

I honestly didn't care at this point, instead my main concern driving there was how others would see me. A lot had changed since my last visit and I didn't want people thinking I was being lazy if I was struggling or that I was in some way slow because of my memory and cognitive skills being so bad. That's the kind of effect anxiety and paranoia have when a brain injury is involved, more so when you spend so much time trying to ignore it.

Later that day I got a message from Michelle, it was a long message that explained that although she didn't agree with my recent actions over the past couple of months (having Miek over, binning my WTM gear and being in SA) she was still there for me and wanted to help me. She told me how upset she was that I felt like I couldn't tell her that I'd booked to come back to Riverside but was still there for me regardless. I honestly could have cried reading that message - I never told her at the time but that message broke me, I felt like an utter prick and I guess I kind of was.

When we first arrived at Riverside I could see Miek sat in the Georgie enclosure. All the volunteers in the area came over to say hello - all except Miek that was. A part of me had hoped we could talk and at least be friends but I realised at that moment that wasn't going to happen.

The purchase of alcohol had been banned during South Africa's lockdown, so I had brought a bottle of Jäger with me and that night, just like the last two visits, I got little worse for wear but was starting to think I'd made a good decision coming back.

The next morning, I woke up early and went for a run, thinking it would set me up for the day but nobody had mentioned that an alarm system had been set up by the gates leading to the main entrance. It was about 5:30am when I ran through to the main gates and set the alarms off, waking up everyone who was asleep in that area. I looked and felt like a twat but it was a simple mistake and nobody seemed to mind.

When I got back I discovered that I had been put on food prep for my first morning and was working tables with Miek which felt ridiculously awkward.

By now I was a third time volunteer so there was an expectation that I had some idea of what I was doing - I didn't! I couldn't get my head around what food went into what crates or what sizes it needed to be cut in to. All things food prep at Riverside are simple and straight forward, yet here I was, struggling with the basics of a piss easy job.

I remember around my second or third night, I was sat in bed just flicking through photos of Jack and Billie when I noticed something in the corner of my eye by the door. I looked up and realised it was a snake - black and about 30cm long. I knew that it was either a stiletto snake (venomous) or a garden snake (harmless).

My first instinct was that I needed to get a photo of it just in case nobody believed I'd found a snake in my room. (Yes, I see the stupidly now...).

After taking a few shots it was time to get rid of it; so I tried to scoop it up with the bin but that failed and only seemed to piss it off, I soon gave up, realising that my only opinion was to ask for help.

On my way into my dorm I'd passed Miek who was chilling out in the hammock I'd left outside so I took a deep breath and went outside to see if she was still there – she was and eventually came in to evict it leaving me feeling like a complete idiot. Just to make it even more embarrassing it turned out to be a harmless garden snake too.

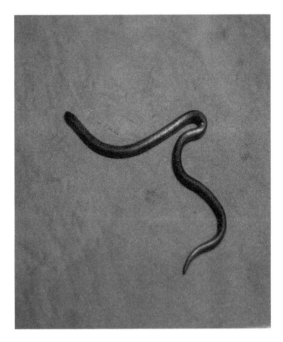

The snake I found in my room

As the days went by, I soon found myself feeling exactly how I felt before I booked my flight - I was avoiding spending time with other volunteers rather than sitting and chilling out with them and instead would disappear and do my own thing; I was beginning to feel like I'd made a mistake in coming back after all.

One morning before work started, just as this feeling started to really hit me, Miek came over and asked what was actually going on. I'd been trying to avoid her whenever I could up to this point and had convinced myself that she hated me and wasn't happy with me being there. So, seeing her come over that like that was definitely awkward, I didn't have a clue what to say.

As I tried to tell her I thought I'd made a mistake coming back, I found myself getting emotional. I knew by now that my focal seizures were triggered by stress and emotion and the last thing I wanted was to have a bloody focal seizure in front of Miek of all people.

Before I knew it the left side of my face had begun to twitch and I told her I couldn't talk. Thankfully she seemed to realise I was going break down so she said we'd talk properly during lunch.

So later that day we headed over to food prep so we could talk in private. She started by saying something like.

"I want you to know that I still care about you" that comment caught me off guard.

I'd spent my time up to this point thinking that she hated me and I'd been avoiding her mostly for that reason. I was half expecting a short conversation that essentially told me to man up or go home but instead we had a really good talk.

Rather than just giving me sympathy and feeling sorry for me or telling to fuck off home, she challenged me on most of the problems I'd described that had brought me back to Riverside, not in a negative way but much like a counsellor would and by the end of our talk, I realised just how much of a dick I must have looked to everyone else. I knew at that point that things started to change so I decided to start by engaging more with the whole Riverside experience again.

In my first week there one of the baby baboons, Frankie had become obsessed with me - whenever he saw me he'd charge at me, jump up and cling on to me. Just like Becca in the last visit, I'd been chosen as this furry little guy's human.

Of course I'd bought my camera with me for this trip and would spend as much time as possible taking photos of the animals and people alike. Once again, I wanted natural shots of people working and of the animals to give a good idea of what day to day life at Riverside really looked like.

No matter how crap I felt during the day, I loved being able to crack on with my photography, I loved feeling like I was actually doing something of some use for once.

I'd take my camera everywhere with me to make sure I wouldn't miss "that perfect shot" then spend my free time at lunch and after work editing the days photos and sending any out that I had of other volunteers.

I remember being in the hide one night in early January, we were all getting ready to head down to the dorms. Just as I began to walk out, Abbie, one of the volunteers looked at me and said.

"Do you really want to leave your laptop in here over night Matt?"

I was going to leave it because I really couldn't be bothered to move it in to the locker room but I took it as a polite way of telling me to lock it up like I was supposed to so, I took it over to the locker room. My photography rucksack however, was still in the hide as I decided that could stay there. It'd save me only having to carry it back up again in the morning.

That night there was an incredibly bad storm that lasted the entire night, When we woke the next morning we made our way up to the hide to get ready for the day's work and it very quickly became apparent that the hide had been broken into during the night. All of the cables that had been left in there, all the food and remaining alcohol we each had had been stolen and obviously, my photography bag had been taken too.

I had all of my photography equipment in that bag and thanks to my sheer stupidity and laziness, I'd lost it all. At that point I felt myself spiralling again and just walked off - I was done. The one thing that I was actually good at had just been snatched away from me and I couldn't blame anyone but myself. I went back down to the dorms, I needed to be on my own. I was so angry and last thing I needed or wanted was people to see me get into a state.

After a while, I realised I had no choice but to accept that the kit had gone, it was my own fault and I just needed to crack on. I hadn't come to Riverside to get photos after all, I was there to get my head back in shape.

Over the weeks I had a combination of good days, bad days and incredibly shit days but one day in mid-January I'd had enough of people back home thinking I was just on a holiday having the time of my life. Obviously, there were people who made it clear how much they disapproved of me being overseas during Covid. So I once again took to Facebook to rant! It wasn't like that at all - I'd gone from a job that involved me helping people, a job where I'd saved thirteen lives over five years and actually felt like I was needed - only to end up in a state where I felt useless and pathetic. Being at Riverside was making me feel like I had a purpose once more. I ended the status by telling people that had I not come to Riverside, I'd have killed myself. A few people acknowledged what I said and agreed with me but there was one person who strongly disagreed and decided to try and take a shot at me over the status in a group chat saying something stupid like.

"Matt that is bullshit!"

Had she acted like a grown up and sent me a message directly, I would have talked to her about it but taking a shot at me in a group chat like that? Nope! The gloves were coming off. I was not in the mood for someone to try and call me out so I fired a fairly harsh reply back, reminding her that she was more than welcome to act like a grown up and discuss the issue with me directly.

She soon did and in short told me that a lot of people suffer with mental health and that they just get on with it, why should I be any different? She made a point of telling me how selfish I was for heading to SA. It was an incredibly long message that was essentially all about her. I quickly shot her down, blocked her and moved on – clearly, she didn't quite understand how mental health worked.

Just like the last visit, I loved going for a run at the end of the day, it was only a 5k run with no pressure on getting a good time. I just appreciated the run and being able to properly unwind.

It wasn't long though before I was becoming more and more stressed out again. I'd not had a job in over a year before coming back to Riverside and now I was starting to see and feel why that was the case - my anxiety was working overdrive. I genuinely felt like people looked at me as some kind of idiot, like someone with learning difficulties. The constant feeling of being looked at like this would not go away. I wasn't sleeping and I was barely eating so decided that I had had enough and started to look for flights back home. I had a few days before I was due to be paid so decided to use that time to think about whether I should stay or go. I felt like it was what everybody else wanted anyway.

Me with baby Frankie after prepping him for bed

I'd been at Riverside for about three weeks by this point and not one baboon would come to me during the baboon walks. It was unusual to go that long without a baboon taking to you but I just put it down to them being able to sense I was in such a foul mood. Only one of the baby baboon's had taken to me so far, Baby Frankie.

I remember being on a baboon walk on one particular day, Frankie had clung on to me on the way down before leaving me when we got to where we would normally go. Like always, I went to sit down by a tree, on my own, trying to plan out how I was going to leave and if I really wanted to. Not long after I'd sat down, a baboon came over to me and clung on to me while all the other baboons continued to forage and play. The baboon was Laura and she quickly fell asleep on me for the rest of the time we were on the baboon walk. I soon realised she'd taken to me and that moment was a special one for me and offered me a moment of clarity. It was then that I decided I was staying.

The day Laura "choose" me

One day not long after that, during an afternoon off, I was sat in my dorm, when there was a knock on my door. I figured it would be Alex, the kid opposite my room but nope, it was Miek.

"Do you want to hang out?"

She came in and we got talking, I can't remember what exactly was said but I mentioned that the feeling of being a "bit slow" was something that was fucking with my head. Before I could any further, she stopped me.

"Matt, you're not a retard" I gave her the smile and nod treatment and carried on with what I was doing.

"Matt, are you listening? You're not a retard"

Something about the way she said it struck a chord and I took that on board for sure. It's amazing how just one sentence can change an entire way of thinking.

Like I said before, I had good days and bad days while at Riverside but by late January I had completely relapsed and fallen back into every day being a bad one and I started self-harming again. I can't explain how or why it would help but just like every other time I relapsed, my mind was in a state.

What annoyed me then and still does now, is that I had gotten myself into that state through ignoring offers of help and pretending to be ok when I knew I wasn't, I had made myself worse. I knew then that it was my own fault.

I did everything I could to make sure nobody would find out about the self-harming. This was my problem, my issue and I needed to sort it out myself. I thought I'd done a decent job of hiding it too.

After a few days, things slowly seemed to be getting better when there was a day I found myself stood around with Miek while we waited to go on our baboon walk. The area we were in had a tree that people would sometimes use to do pull ups. While we were waiting for everyone else to come over, we started to have a bit of banter when she started doing pull ups. After doing a couple, I started taking the mick out of her and did the whole, "you're meant to do them like this" act jumping up and starting to do pull ups.

Lost in the moment, I hadn't thought that my sleeve would roll down as I did them but after a couple I felt my sleeve drop just enough for me to know that I needed to stop. I only had to look at Miek's face to know that she had seen the state of my arm - it definitely killed the moment there and then.

I was humiliated, more so when she told me that other people had noticed my arm too. I thought I'd been smart by only focusing on my upper arm, close to my shoulder but what I hadn't thought about was when I was stretching to pick things up, especially during food prep, people would notice.

Realising that people knew how fucked I was just made things worse and once again I was starting to question what I was actually doing with my life.

A few days later on the way up to the hide I spotted Steve running into one of the vervet monkey enclosures.

"Steve, what's up!?" I shouted over but he didn't answer me. When something like that would happen back at the hostel I quickly learnt to just follow the person running, knowing that there must be some kind of emergency. You don't stop and think, you just go. So I dropped my bag, entered the gate ran after him expecting there to be some kind of emergency involving the vervet's.

After getting inside the main part of the enclosure, Steve came walking back towards me with a dead vervet in his arms. It had died and he didn't want the girls to see it and get upset. As I walked away, towards the gate, I remember feeling this almighty crack across my face before everything went black.

The next thing I knew, I was on the floor. I didn't know how I'd gotten there and was pretty confused. I could hear Steve shouting my name, asking if I was ok as he was running over to me. As I stood up, I realised my face was bleeding - a lot. I went to the office to get a plaster, thinking I'd only cut my face but Debbie only had to have a quick glance to realise that it wasn't a cut at all, it was in fact - a hole.

It turned out that as I had walked towards the gate of the enclosure I'd passed out, face planted the electric fence and shoved my face into the barbed wire fence as I went down. Debbie knew that the wound needed to stitched or at least glued but all I wanted was a plaster.

The money I had left wasn't nearly enough to cover the cost of seeing a doctor over there but Debbie wasn't having it and offered to lend me the money to cover the costs. She wasn't going to back down so I agreed to go to the doctors and get it checked.

After explaining what had happened to the doctor and being looked at like I was an idiot, he told me that he needed to glue the wound back together. Once done, his parting advice was to avoid electric fences in the future.

The bill came to Rand1000 - about £50 - for some bloody glue! I was also left with a not so glamorous scar on my face as a result of that little incident.

Being at Riverside this time around was nothing like my previous experiences. Previously I "found myself" through positive interactions with people and animals but this time around I felt as though the only way I could do that was through far less positive experiences and much soul searching.

One of these moments in particular stands out to me - I was working in Baby Kitchen one morning where part of my job was to mark down which babies had been fed by the other volunteers and exactly how much they'd had. I was struggling to find one of the babies names in the folder but while I tried to more and more volunteers were coming in and asking me to mark down another baby they had fed had x amount of milk. After a few minutes I had a back log of names and amounts that I was struggling to remember while still struggling to find what I was looking for.

I started to feel like I was burning up, sweating and panicking. I remember feeling like I was about to break down when the left side of my face was beginning to twitch. I have been told by a few people that when this happens it is by no means as noticeable as I think it is but that doesn't stop me being extremely conscious of it – I couldn't stand the thought of everyone seeing me like that so I just stopped what I was doing and walked off as fast as I could. I didn't tell anyone what was wrong so nobody really knew what was going on or what was up. But I just rushed to the toilet, locked myself away and broke down crying.

I almost felt like I'd had an anxiety attack but this was also somehow very different at the same time. I'd soon learn that the actual term used for what I had experienced was "sensory overload" Although I had no doubt experienced these before, this was the first time I had been able to identify what it was and therefore understand it which made the whole thing easier for me to process.

As well as learning a lot about myself and my ever changing symptoms I also managed to form some new friendships – one of which was with another girl named Michelle who was from Germany and spoke perfect English. We'd sometimes spend time watching movies or crappy TV shows on my laptop or just sit and chat on a night outside the dorms. Little moments like that are the kind of moments that I can look back at now and smile.

Me and Michelle sat in Georgie with the baby velvets

I used to love spending an hour or so on a night after everyone had gone to bed just sat outside, listening to a chilled playlist and looking up at the stars. It didn't matter what kind of day I'd had, it was just so nice to be in the moment.

Towards the end of my trip things finally started to improve and I started to focus more on what I wanted when I got back home. In all honesty the thought of going back home to another lockdown left me quite anxious, I was worried that I would slip back in this relapse and not be able to get out of it. I soon found that focusing on an action plan for when I got home was the best thing to keep my mind busy and surprisingly it worked.

Even though that was the case things were going well now at Riverside so I decided that I was going to extend my trip and stay a little longer bringing my trip to a total of twelve weeks. However, a couple of days after I'd told Lynne this the government in UK started to talk about introducing a forced ten-day hotel quarantine for travellers returning home from countries that had high infection rates and new strains at a cost of almost £2000 per person. As South Africa fell into this category it didn't take me long to realise that I couldn't afford that so whatever happened, I needed to get home.

I had extremely mixed emotions about this - A part of me didn't want to leave but I knew I had to go, I needed to go home and face my demons head on.

On the last morning, I spent some time helping out at food prep before going back to the dorms to sort my kit and grab a final shower.

Because of the rising situation back home it wasn't just me leaving, another UK volunteer, Davina had decided that she didn't want to risk the hotel quarantine either and opted to leave with me.

As we both said our goodbyes to the other volunteers, I began to get emotional. I'd hugged every volunteer except Miek. Not wanting people to see me cry I choose to walk away, knowing I'd look like I was avoiding her. I went to the side of our bus, sat on the step and cried my eyes out. It was like everything that had happened over the past three years all came back and sucker punched me. This trip was the end of us something huge.

Just as I was trying to pull myself together Miek came around the corner.

"Want a hug?" she said.

"Sure do!" I said.

With that I got a hug that I so desperately needed at that moment in time and she told me to message her if I ever wanted to talk, before walking away. I felt like I'd made things awkward or hard for Miek for a lot of my time there, I felt as though she hated me at times so had gone out my way to avoid her, sometimes causing an obvious atmosphere. In that moment, I realised how much a prick I must have been.

With that it was time to leave - I jumped in the bus, sat in the back corner and just cried most of the way to the Airport, leaving Riverside was harder than I thought it would be.

When we got to the airport, my attitude soon changed, now I needed to focus on getting home and start my recovery. Only this time - I needed to get it right so I decided to use the next twenty hours of travel time to think about an action plan that would keep me busy when I got home.

Kris had brought Charlie home for me a couple of hours before I got home - I might have missed the hotel quarantine but I still needed to isolate for ten days, meaning no face-to-face contact with anybody when I got home.

Coming home and seeing Charlie again and how ridiculously excited he was to see me made me realise that I was happy to be home.

After some much-needed sleep, the next day I made a list; a list of things I needed to work on to keep me busy and focused. No more feeling sorry for myself, no more avoiding my issues and not working on my recovery -I had work to do!

Being at Riverside was for those six weeks, although at times mentally challenging, by struggling and seeing myself fail where I did, I was able to identify some of the main issues I had been ignoring since my brain surgery and since leaving work whereas being at home, most often alone, had only served to help me hide from my demons and in turn, let them win.

Back in South Africa, Riverside were struggling to remain open, thanks to Covid. They needed every volunteer they could get to keep the place running. Being there was the first time since leaving work, that I actually felt like I was needed and I that I was making a difference. I did help make a difference. By the end of the trip, I realised that my recent struggles had only served to aid in my recovery.

Within a week, I could see and feel the change, the mental change in myself and it was amazing.

After explaining what had happened the last time I tried to go to college to the tutor, I was able to sign up for college again with a start date for that week. All I had to do was start and finish my Maths and English and then I'd be eligible to start my paramedic course.

I managed to track Billie's mum down and after some talk about what we both wanted and what we each thought was best for Billie, she finally agreed to allow me to be part of Billie's life again. I don't know what changed, how or why but seeing Billie again after so long is a feeling I can't justify with words.

With this fresh motivation and knowing that I had the power to make positive changes I reached out to Jack's mum's partner (again) and this time Jacks mum herself responded. She was happy to restart contact but once again it had to be on terms she set. To me they felt quite restrictive - no visits without her being present, no overnight stays at all as apparently that didn't suit Jack's routine. I now felt that the only real option left was to move towards the legal route. I'd sorted the situation with Billie and now it was time do the same for Jack, no matter how hard his mum didn't seem to want that.

Going back to Riverside had actually helped change me for the better once again. I'd come home with more energy, motivation and determination to win. To win at life. No more falling down and not being able to get up again. Now I knew that when I did fall, I'll be back up again in no time at all!

I feel as though the best way to look at my life now was like this - forest fires are devastating to watch them unfold in real time but once the flames are extinguished, once the smoke has cleared and the healing process begins - in time you'll see a much bigger and more beautiful forest grow in its place.

My life post brain surgery is that forest fire and the final few weeks at Riverside was the beginning of that fire being extinguished which meant the next step for me was to finally see that there really was an end to this "road to recovery"

Final thoughts.

It's now been three years since I had my brain surgery. Since coming home from Riverside in 2021 and taking some actual time to focus on me and my recovery, I've started to understand the side effects of this brain injury of mine. I've learned to look at this journey of mine - particularly the years after my surgery by using the "Kübler-Ross model. (The five stages of grief).

Denial, Anger, Bargaining, Depression and Acceptance. I've definitely been through each of these emotions post diagnoses.

Denial - Refusing to believe that a tumour could and would cost me my job and denying that I needed help.

Anger - I was angry with those who were trying to help me thinking that they thought I was weak.

Bargaining - Doing everything I could to keep my job and not end up losing it.

Depression - with hindsight, it's incredibly scary to see just how close I came to killing myself. My arms are now riddled with scars that will be with me to the day I die. If I had reached out and asked for help when I clearly needed it, I may have followed a better path.

Acceptance - I've come to learn and accept that my brain injury is here to stay. Not only do not need to fight it anymore, I never have. By accepting that I have it, I'm now able to ask for help. I know that I'll have bad days but I also know that I'll have better days too. I understand and accept that at some point in my lifetime, this tumour most likely will grow back. That's fine - if and when that does happen, I'll kick the fucker's arse just like I did with this one!

Do I have regrets? Yes, of course I do but my regrets are outweighed by the things I've achieved, seen and done over the past ten years.

So - just where am I at with this "road to recovery?"

Well, on the physical side of things, I tend to struggle with my balance while walking at times - I've even had a few occasions where people have asked me if I'm drunk because I struggle to walk in a straight line.

I still have focal seizures but have seemingly been full seizure free for a while now.

Every so often, I'll get random headaches or sensations around the area where the tumour originally was but these days it's more of an inconvenience than anything.

On the mental and cognitive side of things, I do seem to struggle more often than not. I sometimes find that simple/basic tasks are more of a struggle than they used to be. I struggle to watch movies and be able to follow the story and the same goes for video games. My short term memory is shocking. I find that if I'm given more than a few tasks to complete without having it written down I start to panic and stress because no sooner than I hear the second instruction, I've already forgotten the first. This is when anxiety starts to become an issue but over time, I'm learning new ways of coping - such as breathing techniques.

I still struggle with my emotional responses and my emotions in general but I now have a better understanding of my emotions and have finally learned that I can and should reach out and ask for help if I see that I'm heading back towards a relapse. I also now have the support network I need to do that and friends who are more like family.

I now better understand my brain injury and know that it will always be around but I refuse to let it define me. I live with it and accept it.

Some final thoughts and some parting advice before you put this book down...

Forget about yesterday, you can't and won't change what happened.

Forget about tomorrow because anything could happen between now and then. Hold on to now. Right now. You have full control of now and what you do now is what matters.

Life is far too short and far too unpredictable to spend time focusing on anything but the here and now.

Life is far too short. I was at the peak of my fitness level when I keeled over at work with a stroke/seizure. I spent eight years walking about with a brain tumour that could have killed me at any moment. If luck and good timing didn't play its part when it did, I probably would have died, having spent the last few weeks of my life obsessing with work. What a waste...

Start a bucket list and learn to accept that you will have bad days but you'll also have better days if you allow yourself to have them!

Life is too short so live it! Too many people say that we only live once but that's not actually true – we only die once – we live every day!

Lightning Source UK Ltd.
Milton Keynes UK
UKHW051316280122
397737UK00007B/78